Men of Business and Politics

Men of Business and Politics

The Rise and Fall of the Quaker Pease Dynasty of North-East England, 1700–1943

M. W. Kirby

Lecturer in Economic History, University of Stirling

London
GEORGE ALLEN & UNWIN
Boston   Sydney

George Allen & Unwin (Publishers) Ltd,
40 Museum Street, London WC1A 1LU, UK

George Allen & Unwin (Publishers) Ltd,
Park Lane, Hemel Hempstead, Herts HP2 4TE, UK

Allen & Unwin, Inc.,
9 Winchester Terrace, Winchester, Mass. 01890, USA

George Allen & Unwin Australia Pty Ltd,
8 Napier Street, North Sydney, NSW 2060, Australia

First published in 1984

British Library Cataloguing in Publication Data

Kirby, M. W.
  Men of business and politics.
1. Pease (*Family*)   2. Society of Friends
—Biography
I. Title
289.6′092′2   BX7795.P3
ISBN 0-04-941013-X

Library of Congress Cataloging in Publication Data

Kirby, M. W.
  Men of business and politics.
Bibliography: p.
Includes index.
1. Businessmen—Great Britain—Biography.   2. Politi-
cians—Great Britain—Biography.   3. Pease family.
4. Great Britain—Economic conditions.   I. Title.
HC252.5.A2K57 1984   338′.04′0922 [B]   84-10957
ISBN 0-04-941013-X (alk. paper)

Set in 10 on 11 point Plantin by Preface Limited, Salisbury
and printed in Great Britain by Billings and Sons, London and Worcester

Contents

For my brother – a true Darlingtonian

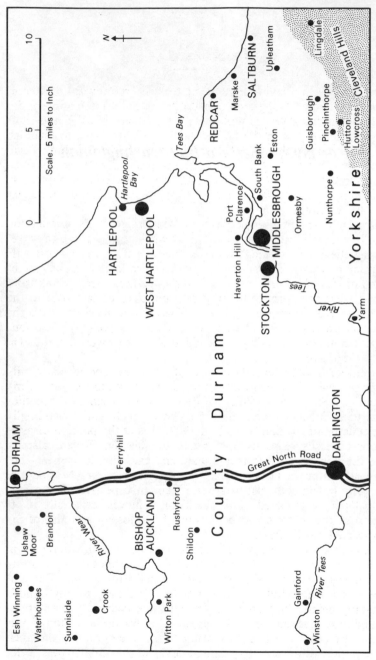

Map of principal places mentioned in the text.

Foreword

Dr Maurice Kirby, having invited me to write a foreword to *Men of Business and Politics*, suggested that I may wish to use the opportunity to criticise anything he has written. That is a very unusual and most generous gesture, but in the face of such careful research to establish truth and balance, and to avoid speculation, there is nothing I can possibly want to say in criticism. On the contrary, this book has given me enormous pleasure, and from a family point of view the controversy surrounding the final stages of the saga has, I feel, been fully, independently and authoritatively put straight.

When Dr Kirby first approached me with a view to an examination of family papers I had very little idea of what he was going to write. Though believing myself to have full possession of the facts, I had little perception of what someone else, detached from family loyalty, might pull out of it all. Hitherto, an inner conflict had made me shrink from allowing what was 'private' as well as 'public' to be laid bare to the critical and searching eye of others. Then, more recently, with the passage of time and when all are gone to whom any possible censorious comment could be wounding, it seemed that Dr Kirby came forward at the right moment.

The author has scrutinised the years of steady but spectacular family entrepreneurial achievement in a range of industries to the time of my grandfather, Sir Joseph Whitwell Pease, when business difficulties became enduring and, compounded by distressing litigation, led finally to the collapse of the family bank in 1902. It is at the point of disaster that one naturally stops to ponder and to question. When calamity strikes there is the need to recapitulate and examine the causes – not only to search for the facts in order to make an objective assessment of what went wrong, but also to attempt an introspective view of the principal people involved. This the book achieves, especially in its appraisal of the motives and behaviour of Sir Joseph and also of my father, Sir Alfred E. Pease.

My childhood was spent with a brother and sister at Pinchinthorpe in what was then the North Riding of Yorkshire, within two miles of my grandfather's old home, the very much larger Hutton Hall. Pinchinthorpe was a wonderfully happy home, as it had been for my father's first family before the turmoil. To recall these places as they were in my childhood gives me an enduring sense of warmth. Hutton, I was reminded by a cousin, was a place where 'on summer evenings the smell of hot heather swept down from the moors' and the night air was 'a riot of pine'. The personal value to be placed upon this kind of experience is immeasurable and it was important in my father's view that whilst he lived his second family should also share this experience from the home that was almost lost in the midst of his financial ruin. To have been deprived of that childhood experience during formative years would have left me with a greatly diminished sensibility of that particular dimension of things.

The history of the Pease family is a contrasting one of extraordinary success and failure. It is true that without disaster the story would have had less merit for its telling, but as it unfolds it serves as a reminder of the immense influence that my forebears wielded, for better or worse, in the industrial and political development of north-east England.

J. GURNEY PEASE

Preface

I began work on this book in the summer of 1975 during the final stages of research for an earlier volume on the British coal industry. I was examining the private papers of Joseph Albert Pease, first Baron Gainford of Headlam, and although my primary interest was in Lord Gainford's role in industrial politics after 1918 I soon became aware that his papers contained the core of a fascinating story. As a former resident of Darlington I was well aware of the Peases' involvement in founding the Stockton and Darlington Railway in 1821, an event which presaged the opening of the railway age. I knew also that their early industrial fortunes had been based upon the woollen and coal-mining industries of south Durham. But beyond that I was ignorant of the family's history. To me the Peases were remote figures who hardly merited a book-length study. The Gainford papers, however, forced me to revise this opinion, for they contained the outline of the rise and fall of a family dynasty which in its heyday had wielded immense influence in the north-east of England. Far from their interests being confined to the coal and textile industries and a particular episode in the development of railway enterprise, the Peases' entrepreneurial activities also embraced ironstone mining, limestone quarrying, locomotive construction, iron founding and banking. The family's history in the nineteenth century, therefore, was inextricably linked to the rise of the British industrial economy. The more I read about the Peases, the greater was my conviction that their experience provided a view of this process in microcosm, in a distinctive region of the country which in the decades after 1850 enjoyed extraordinarily rapid economic growth based upon the exploitation of key industrial raw materials. As an economic historian, I was instinctively attracted to this side of the Peases' activities but I very soon came to realise that there was far more to their story than the exercise of vigorous entrepreneurship. With the aid of further archive collections I was able to build up a picture of considerable political involvement. In the same way that the fortunes of the family mirrored those of the national and regional economy, so in the political sphere they reflected some of the most important developments in modern British history. The identification with Dissent and the challenge to traditional landed influence, the emergence of oligarchical political control in an urban context, the Home Rule split in the Gladstonian Liberal Party and the rise of the Labour Movement – all of these were critical factors in moulding the political environment of the nineteenth and early twentieth centuries and they were part of the direct experience of the Peases. It seemed, therefore, that a study of the family, concentrating on economic developments but embracing political themes as well, could shed valuable light not only on the history of north-east England but also on that of Britain as a whole and it is in this spirit that I have written the book. Within this broad framework, I hope, too, that my comments on the decline of 'Friendly discipline' in the family as the process of 'conformity to the world' gathered pace after 1850 will help to illuminate a notable aspect of Victorian Quakerism and one which cannot be divorced from the accretion of economic and political power. My major concern, therefore, has been to emphasise the paradigmatic quality of the Peases' experience whilst charting the history of a family whose story is interesting in its own right. Although many people in the north-east of England with a knowledge of local history will be aware of the Peases' influence on the development of a regional railway system and their activities in promoting urban and industrial development on Teesside, there can be very few who possess any knowledge of the distressing events which led to the failure of the family bank, J. and J. W. Pease of Darlington, in 1902, a disaster which foreshadowed the collapse of the dynasty. Fewer still will be aware of the extraordinary Portsmouth affair and its devastating financial consequences for the then head of the family, Sir Joseph Whitwell Pease, who found his reputation for honour and integrity impugned in the Chancery Division of the High Court. As a story, therefore, as opposed to a strictly academic history, the book contains elements of tragedy – the near-bankruptcy of the head of the Pease dynasty, the ruin of his public reputation and the destruction of his sons' inheritance.

I am indebted to many people for easing my path in the preparation of this book – to Josef Keith of the Friends House Library, London, for directing me to the Hodgkin Papers, to Miss Kathleen Bryon and Miss Dorothy Hutchinson for guidance through the archives of Barclays Bank in London and Darlington respectively, and to my parents for carrying out the greater part of the research at the Durham County Record Office. I am also grateful to Professor R. H. Campbell and Dr D. W. Bebbington for reading and commenting upon the manuscript; I owe to them a considerable improvement both in the clarity of exposition and structure of the book. Needless to say, the author alone is responsible for any errors of fact or interpretation. The Social Science Research Council awarded a grant in support of my research and this was supplemented by financial assistance from the University of Stirling; without that support the book could not have been written. I owe a special debt of gratitude to members of the Pease family. Lord Wardington gave much encouragement in the early stages of my work and Sir Richard Pease responded generously to a request to examine potentially sensitive papers in the archives of Barclays Bank. Lord Gainford's enthusiasm for the project never wavered and he provided a great deal of information on the history of his family. Historians are in debt to him for his decision to deposit an important collection of family papers in the library of Nuffield College, Oxford; it will be obvious to the reader that the Nuffield papers form one of the twin pillars of the research base for the book. My other major source of primary material has been the extensive collection of diaries and correspondence in the possession of Mr J. Gurney Pease. Gurney Pease's involvement in this project has been of particular value: his attempts over many years to rescue dispersed family papers have been painstaking and I have made full use of the fruits of his labours. Like other members of his family, Gurney Pease has given every encouragement to my work and during the last two years we have been engaged in a voluminous correspondence on various aspects of the Pease family history. I am deeply grateful to him. My thanks are also due to Miss M. E. A. Hendry, who typed the manuscript with her customary efficiency and good humour. Finally, I wish to acknowledge my wife's patience in examining innumerable boxes of papers at Nuffield College. Her endeavours helped to accelerate the pace of my early researches but, thereafter, as I am sure she will cheerfully admit, her contribution waned as her parental responsibilities increased.

Dunblane, May 1983

Illustrations

Men of Business and Politics

1
The Founding of the Dynasty

Little is known of the Pease family before 1750. Joseph Pease, who was born in 1665, is recorded as being a descendant of landowners in Essex in the late fifteenth century, one of whom settled at Sikehouse in south Yorkshire at some time during the reign of Henry VIII. By the end of the seventeenth century the Peases had moved on from Sikehouse with Joseph well established as a small landowner at Pease Hall, Shafton Green, in the parish of Felkirk in the West Riding.[1] In 1706 Joseph contracted a marriage that was to be of the utmost significance. His partner was Ann Couldwell, 'heiress in her issue of her brothers, William Couldwell of Cudworth and Thomas Couldwell of Darlington', both of whom were wool-combers.[2]

Joseph and Ann Pease had three sons and two daughters, and it is the second son, Edward, born in 1711, whose career is of most interest. According to tradition in the Pease family, Edward was turned out of his home for becoming a Quaker, but since he was only eight years old when his father died in 1719 and his mother was herself of Quaker stock this can hardly have been the case.[3] The origins of this story are unknown but it is worthy of note that in 1735 Edward married Elizabeth Coates, a member of a Quaker family from Caselee and Langleyford in Co. Durham. The marriage took place at Raby Meeting House near Darlington and it is legitimate to conclude that Edward was by then a member of the Society of Friends.

At the time of his marriage Edward's status is unknown. His elder brother had inherited the property at Felkirk, but by 1744 Edward was in residence at Darlington, having entered the wool-combing business of his uncle, Thomas Couldwell.[4] On the latter's retirement in 1760 Edward formally took over the business, at the same time offering employment to his younger brother George, a non-Quaker, who had joined the army in 1740 and fought at Culloden. Thomas Couldwell of Darlington was therefore the founder of the commercial fortunes of the Pease family.

In the mid-eighteenth century when Edward Pease was establishing himself in business, Darlington was the principal market town serving the rich agricultural district of the vale of Tees. Indeed, as early as 1538 it had been described as second only to Durham as a market centre in the entire country palatine.[5] Darlington's importance, therefore, was not so much the product of its early ecclesiastical status, as reflected in the collegiate church of St Cuthbert, but far more the result of its location – at the head of the Tees valley at a point where the Great North Road passes over the River Tees from Yorkshire into Co. Durham.[6] In the late 1760s it is likely that a majority of the town's 3,300 inhabitants were dependent upon manufacturing industry utilising the products of the local agricultural economy. The woollen and worsted industries in their various branches were an obvious example of this, but so too was the tanning industry and, more especially, the manufacture of linen.[7]

As a textile centre Darlington was better known for linen than wool in the period before 1800 and it is possible that by 1790 it was the most important producer of linen in England, supplying yarns to manufacturers in Durham, Yorkshire and Cumberland.[8] In the previous half-century, however, the woollen industry had also experienced rapid development in the town. This was in conformity with the national trend. On the eve of the Industrial Revolution, the woollen industry was Britain's most important manufacturing sector, and between 1740 and 1780, in the country as a whole, it enjoyed a sustained expansion in output.[9] It was eclipsed thereafter by the more rapid growth of the cotton industry but it is important to note that numerous, if modest fortunes had been accumulated in the more traditional textile industries before the end of the century.

For the Pease family the year 1752 marked a significant stage in the growth of their own prosperity. Before this date much of the business of wool-combing was given out on commission and Thomas Couldwell's 'mill' was principally a centre of exchange in manufacture. But from this point onwards Edward Pease took over the active management of a more ambitious concern, embracing not only the preparatory processes of sorting and combing but also weaving and dyeing. Whilst the transition from the 'domestic' or 'putting out' system of manufacture was protracted, an increasing proportion of the business was henceforth carried on at an extended mill complex in Priestgate adjacent to the River Skerne and at a smaller mill located in the Leadyard.[10]

Edward died in 1785. His will, made shortly before his death, directed the sales of 'Messuages, Tenements, Dwellinghouses, Shops, Warehouses, [and] Work-houses', and the division of the proceeds among his five sons and two daughters. He left his silver plate to his children collectively, while each son was to receive the contents of one room of the family home and the daughters were to divide 'the china and delft ware' between them. The value of these legacies amounted to £3,900. The principal beneficiary of Edward's estate, however, was his oldest son Joseph, who was the sole successor to the family woollen business.[11] According to one of his descendants, Joseph was 'the least interesting of the Peases . . . a hard working man of business . . . mixing little socially with any outside his own circle'.[12] Although he was a member of the Society of Friends, he seems to have been irritated by his wife's strict observance of Quaker rules in matters of speech and dress, an attitude which contrasted markedly with the more liberal stance of his great uncle, Thomas Couldwell. To the historian, however, as opposed to the family chronicler, Joseph Pease is far from uninteresting, for as well as expanding the woollen enterprise (it became known as Joseph Pease and Sons some time after 1785) he also carried on a modest banking business which in the eighteenth century was known as Pease Partners' Bank. In the period 1765–99 the bank handled 109 accounts and paid an average rate of interest of $4\frac{1}{2}$ per cent per annum. Some accounts were held within the Pease family, but the great majority were scattered throughout the adjacent villages of south Durham and north Yorkshire.[13] In a business such as woollen manufacturing, with several separate but dependent stages of production, a commercial arrangement of this kind could be highly beneficial. In the latter half of the eighteenth century, when the currency system was in a chaotic state, an employer in a labour-intensive industry with a persistent cash shortage required a reliable supply of small change and, in addition, access to credit in order to finance the waiting between the various stages of manufacture – from the first act of wool-buying to the final sale.[14] By integrating banking with manufacturing, Joseph could both advance credit to customers and receive it from suppliers and so more easily sustain the expansion of his woollen business.

As a small country banker Joseph Pease was not untypical of many entrepreneurs in the eighteenth-century economy who combined industrial ventures with banking. The Quaker Lloyds of Birmingham and the Gibbons family of Wolverhampton provide excellent illustrations in the metallurgical industries, whilst in mining there are several cases in the north-east of England.[15] In textiles, perhaps the best known example is provided by the Gurneys of Norwich, a Quaker family with a banking tradition going back to the early seventeenth century, but which also developed a thriving trade in woollen yarns in the first half of the eighteenth century.[16]

In Darlington itself Pease Partners' Bank was not unique. In 1774 James Backhouse, flax dresser and linen manufacturer, founded the banking firm of J. and J. Backhouse in partnership with his eldest son Jonathan. Already, in 1759, James had acquired the agency of the Royal Exchange Assurance Company and as the local linen industry went into decline after 1800 the Backhouses easily made the transition to full banking.[17] Coincidentally, in 1774 Jonathan Backhouse married Anne Pease, Joseph's younger sister, thus inaugurating a family alliance which was to be of considerable importance in later years. Like the Peases, the Backhouses were members of the Society of Friends, and if the Quaker antecedents of the latter were more impressive it should be remembered that both Joseph and Anne were birthright members of the Society, albeit in the first generation.[18]

The alleged role of the Protestant ethic in fostering 'the spirit of capitalism' as an essential precursor to the Industrial Revolution has given rise to a vast and complex literature.[19]

Although the original thesis, propounded by Max Weber, is vulnerable to the criticisms that there can be only tenuous links between an acceleration in the rate of growth in the eighteenth century and the Protestant Reformation, and that seventeenth-century Puritanism, in encouraging thrift and diligence as part of the 'daily effort for salvation' was hardly conducive to the amassing of large business fortunes, it is undeniable that Protestant Nonconformists, and Quakers in particular, are overrepresented in the ranks of the most successful entrepreneurs in the eighteenth century. Among historians of Quakerism there is a great deal of consensus as to why this should have been so. Under the Toleration Act of 1689 the Society of Friends was given its liberty of worship, and whilst the payment of tithes and other ecclesiastical demands remained as major irritants to Quakers the worst days of persecution by the state were at an end. Following the Affirmation Acts of 1696 and 1722 the Society was free from the burden of legal oaths and its form of marriage was tacitly recognised by the law. Thus, by the end of the seventeenth century the religious fervour and social radicalism which had characterised the period of George Fox's founding ministry were lessening in intensity and the body of Quakers, dominated at that time by artisans, small traders and yeomen, was about to settle into a long period of 'quietism' distinguished from other groups in society by increasingly formalised peculiarities of speech and dress. As Braithwaite, the leading historian of Quakerism, pointed out:

> With the accommodation of the Affirmation question . . . Friends . . . had passed from being the outlaws of the State into a position of privileged security. They were rapidly acquiring that savour of respectability which attaches to estimable characters, known to be free from disturbing enthusiasms. The State had learnt how to silence their obstinate witness by prudent concessions . . .[20]

For Braithwaite the acquisition of 'respectability' was clearly a cause for regret, but the economic implications of these developments were highly significant. By the beginning of the eighteenth century Friends had already established a reputation for honesty and scrupulosity in business dealings – a legacy of the fixed or 'just' price – and members of the sect engaged in industry and commerce were well placed to take advantage of such business opportunities as were consistent with their austere and censorious religious discipline. The Quaker lifestyle was marked by frugality and personal abstention: capital was to be ploughed back into a business and the stigma of bankruptcy avoided, if only to remove the threat of disownment. The Quaker entrepreneur may have been a cautious man but at a time when access to credit was of increasing importance as a prerequisite for remaining in business this very caution, when sustained over a number of generations, could make a positive contribution to the accumulation of wealth. In short, 'Quaker credit was very good, people trusted money with them, were ready to share in their enterprises, were eager to be employed by them. In all these ways Friends stood for security.'[21]

In addition to the Quakers' strict personal probity and honesty, the organisation and structure of their sect was geared to business stability and confidence. The mechanism of trade could only benefit from tours by travelling ministers and from the regular monthly, quarterly and yearly meetings of the Society of Friends. At these meetings, many of which involved considerable travel and lengthy periods away from home, it was not unnatural for Friends with commercial and business interests to discuss the state of trade and also perhaps to discuss the possibility of partnership in joint ventures.[22] As a close-knit sect the Society of Friends resembled an extended family group and as the eighteenth century progressed a chain of credit was forged throughout the Quaker business world, not unlike the 'web' of credit which emerged in the Lancashire cotton industry after 1780. But the Quaker credit network was nationwide and even extended overseas, notably to North America. The strength of the chain was reinforced at frequent intervals by intermarriage – again on a nationwide scale – especially in the iron and textile industries and banking.[23] This is not to suggest that all members of the sect were rapacious capitalists possessing a single-minded dedication to the pursuit of profit. On the contrary, the bulk of the membership with commercial interests continued to be dominated throughout the eighteenth century by small farmers, shopkeepers and craftsmen-manufacturers who remained committed to the original Quaker code with its insistence on spiritual priorities. Neither should it be thought that all Quaker marriages were the product of narrow business calculation, merely that in the restricted world of the Society of Friends and when 'marrying out' led to immediate disownment the pressure to contract marriages with those from similar backgrounds, sharing common perceptions and beliefs, could prove irresistible. In the context of the small and well organised community of Darlington Quakers, numbering about 160 in 1774, it is possible that a marital alliance between the Pease and Backhouse families was unavoidable before 1800.[24]

The practical result of an increasingly close network of family relationships was to mitigate the high risks and uncertainty of eighteenth-century business transactions. In an era which awaited the arrival of a more sophisticated institutional structure, both in terms of access to capital and the ownership and management of commercial enterprise, firms in difficulties could be helped by numerous 'cousins'.[25] The staying power of many of the Quaker business dynasties which were founded during the course of the eighteenth century was remarkable and it can be explained in part by the structure of Quakerism and ties of kinship.[26]

Apart from these positive aspects of Quakerism there were negative factors which made the Society of Friends a fruitful source of entrepreneurial talent. Whilst Quakers had obtained their religious liberty, they still laboured throughout the eighteenth century under civil disabilities which restricted their employment opportunities. The Test and Corporation Acts, for example, barred Dissenters from municipal corporations, whilst the Quakers' refusal to take the parliamentary oath and to subscribe to the thirty-nine articles of the established church led to their exclusion from the House of Commons and the ancient universities.[27] It has been claimed that the effect of these restrictions was to make Quakers more assertive and effective in non-political careers and that the world of business provided a safe environment for those who, through religious conviction, suffered from a sense of social alienation.[28] The irony in all this is that the long-term result of a combination of Weberian economic virtues and civil disability was to produce an interrelated group of merchant-manufacturing-banking family dynasties who could rival the ruling elite of landowning society in wealth and ultimately aspire to the social and political status enjoyed by the lower echelons of the British aristocracy itself.

When Joseph Pease died in 1808 his family still had some distance to travel before joining the established Quaker dynasties, dominated by the Barclays, Bevans, Gurneys and Lloyds. The Peases' significance was local, and whilst the family woollen enterprise was prosperous and profitable (the spinning of worsted yarn by machinery had commenced in 1796),[29] with trading links stretching into central Scotland and the west of England, the banking business was still operated on a small scale without a note issue and, unlike their Backhouse cousins, no plans for expansion into full-scale branch banking. Indeed, the Peases would have remained as undistinguished representatives of the numerous Nonconformist entrepreneurs of the Industrial Revolution had they not become involved in the financing and promotion of a long-standing project to link the small landsale collieries (i.e. collieries trading only in inland markets) of south Durham to a navigable point on the River Tees. The member of the family responsible for this decisive development in its history was Edward, Joseph's elder son.

Edward Pease was born in 1767 and after attending dame-schools in Darlington he was sent, at the age of eleven, to the Quaker boarding-school of Joseph and Sarah Tatham at Leeds. He returned home at the age of fourteen, a typical product of eighteenth-century Nonconformist schooling, 'well educated in English, with a very fair knowledge of Latin, proficiency in French, and able to draw and paint a little'.[30] To judge from the neat and precise private ledgers he kept later in life, Edward was also highly numerate. As was to be the custom with all the eldest sons in the Pease family, he entered the world of business in a position of low standing but by the time he was eighteen he was well acquainted with most of the processes of manufacture in the woollen and worsted business and was by then 'travelling on horseback from place to place buying and selling with energy and prudence'.[31] In common with other industrial pioneers, Edward Pease was to be the subject of considerable literary attention in the years following his death in 1858 in his ninety-second year. Yet despite the close scrutiny that his business activities were to provoke, especially in the writings of Samuel Smiles, the arch-apostle of nineteenth-century industrialism,[32] to the historian his character remains elusive. Such mid-nineteenth-century designations as 'the father of the railways' and 'a man who could see a hundred years ahead' combined to produce an image of foresight and purposefulness which Edward would have found difficult to understand. A close reading of his edited diaries[33] shows that, although he was a fervent advocate of the steam locomotive, his vision of the future was limited and circumscribed by eighteenth-century perspectives. In matters of religious faith, for example, he was certainly sympathetic to the anti-quietist tendencies at work within the Society of Friends after 1790, but despite his enthusiasm for the anti-slavery cause – even to the extent of making personal representations to senior French Cabinet ministers in the 1820s – his support for evangelical Quakerism was essentially lukewarm. Edward was in fact a very 'plain Friend' with strictly orthodox views on Quaker speech and dress.[34] His marriage in 1796 to Rachel Whitwell of Kendal, a deeply serious woman who was to become a minister in the Society of Friends, merely intensified a predilection for religious piety in everyday life which had first manifested itself in his early twenties when he consciously abandoned such frivolous and youthful diversions as field sports and the reading of 'pernicious books of novels'.[35] In the sphere of business he was undoubtedly an entrepreneur in the classic Schumpeterian sense,[36] but he failed lamentably to foresee the social and political pressures that the accumulation of wealth would place upon Quakers in general and individuals within his own family. In both of these respects, the religious and the secular, Edward Pease straddled two worlds: a woollen merchant and railway promoter who 'worshipped cent for cent'[37] and the sanctimonious Quaker elder who could lament that 'the accumulation of wealth in every family known to me in our Society carries away from the purity of our principles, adds toil and care to life and greatly endangers the possession of heaven'.[38]

By 1817 Edward had greatly curtailed his involvement in the management of Joseph Pease and Sons. With advancing years his commitment to the Society of Friends deepened and philanthropic causes, notably the anti-slavery agitation, began to claim more of his attention. At first sight, therefore, it is all the more remarkable that at the age of fifty, and in the midst of coping with a disastrous fire at the Priestgate woollen mill, he chose to become directly involved in the arduous process of railway promotion. In the absence of diaries for the period his reasoning can only be guessed at. As the most influential employer in Darlington's leading manufacturing industry he could hardly stand aloof from a project which could have significant implications for the local economy. Perhaps, too, the involvement of his Backhouse relations, especially his banker cousin Jonathan, was a contributory factor. He may also have been spurred on by feelings of territorial loyalty – the fact that much of the impetus for improved communications in south Durham came from the neighbouring town of Stockton located further down the Tees valley. A more plausible explanation is that of direct interest. Although no primary sources have come to light which provide direct confirmation of the fact, in 1814 the Peases had possibly acquired an interest in a colliery at Witton near Bishop Auckland.[39] Nevertheless, Edward's influence on the events which were to lead to the opening of the Stockton and Darlington Railway in 1825 was persistent and at times decisive.

In the eighteenth century coal mining had risen to prominence as the principal industrial activity in the north-east of England. It may be an exaggeration to claim that 'In Britain every landowner dreamed of finding coal, iron, copper, lead or some other valuable ore on his property',[40] but the Great Northern Coalfield, dominated by the Grand Allies – a combination of noble and gentry landowners – provides an excellent illustration of aristocratic involvement in the exploitation of mineral resources.[41] The desire to augment the capital values of estates and the search for *rentier* income had led by the beginning of the nineteenth century to a thriving coastwise coal trade, based upon the Tyne and Wear, to London. The expansion of this trade had been facilitated by the willingness of those landowners with mining interests to invest in improved technology. The most spectacular development was the introduction of steam power for pumping, which gave access to deeper seams, but no less significant was the more extensive use of improved waggon- or tramways linking inland collieries with the numerous shipping points on the Tyne and Wear.[42]

Further to the south, the expansion of the Auckland coalfield had long been inhibited by the inadequacy of the Tees as a navigable river. The port of Stockton at the highest navigable point was 25 miles away from Bishop Auckland, the nucleus of the coalfield. A horse-drawn waggonway of this length would have been unusual and it is hardly surprising that the initial interest in improving the district's transport facilities centred on the possibility of a canal. This was first mooted in Darlington in 1767 when a group of thirteen potential promoters, among whom were Peases and Backhouses, agreed to fund a survey for a canal. This was carried out by Robert Whitworth acting for James Brindley, the foremost canal engineer of the day. The route of Whitworth's proposed canal was to lead from Stockton by Darlington to a point on the north bank of the Tees at Winston within reasonable distance of the coalfield. Together with a feeder network stretching into the North Riding, the total length was more than 33 miles with an estimated construction cost of £63,722. Although coal was to be the principal item of carriage, in addition to lead, alum and lime, it was not envisaged that the canal would be used to develop a coal shipping trade in competition with the Tyne and Wear: the market was to be primarily a local one, dominated by Darlington and Stockton, and the North Riding of Yorkshire in and around the small market town of Yarm.[43] The project was a costly one for a sparsely populated district to support and due to a marked lack of public interest it was allowed to lapse. There were signs of a revival of interest in the 1790s[44] but serious consideration of the project had to wait until 1810. This was the year of the opening of the Mandale cut, a straight channel of 220 yards, which shortened the distance from the mouth of the silt-choked Tees to Stockton by more than two miles.[45] Whilst Edward Pease and his father were directly interested in the Mandale scheme, the Tees Navigation Company, which had been formed in 1805 as the sponsoring organisation, was mainly the product of Stockton initiative. This was not a surprising development, since at that time the town had a population of 4,000, and rivalled Darlington in prosperity, as evidenced by its numerous 'quays, granaries, warehouses, roperies, sail-cloth workshops, lead works, shipbuilding and timber yards'.[46] The opening of the cut was in fact celebrated by a dinner held in the town hall of Stockton in September 1810. It is not known if members of the Pease family were present, but Leonard Raisbeck, the Recorder of Stockton, took the opportunity to inaugurate a project for 'the construction of a railway or canal from Stockton by Darlington to Winston, for the benefit of the mineral and other traffic of South Durham and North Yorkshire'.[47]

The events which followed Raisbeck's announcement have been told on many occasions and it is unnecessary to reiterate in detail a story which in its broad outlines is well known.[48] It is sufficient to point out that although the interested parties in Stockton and Darlington were at first united in their advocacy of a canal to follow a route projected by the eminent engineer John Rennie in 1813, they eventually drew apart both in respect of the route to be followed and the mode of conveyance. The catalyst for dissension was provided by Christopher Tennant, a leading merchant of Stockton. In 1815 Rennie's scheme had been abandoned in the aftermath of several bank failures in Co. Durham[49] and three years later Tennant funded, at his own expense, a survey for a canal to the Auckland coalfield via Rushyford, well to the north of Darlington. Although such a route would have required fifty locks, presenting significant engineering problems, it was judged to be commercially sound because in veering northwards away from Darlington it provided a shorter link to the coalfield than the Whitworth and Rennie schemes. Tennant also held out the prospect of securing a portion of the lucrative coastal trade in coal and his proposed scheme, with an estimated construction cost of £205,283, was endorsed at a public meeting held in Stockton in July 1818. In November he led a deputation to London to raise the necessary four-fifths of the cost of construction so that parliamentary authorisation could be obtained.

The new initiative from Stockton was greeted with some dismay in Yarm and Darlington, and the response was swift. Even before Tennant had departed for London a rival scheme designed to reconfirm Darlington as the focal point of the line of communication had been initiated. In September commercial interest in both towns 'directed estimates to be made for a line from Stockton by Darlington to the collieries, with branches to Yarm, Croft and Piercebridge, as well as by the joint mode of having a canal and railway as by railway the whole distance'.[50] The wording of the resolution was a direct reflection of considerable uncertainty among the promoters over the mode of conveyance. Thomas Meynell, the leading representative from Yarm, and Jonathan Backhouse were strongly in favour of a canal from Stockton and Yarm to Darlington and a rail or tramway from the latter to the coalfield.[51] Another group led by Edward Pease and Richard Miles of Yarm were equally adamant in their advocacy of an unbroken line of communication by railway on the grounds of technical feasibility and, more especially, lower operating costs. George Overton, a Welsh engineer with considerable experience in laying down tramways in the colliery districts of South Wales and a relative by marriage of one of the Yarm promoters, was engaged as surveyor. His report, which was in readiness by the end of September 1818, indicated that a continuous line of railway, roughly 27 miles in length with an estimated construction cost of £124,000, would prove to be the most efficient and economical form of communication.[52] The views of Edward Pease were vindicated, but there was no rancour on the part of Backhouse or Meynell. This was confirmed at the public meeting held on Friday 13 November in the town hall of Darlington to consider Overton's report, when Backhouse made a highly impressive speech in favour of a railway, citing 'fact and figures which he used with sledge-hammer effect to demolish the arguments and calculations' of those who were still inclined to support Tennant's 'northern' canal scheme.[53] In holding out the prospect of a 25 per cent return on a capital investment of £120,000, Backhouse seems to have been carried away by his own enthusiasm and it was left to Edward Pease to instil a greater sense of reality in the meeting. Basing his calculations on the tolls payable on the existing coal-road from Darlington to the Auckland coalfield, Edward argued bluntly that a railway was assured of a certain 5 per cent return from this traffic alone:

> You need not go any further. This quite satisfies me. That revenue on this short piece of road yields me 5 per cent. on the outlay, and this is enough . . . Some perhaps can make it out to be 6, or 8, or 10 or 12 per cent. – I do not know how much –but there is ample room for calculation; but I am quite satisfied with my 5 per cent.; and I have only made this statement to show that by one single article we can make a sufficient rate of interest by this undertaking, and all the rest may be taken as profit over and above 5 per cent.[54]

Overawed by this dual denunciation of a canal scheme at the hands of two of Darlington's most sober and respected inhabitants, the meeting concluded by appointing a 40-strong management committee composed of all those prepared to subscribe a minimum of £500 to the project. Its principal task was to draw up a prospectus preparatory to making an application for an Act 'for a tramway, on the plan and estimates given by Mr Overton'.[55] The prospectus, which was devised in large measure by Edward's second son Joseph, then aged nineteen, was issued on 15 November 1818 and within a week £25,000 had been raised.[56]

The subscription list for the projected Stockton and Darlington Railway was closed on 26 December 1818. Of the 1,209 shares of £100 each the majority were subscribed locally.[57] The Backhouse family were prepared to invest £20,000 and the Peases £6,200. Other large subscriptions came from the Quaker Benjamin Flounders of Yarm (£5,000), Colonel William Chaytor of Croft (£5,000), Thomas Meynell of Yarm (£3,000) and Leonard Raisbeck, one of the few subscribers from Stockton (£1,000). But whilst the bulk of the subscriptions were local (two-thirds) there was significant 'external' interest in the Stockton and Darlington project. It was principally from within the Society of Friends. The Gurney family of Norwich and London were committed to the extent of £20,000 and Thomas Richardson of London to £10,000. The implications of this pattern of prospective shareholdings were threefold. In the first instance it implied that the projectors of the Stockton and Darlington Railway could not rely on local sources of finance alone. This was recognised formally in the prospectus which provided for the appointment of a separate committee of bankers and financiers (mainly Quakers) in London charged with the task of obtaining subscriptions.[58] Secondly, the preponderating influence on the whole enterprise was vested from the outset in the Society of Friends. Jonathan Backhouse himself was married to Hannah Chapman, the elder daughter and co-heiress of the largest single subscriber, Joseph Gurney of Norwich, while Thomas Richardson of London, partner in the bill-broking business of Overend, Richardson and Co., was both a cousin and close friend of Edward Pease.[59] This in itself is an excellent illustration of the Quaker 'chain of credit' alluded to earlier and in the context of subsequent railway development it meant that the Stockton and Darlington venture was a special case – a public joint stock company with a capital of £100,000 which was, in effect, a close family partnership.[60] It is significant that Christopher Tennant's mission to London in November 1818 in support of his rival canal project proved abortive due to his failure to raise the necessary capital. This leads to the final point. Quaker financiers in Norwich and London were prepared to invest in the unfamiliar venture of a public railway because the risks were mitigated by the commitment of their Quaker 'cousins'. The involvement of the Gurneys and Thomas Richardson was an indication of the confidence that they placed in the sound judgement of their Darlington relatives. Even if Tennant's scheme had been practicable he could not have competed with a private capital market bound together by ties of mutual trust and kinship.

After the necessary subscriptions had been obtained the next hurdle confronting the projectors was the passage of a parliamentary Bill of incorporation. Although the company form of organisation in manufacturing industry was virtually prohibited after the Bubble Act of 1720, public utilities, principally canals, had been able to avail themselves of the benefits of incorporation, namely the raising of capital publicly and the receipt of compulsory powers to purchase land. There had, of course, been numerous Canal Acts in the eighteenth century but the negotiation of rights of way remained a sensitive issue. Landowners who objected to a canal traversing their property could create severe difficulties for canal promoters in Parliament and unless they had a direct pecuniary interest their opposition had to be bought off, often at considerable expense. Waggonways for the transport of coal were potentially subject to the same disability and it was fortunate that the short waggonways of the Tyne and Wear invariably ran over the property of landowners who were themselves colliery proprietors. Because of its length, however, the Stockton and Darlington line was exceptionally vulnerable, and all the more so because Overton's route cut deeply into the estates of the two most influential landowners in the district – the Earl of Darlington (later first Duke of Cleveland) and the Earl of Eldon, at that time Lord Chancellor in Lord Liverpool's administration. The resistance of both magnates to the Stockton and Darlington project is well known. Whereas Eldon was eventually bought off, Lord Darlington remained implacable in his opposition to a scheme which in his view was 'harsh and oppressive to the interests of the country through which it is intended the railway shall pass'.[61] Unlike Eldon, Lord Darlington had no interest in industrial activities and his real concern, almost to the point of obsession, was the damage that the railway would inflict upon his fox coverts.

The first Stockton and Darlington Railway Bill was defeated by 106 votes to 93 on 5 April 1819. An unidentified member of the House of Lords subsequently commented: 'Well, if the Quakers in these times, when nobody knows anything about railways, can raise up such a phalanx as they have on this occasion, I should recommend the county gentlemen to be very wary how they oppose them.'[62] To put it another way, the closeness of the vote was not so much the product of a new awareness among 93 members of the House of Commons of the virtues of railways. It was far more the result of the highly effective lobbying carried out by Edward Pease and his fellow promoters in February 1819 when they descended on London to canvass the support of MPs, calling in pairs at their homes. They were considerably aided in their task by the network of Quaker financial connections in the capital, but even so the first solicitor to the Stockton and Darlington Railway, Francis Mewburn, was moved to remark in later years that 'The difficulties, pain and anguish which I endured during my sojourn in London while soliciting the Bill can scarcely be imagined'.[63] Mewburn was a rather sensitive individual, but his legal responsibilities to the promoters cannot have been eased by the evident failure of Lord Eldon, in his capacity as Lord Chancellor, to comprehend some of the technical details in the Stockton and Darlington Bill.

The promoters were far from discouraged and the very closeness of the vote spurred them on to greater efforts. A second survey was commissioned from a somewhat irritated Overton with the object of avoiding Lord Darlington's estates as far as practicable and also of appeasing other objectors, notably the trustees of the turnpike on the Auckland coal-road.[64] All of this was accomplished at some expense and after a local campaign of propaganda, during which Lord Darlington attempted, without success, to bankrupt Backhouses' Bank,[65] the promoters renewed their application to Parliament for an Act of incorporation in the session following the death of George III in January 1820. On this second occasion the lobbying was even more intense than in 1819. J. S. Jeans, the 'Jubilee' historian of the Stockton and Darlington Railway, was guilty of only slight exaggeration in his claim that 'Every member of Parliament that could be influenced, directly or indirectly, was pressed into the service of the promoters. Every peer that was known to have any doubt or hesitation was seized upon and interviewed until he became a convert, while those who looked upon the measure with favour were confirmed in the faith.'[66] Yet despite these efforts, which even included attempts to influence the selection of parliamentary candidates in the north of England, the Bill was nearly lost due to a failure to comply with the standing orders of the House of Commons which required the subscription of four-fifths of the share capital of a projected public company before a Bill could pass to the committee stage. Mewburn, who was once again responsible for soliciting the Bill, panicked when he found that no more funds were forthcoming from Norwich and London and in desperation he contacted his colleague Leonard Raisbeck in Stockton. With only a few days to spare, Raisbeck was able to obtain the extra subscription, amounting to £7,000, from Edward Pease.[67] It was this gesture of confidence in the enterprise at a critical moment which marked the real beginning of the ascendancy of the Pease family over the conduct of the Stockton and Darlington Railway. Henceforth, it was known as 'the Quaker line', much to the disgust of Colonel Chaytor, who resigned as chairman of the promotion committee in protest at the growing domination exercised by the Pease-Backhouse alliance.[68]

In the years preceding the opening of the Stockton and Darlington Railway in September 1825, Edward Pease's influence on the project was persistent and beneficial. The Act of 1821 was 'for making and maintaining a railway or tramroad from the River Tees at Stockton to Witton Park Colliery with several branches therefrom, all in the County of Durham' with 'men and horses' as the sole means of conveyance. The tramroad option was abandoned following Edward's historic meeting in April 1821 with George Stephenson, the self-consciously brilliant engineer in the employment of the Grand Allies at Killingworth Colliery.[69] It hardly needs to be reiterated that Stephenson proved to be a highly effective advocate not only of a railway but also of locomotive engines. Since the speed of the crude and unreliable engines of the early 1820s offered no great advantage over conventional means of transport, and their superior economy in operation had yet to be demonstrated, it was an indication of Edward's influence that he was able to persuade his fellow directors to introduce locomotives on to the Stockton and Darlington line as a complement to horses and stationary engines and also to permit Stephenson to re-survey and modify Overton's original route. Although Thomas Meynell was elected chairman of the company, as befitted his status as a gentry landowner, it was Edward Pease who was approached for advice from other aspiring railway promoters and who also conducted the detailed correspondence with Stephenson, ultimately securing his appointment as engineer to the line. Edward's interest in the project was in fact incessant: he insisted on discussing the gauge of the rails with Stephenson and arbitrated between the obstinate engineer and his fellow directors over the proportion of malleable to cast iron rails to be laid down on the 27-mile route.[70]

1 Edward Pease (1767–1858) in old age, *c*. 1850.

Edward's energy in a period when his commitment to the anti-slavery agitation was moving to its climax[71] was to earn for him the designation of 'The Father of the Railways', the man whose 'amazing foresight' in advocating 'the necessity of unbroken communication by railways' had been the means of 'opening fresh avenues to science, encouraging every branch of trade and commerce, employing large bodies of operatives and ameliorating the condition of all classes of society'.[72] These remarks, contained in an address presented to Edward in 1857 by the leading residents of Darlington and other well-wishers (see below, p. 48) expressed sentiments typical of an age which accorded the highest acclaim to industrial pioneers.[73] But although the Stockton and Darlington Railway was the first public railway to utilise steam locomotives it is only with the benefit of hindsight that its unique position in the history of railway development is assured. The fact remains that the Stockton and Darlington line did not inaugurate the modern railway era. The combination of stationary and locomotive engines with horses did not provide conclusive evidence of the advantages of steam traction, and in leasing the line to contractors for the conveyance of passengers the promoters revealed the true limits of their conception – an extended waggonway for the transport of coal and other minerals with locomotive haulage and the carriage of passengers essentially as afterthoughts.[74] Even in respect of the coal trade the line was restricted in its objectives. Although the shipment of coal for export was to be the major source of revenue after 1830, both Edward Pease and Jonathan Backhouse initially contemplated only the landsale of coal along the line. Of the 29,000 tons of coal that the promoters envisaged would be transported to Stockton each year it was expected that over 14,000 tons would go into Cleveland to the south with only 10,000 tons as shipment for ballast.[75] When the powerful Tyne and Wear exporting interests succeeded in obtaining a statutory limitation of the cost of transport of one halfpenny per ton-mile for coal exported from Stockton (compared with twopence per ton-mile for landsale coal), this merely reinforced the promoters' belief that they had been right to question Christopher Tennant's claim that a coastwise trade based upon Stockton could be remunerative. This attitude was to change dramatically in the period 1825–6 (see below, p. 20), but the promoters' original views demonstrated their failure to appreciate the extent to which cheaper and speedier transport on the railway could create *extra* traffic over and above that which already existed on the local turnpike system – an attitude exemplified by Edward's simple acceptance of a 5 per cent return on the capital invested.

Nevertheless, the Stockton and Darlington line demonstrated what was possible and in so doing paved the way for the more spectacular Liverpool and Manchester Railway whose opening in 1830 marked the true birth of the railway age. It was George Stephenson who was appointed engineer to the latter and it was his own locomotive – the *Rocket* – which vindicated his faith in the speed and efficiency of the steam locomotive. Unlike the proprietors of the Stockton and Darlington line, those responsible for the Liverpool and Manchester Railway opted for complete mechanical traction and did not make recourse to the granting of leases to the owners of horse-drawn carriages.

The *Rocket* itself, together with the four locomotives that were ordered for the new railway after Stephenson's success in the Rainhill trials in October 1829, was manufactured at Newcastle upon Tyne at the Forth Street works of Robert Stephenson and Co. This firm had been founded in June 1823 to manufacture locomotives, stationary winding engines, waggons and trackwork, and it was the product of Edward Pease's confidence in the engineering abilities of George Stephenson. The company was formed as a co-partnership between George and his son Robert, together with Thomas Richardson, Michael Longridge and Edward.[76] As the owner of the Bedlington Iron Works which produced the malleable iron rails for the Stockton and Darlington line, Longridge clearly had a vested interest in the Stephensons' success (in December 1824 he agreed, albeit reluctantly, to become executive partner of the firm) but it was Edward Pease who subscribed the bulk of the capital of £4,000. His share amounted to £1,600, but he also loaned Robert £500 towards his own subscription.[77] Whatever Edward's motivation – a vision of a communcations system transformed by steam traction, or the more immediate concern of obtaining an assured supply of reliable locomotive and stationary engines for the Stockton and Darlington line itself – this was the beginning of a long and fruitful business partnership between the Pease and Stephenson families until the onset of managerial difficulties in the company after 1880 (see below, p. 79).[78] In later years Edward's religious scruples would conflict with this interest from time to time, as in 1853 when he declined to accept his portion of the profits arising from the manufacture of 'war steamers for the King of Sardinia'.[79] His diary entries, however, frequently refer to the income earned from his Forth Street investments, especially in the 1840s when the railway construction boom was at its height.[80]

On the eve of its opening the financial condition of the Stockton and Darlington Railway was far from sound. A shareholders' report issued on 9 September 1825, only three weeks before the official opening, raised doubts about the line's ability to pay the minimum dividend of 5 per cent demanded by its leading promoter.[81] The problem of mounting debts was a serious one. Even before the completion of coal drops, engine sheds and depots the company had had to borrow £40,000 from the Gurneys and £20,000 from Thomas Richardson – all on the basis of its promissory notes – to help meet the cost of land purchase. At £25,000 this was £7,000 more than had been estimated. Far more serious, however, was the totally unforeseen amount of £32,000 which had been expended in successfully opposing the rival Tees and Wear Valley railway project in 1824. The company even owed the sum of £9,342 to its treasurer, Jonathan Backhouse, in respect of his personal expenditure in acquiring land on behalf of the management committee.[82] Once more Edward came to the rescue of the Stockton and Darlington Railway when he agreed to meet the company's wage bill until new loans had been secured.[83] Fortunately, these were soon forthcoming when it became increasingly obvious that the company was going to exceed the financial targets laid down in the original estimates of 1819. In the first year of operation a $2\frac{1}{2}$ per cent return was paid out of a revenue of £9,194, but thereafter the company went from strength to strength. The total revenue in the second financial year (1826/7) amounted to £18,304, of which £14,455 was accounted for by the carriage of coal. The equivalent figures in 1829/30 were £23,727 and £20,951 respectively, sufficient to pay a dividend of 5 per cent.[84] In 1826/7, 80,446 tons of coal had been carried on the line, and, in the operating year 1829/30, 147,570 tons.[85] These tonnages greatly exceeded the hopes of Edward Pease and his fellow promoters. Between 1825 and 1830 the average price of a ton of Auckland coal at Stockton fell from 18 shillings to 8s 6d, a spectacular testament to the economies in transport costs brought about by the railway.[86]

In 1827, with the market price of shares in the Stockton and Darlington Railway rising from £120 to £160, Edward Pease terminated his active business career 'with a resolution never to enter a railway meeting again'.[87] The remainder of his long life was devoted to the affairs of the Society of Friends. He was a regular attender at the London Yearly Meeting until well into old age and he travelled extensively between the quarterly and monthly meetings of the Society in England, visiting his many Quaker relatives and attending innumerable funerals.[88] Until his death he continued to reside at the modest plain-fronted house he had occupied since 1798 at 73 Northgate, near to the centre of Darlington. It was here that he cultivated his highly prized plums, apricots and apples, tended his greenhouse and provided infrequent dinner guests with 'a most excellent table' accompanied by 'heavy cut-glass decanters of port, Lisbon and Madeira and Bucellas wines'.[89] These were the only private indulgences which brought pleasure without guilt. To his family and friends Edward was outwardly cheerful, the epitome of a kindly and generous patriarch. He was a venerated but popular figure in the local community and this was reflected in his nickname – 'Neddy Pease'. His diaries, however, provide a depressing record of morbid self-examination, of deep mourning for his wife who died in 1833, of failure to overcome his youthful addiction to 'popular' literature (the *Illustrated London News* in particular) and agonies over the conflict between deeply held religious convictions and the steady accumulation of wealth. But as a plain Quaker his principal source of anguish was the erosion of 'Friendly discipline' that year by year became more apparent in the conduct of his descendants. The irony, as Edward himself appreciated, was that his own 'unwatchfulness in entering into public concerns' was partly to blame for this.[90]

2
Speculative Enterprise

It has already been noted that the Stockton and Darlington directors had dismissed the prospect of a coal-shipping trade based on the Tees in the early stages of their railway project. It is significant, therefore, that in the summer of 1825, immediately before the opening of the line, Thomas Richardson, with encouragement from Jonathan Backhouse, began to explore the possibilities of developing a coastal trade in coal. The result of Richardson's deliberations was the formation of the Tees Coal Company later in the year in association with Thomas Harris and Joseph Taylor.[1] After an uncertain beginning, with the company sustaining operating losses of £2,000 in the financial year 1825/6, it very soon became obvious that a substantial coastal market for Tees coal awaited exploitation – despite the statutory burden of a significant differential in the rate of carriage for landsale and sea-sale coal. In 1825/6 the railway carried 7,296 tons for shipment and in 1827/8, 54,290 tons. Even a severe diminution in this rate of expansion would have led to port congestion if Stockton remained the sole shipping point. The dockside was already overcrowded in 1827, and the difficulties of navigation were exacerbated by shoal water in the upper reaches of the river.[2] What was required was a new port down river where deeper water was available. This would, in turn, necessitate the extension of the railway.

As early as February 1826 the Stockton and Darlington directors had considered Haverton Hill on the north bank of the Tees as a possible deep-water port. By the autumn of 1827, however, they had decided to apply for parliamentary powers to extend their line to Middlesbrough, a small hamlet on the south bank of the river which was not only nearer to Stockton but also offered equal advantages as a point of shipment. Predictably, the proposed line was opposed vigorously by the Tyne and Wear interests, who claimed that the extension would give the collieries of south Durham an unfair competitive advantage due to the absence of wayleave payments (payments made by colliery companies for the right to transport coal over private property). But even the combined influence of such powerful colliery magnates as Lord Londonderry and the Earl of Durham was insufficient to prevent the passage of the Bill and the Act for the Middlesbrough extension received the royal assent in May 1828. Once again, as in 1819 and 1821, the Stockton and Darlington interests had been able to call upon influential forces of their own, in particular Richard Hanbury Gurney of Norwich 'who being well-known as a hunting man in Leicestershire and his own county, induced a considerable number of Norfolk noblemen and others to come down and support the railway'.[3] It has already been noted that the Gurney family had a large financial interest in the Stockton and Darlington line, but by the later 1820s the kinship ties which had been so important at the beginning of the decade had been further enhanced by the marriage in March 1826 of Edward Pease's second son, Joseph, to Emma, the co-heiress of Joseph Gurney. Emma was the younger sister of the wife of Jonathan Backhouse and it was this new marital alliance, in addition to the Gurney manipulation of the House of Lords, that contributed to the resignation of Thomas Meynell as chairman of the Stockton and Darlington Railway in 1828 in protest at the Darlington Quakers' hold over the company's affairs.

Like his father, Joseph Pease had been educated at Tatham's academy in Leeds but had completed his schooling at the Quaker establishment of Josiah Forster at Southgate near London. He began his career under the strict supervision of his father in the family woollen concern and at the age of nineteen was sufficiently committed to the Stockton and Darlington project to be invited to draw up the promoters' first prospectus. Now in the late 1820s, aided by his Gurney relations and Edward Pease's large financial stake in the company, Joseph was on the threshold of a business career which, through a combination of luck, acute judgement and an overwhelming 'desire to excel', was to secure for himself and his descendants a considerable fortune with its attendant social prestige and political responsibilities.[4] Unlike his father, Joseph was not inhibited by the accumulation of wealth. Such guilt as he felt was more the product of concern for his family at times of commercial crisis and in the midst of business speculations. Although he became an elder and eventually a minister in the Society of Friends his religious convictions, deeply and seriously held as they were, found stronger expression in private diaries than in public action. If Edward Pease's views on the amassing of wealth were inspired by eighteenth-century perspectives then in this respect at least Joseph epitomised the thrusting urban manufacturing-industrial interest which was to transform the economy and society of Britain during the course of the nineteenth century.

Joseph's first independent business venture was as a colliery entrepreneur. From October to December 1827 he was engaged in leasing various coal properties in Co. Durham. These were mainly in the Auckland coalfield at the St Helens and Adelaide collieries. He also travelled further north to inspect coal properties at Pickton near Chester-le-Street and in December 1827 negotiated a lease for the exploitation of coal measures belonging to Sir Thomas Clavering of Durham.[5] It is significant that these colliery interests were being acquired immediately after the decision to extend the Stockton and Darlington Railway to Middlesbrough and, despite Joseph's wish to avoid any 'sanguine anticipations', it is clear that even before the Middlesbrough extension received the royal assent he too, like Thomas Richardson, was looking forward to the development of a coal-shipping trade based on the Tees. His ambitions were confirmed in the following year when he 'took [a] boat and entering the Tees Mouth sailed up to Middlesbrough to take a view of the proposed line of the contemplated extension of the Railway'. After looking at the solitary farmhouse and ancient burial ground that constituted the core of the hamlet he recorded in his diary that he was 'much pleased with the place altogether' for 'Imagination here had ample scope in fancying a coming day when the bare fields . . . will be covered with a busy multitude and numerous vessels crowding to these banks denote the busy seaport'. Since the vista of Middlesbrough from the river was dominated by extensive salt flats, the possession of a liberal imagination was a vital quality for a prospective port developer. But Joseph was nothing if he was not determined: his diary entry for the day concluded with the observation:

> Who that has considered the nature of British enterprise, commerce and industry will pretend to take his stand on this spot and pointing the finger of scorn at these visions exclaim that it will never be? If such an one appears he and I are at issue.[6]

Middlesbrough, therefore, was to be the new shipping point for Auckland coal. Surprisingly, in view of the close interest of the Stockton and Darlington Railway in this development, the company was not directly involved in the purchase of the necessary land. This was undertaken by a small group of Quaker financiers from London and Norwich – Thomas Richardson, Joseph Gurney, Henry Birkbeck, Simon Martin and Francis Gibson.[7] In subsequent accounts of the birth of Middlesbrough, Joseph Pease is commonly identified as the principal founder of the town but, whilst he too is named as one of the original 'Middlesbrough Owners', his contribution (£7,000) to the £35,000 purchase price for the 520-acre estate was loaned by his father-in-law, Joseph Gurney, at a rate of interest of 4 per cent.[8] For the young Joseph Pease this was to be one of his most important and ultimately lucrative investments. His vision of August 1828 was of a 'busy seaport' dependent for its prosperity upon the export of coal. Little did he realise that by the time of his death in 1872 Middlesbrough would be a booming manufacturing town with extensive metallurgical industries and a thriving shipping trade based not upon coal but upon the export of iron manufactures.

In the years following the opening of the Middlesbrough extension of the Stockton and Darlington Railway in December 1830 the Tees coal

2 Joseph Pease (1799–1872), from a study by Sir George Hayter for his painting of the first Reform Parliament, 1832.

trade boomed. From 1821 to 1830 only 110,211 tons of coal had been shipped from the mouth of the river, but from 1831 to 1840 the figure increased to 8,293,984 tons with a further advance in the next decade to 17,019,714 tons.[9] In the late 1820s the growing success of the Tees shipping trade was an important contributory factor in the collapse of the Limitation of the Vend, the organisation of Tyne and Wear colliery owners which had been founded in 1771 to maintain prices in the London market. In December 1828 the vend agreement was not renewed and the cut-throat competition which ensued obliged the Stockton and Darlington company to reduce its dues for the carriage of export coal by a substantial margin.[10] Despite the revival of the vend agreement in September 1829, the company was sufficiently disenchanted with the operation of the free market that it decided to let to Jonathan Backhouse, Joseph Pease and Henry Stobart the tolls arising from coal shipped for export at an annual rate of £5,000 – the value that was currently placed on the Tees export trade.[11] Nevertheless, the reintroduction of the vend was an essential prerequisite for the further expansion of the south Durham coalfield and this was one factor which contributed to the upsurge in exports after 1830. A further stimulus was provided by the Tyne and Wear pitmen's strike of 1831, an event which Francis Mewburn believed 'had the effect of advancing the Tees coal full 20 years in London and the outports'.[12] With only a single line of track, the Stockton and Darlington Railway was hard pressed to meet the demands for shipment, but the true measure of the company's success was the further collapse of the vend in 1833. The railway had promoted the rapid expansion of a new and highly competitive coalfield producing sea-sale coal, and this fact was recognised in 1834 when the vend was renewed following a decision to admit the Tees collieries into the regulation.[13]

In 1833 Joseph Pease replaced Jonathan Backhouse as treasurer of the Stockton and Darlington Railway and this was soon followed by his appointment as chairman of the management committee. From this point onwards he began to acquire a preponderating influence in the running of the company both as a result of direct pecuniary interest and sheer force of personality. It was due to his initiative, for example, that his fellow directors became involved in the promotion of the Great North of England Railway in 1835 for the purpose of 'connecting Leeds and York with Newcastle upon Tyne and forming a continuation of all the proposed lines from the metropolis towards Scotland'.[14] The rationale of this project was twofold: to secure for the Stockton and Darlington interest a strategic position in the developing rail network from London to Edinburgh and to increase the company's mineral traffic by acquiring 'a cheap and expeditious transit of coals into the heart of the North Riding and to the City of York itself'.[15] Following a meeting of the management committee in October 1835 all Stockton and Darlington shareholders were exhorted to subscribe to the new railway.[16]

The immediate result of the launching of the Great North of England project was to provoke a serious clash between the Stockton and Darlington and Clarence Railway companies. The latter, which was the successor to the abortive Tees and Wear Valley Railway of 1824 (see above, p. 18), had been successfully projected by the indefatigable Christopher Tennant in 1828 following the decision of the Stockton and Darlington Company to abandon its proposed line to Haverton Hill.[17] Tennant was still anxious to promote the interests of Stockton and he was convinced that a railway company with its own port of shipment on the north bank of the Tees could compete effectively in the coastal coal trade – but only if it was granted statutory running rights on the Stockton and Darlington line to the Auckland coalfield. The Act of incorporation for the Clarence Company gave these rights and Tennant proceeded with the construction of his line and also the development of coal shipment facilities at Port Clarence on the north bank of the Tees opposite Middlesbrough. Unfortunately, the works were expensive to construct and subject to considerable mismanagement. The line was opened for mineral traffic in 1833 but at an early stage of operation it had to surmount the imposition of a levy on the carriage of its coal on the Stockton and Darlington line. By the middle of 1834 the Clarence Company's financial affairs were so embarrassed that it was obliged to ask the Exchequer Loan Board (to whom it was already deeply in debt) to appoint a new board of directors.[18] Not unnaturally, therefore, Tennant's response to the Great North of England project was bitterly personal and direct: Joseph Pease was using the Stockton and Darlington Railway to 'get possession of the county' in order to ruin his closest competitor.[19] For that reason the Clarence Company would propose a modification to the route of the new line so that it ran nearer to Stockton and would also give its backing to the Durham South-West Junction Railway project which was intended to provide a direct connection between Port Clarence and the Auckland and Coundon coalfields. In the event, the Clarence Company was unsuccessful on both counts: the Great North of England route remained unchanged and the Stockton and Darlington Company was supported in its opposition to the Durham South-West Junction project by the Tyne and Wear exporting interests, ably led by Lord Londonderry. It was also significant – and hardly fair to the Clarence Company – that Joseph Pease, as the parliamentary representative for South Durham, was a member of the House of Commons committee which rejected the Clarence-inspired project.[20]

This episode in the early history of the Stockton and Darlington Company demonstrated a degree of ruthlessness on the part of Joseph Pease which was equal to that of any of Britain's predatory railway pioneers and in this context it is interesting to note that the Great North of England Railway was responsible for the construction of only the Darlington–York section of the line, a policy which brought allegations from shareholders in Durham that the Stockton and Darlington interests were deliberately delaying the construction of the northern section in order to protect their southern markets for Auckland coal. This led to a growing lack of confidence in the Great North of England board on the part of a large number of shareholders and this was reinforced in January 1841 by the resignation of Thomas Storey, the company's engineer, in protest at the long delay in the line's completion and the fact that the construction cost of the Darlington–York section alone was in excess of the estimate for the entire route between York and Newcastle.[21] Since its dividend record was disappointing, averaging only 3 per cent in the first three years of the company's operation after 1841, the Great North of England directors were more than happy in the spring of 1845, under pressure from shareholders, to negotiate a favourable leasing arrangement with George Hudson's Newcastle and Darlington Junction Railway, which then became the York and Newcastle Railway.[22]

If this venture into the highly speculative business of trunk-line development during the country's first 'railway mania' was hardly an example of shining entrepreneurship, then it remains to be said that in its local context the Stockton and Darlington Railway was proving to be an outstanding success. Between 1831 and 1835 the annual dividend varied between 6 and 8 per cent but from 1835 to 1841 'the Company reaped in a liberal measure the reward of a prudent policy and good management'.[23] Between 1839 and 1841 the annual dividend was 15 per cent, the highest by far of any railway in the country. This was a reflection of the prosperity derived from the company's expanding mineral traffic from the Auckland coalfield to the Tees. At a time when other railway companies were dependent upon revenue from the carriage of passengers in the face of the last vestiges of competition for freight traffic from canals and turnpikes,[24] the Stockton and Darlington line was still fulfilling the function demanded of it by the original promoters – a mineral railway with only a secondary interest in passenger and freight transport. The company's dividend record was also reflected in the value of its shares. By 1841 each of the original £100 shares was worth £260 but far from their ownership becoming dispersed the pattern of maintained holdings had exhibited a large measure of stability after 1830. Such share transfers as took place were usually between the principal Quaker holders. In 1840 the largest single shareholder was Thomas Richardson with 141 shares. Four years later he transferred ten of these shares to himself and Joseph Pease jointly and sold the remainder to Joseph and his brothers, John and Henry. In 1842 Joseph had acquired a portion of the Backhouse family holding and with Edward Pease's original investment this meant that the Peases were the largest shareholders, possessing 239 shares, almost 25 per cent of the total.[25] Within a period of twenty years the family's original investment of £13,000 had risen in value to well over £60,000.

In the 1830s the effect of the coal trade on Middlesbrough was profound. At the census of 1831 the population was 154; in 1841 it was 5,463. An entirely new community of railway employees, coal heavers and seamen had been created as a result of railway promotion and Quaker initiative. In 1838 the new settlement, characterised by a symmetrical gridiron street pattern, was sufficiently noteworthy to receive its first royal visitor, the Duke of Sussex, whose congratulations on the 'rising prosperity of your little town' were acknowledged by William Fallows, the agent of the Stockton and Darlington Railway, with the observation that whilst Middlesbrough had yet to acquire the paraphernalia of civic institutions 'yet we have far greater pleasure in seeing those institutions rising up in the midst of us, by our own industry and exertions, growing with our growth and strengthening with our strength'.[26] In 1839 five improved shipping staithes were constructed by the Middlesbrough Owners for lease to the Stockton and Darlington Railway and they were complemented in 1842 by the opening of the Middlesbrough dock, the product of the initiative of Joseph Pease and his financial collaborator, Henry Birkbeck. With ancillary coal drops and railway sidings, the dock was constructed at a cost of £140,000.[27] This impressive installation, capable of accommodating 150 colliers and 1,200 loaded waggons, was also leased to the railway pending its purchase and this was accomplished in 1849 when the ownership of the dock and its associated facilities was vested in the Stockton and Darlington Company for the sum of £160,000.[28]

In the wake of the coal trade Middlesbrough began a slow process of industrial diversification. The first enterprise of any note was the Middlesbrough Pottery, inaugurated in 1834 by Richard Otley, the first secretary of the Stockton and Darlington Railway, and several associates. This was followed in 1835 by the construction of boat and shipyards by John Gilbert Holmes, the leading light of the town's first temperance society and subsequently described as 'the only *gentleman*' resident on Middlesbrough's 'turbulent industrial frontier'.[29] In 1842 the Stockton and Darlington Railway itself opened a workshop for the repair of locomotives and other rolling stock and, with the financial backing of the Peases and Thomas Richardson, extended the line to the mouth of the Tees at Redcar in 1846.[30] But the most significant venture by far was the iron foundry and rolling mill opened by Henry Bolckow and his partner John Vaughan on a modest six-acre site in August 1841 for the manufacture of bar iron, rails and castings. Whatever Joseph Pease's personal involvement in inducing Bolckow and Vaughan to invest in an untried industrial location, it is certainly the case that he was able to secure land and coal supplies for the new company at favourable rates and also to provide the partners with letters of recommendation.[31]

Middlesbrough's early urban and industrial development, together with the growth in population, caused the historian J. W. Ord to characterise the town in 1846 as 'one of the commercial prodigies of the nineteenth century' as evidenced by its 'proud array of ships, docks, warehouses, churches, foundries, wharves etc.'[32] In reality this 'Arabian Nights' vision was premature on several counts. The new town, for example, contrary to the expectation of its Quaker founders and Joseph Pease in particular, was failing to conform to any notion of a 'model' community as the symmetry of the original estate plan was gradually abandoned in the face of the needs of industry and building speculation. Overcrowding was an emerging problem and some areas of the estate were proving to be unsuitable for residential accommodation because of their low elevation and consequent dampness. In the early 1840s, moreover, the pottery enterprise was in severe financial difficulties and the firm had to be reconstituted by Joseph Pease, who not only provided fresh capital but also revitalised the flagging management by introducing the young Isaac Wilson of Kendal, a relative by marriage, to the firm.[33] The predicament of Bolckow and Vaughan, however, was not so easily resolved. Almost from the beginning they were handicapped by the precipitate rise in the price of Scottish blackband pig iron, their major raw material (from under £2 per ton in 1842 to nearly £6 in 1846), under the stimulus of the railway mania of the mid-1840s.[34] This undermined the economic rationale of the location of the Middlesbrough Ironworks and in 1845 Bolckow and Vaughan decided to construct their own blast furnaces at Witton Park in the centre of the Auckland coalfield with the intention of using such local clayband ironstone deposits as were available.[35] These soon proved to be inadequate in quantity and the partners were obliged to seek other ore supplies from south Cleveland. Thus, by the late 1840s Bolckow and Vaughan were in the unfortunate position of having to ship iron ore from Whitby to the Tees for transhipment on the Stockton and Darlington Railway to Witton Park and the resulting pig iron had then to be transported back along the line to the Middlesbrough Ironworks for the final stages of manufacture. Confronted by extremely high transport costs, the company was ill prepared to meet the downturn in the demand for iron which followed the national decline in railway construction after 1847 and the commercial crisis of 1847–8 when the Bank of England raised its discount rate to the punitive level of 8 per cent in order to restore bullion stocks in the face of unusually high grain and cotton imports. At this time the company was in the process of laying off large numbers of workers and was saved from the prospect of bankruptcy by the personal intervention of Joseph Pease, who persuaded his fellow Stockton and

Darlington directors to stand security for a loan of £20,000 from London bankers.[36]

These unfortunate developments in the iron trade were compounded by the growing competition of Hartlepool and West Hartlepool as coal-exporting ports with good docking facilities at the northern end of the mouth of the Tees. The Hartlepool dock had been constructed in the 1830s to serve local collieries, but the West Hartlepool project, which was completed in 1847 as the brainchild of Ralph Ward Jackson, was the final link in a rail network capable of competing far more effectively than the Clarence Railway for a portion of the Auckland coal trade. All of this had not gone unnoticed in Darlington. Indeed, the Middlesbrough dock was constructed by Joseph Pease in order to enhance the competitiveness of Middlesbrough as a port.[37] Ironically, the usefulness of the dock was impaired in the later 1840s by a serious decline in the navigable state of the river due to the good intentions of the Tees Navigation Company, whose admirable policy of constructing jetties to contain the channel had produced the perverse effect of rendering the bed of the river uneven.[38] To make matters worse the Stockton and Darlington Railway had leased the dues of the Navigation Company for an annual rental of £8,200 in 1845. At first sight this was a shrewd move in the company's efforts to undermine the position of its northern rival, the Clarence Railway, which had had its own shipping point at Port Clarence since 1833. The advantage of the leasing arrangement for the Stockton and Darlington interest was that the more dues which were paid at Port Clarence the less rent the company would have to pay. The flaw in this plan was exposed when the Clarence Railway was linked to the new harbour at West Hartlepool. This virtually ended coal shipments from Port Clarence and therefore threw the whole burden of the rental on to the Stockton and Darlington Company. The situation could not easily be resolved by the termination of the lease since this would invoke a penalty payment of £3,000 which the Stockton and Darlington Company could ill afford. The only solution was a transfer in the control of the river, a policy which was actively canvassed by Joseph Pease after 1849 and which eventually bore fruit in the establishment of a statutory body – the Tees Conservancy Commission – under Admiralty auspices in 1852.[39]

The period between 1847 and 1851 was one of severe crisis and uncertainty for the Stockton and Darlington Company. Whilst the unfavourable situation at Middlesbrough cast a shadow over its future, a further source of weakness was to be found at the opposite end of the line. In October 1847 the company had taken a 999-year lease of both the Middlesbrough and Redcar Railway and the Wear Valley Railway at a rental equivalent to 6 per cent of their respective share capitals.[40] The Wear Valley Company, which had been formed in 1845, was itself the product of other Weardale lines which had been projected by groups of

Stockton and Darlington directors after 1840 to exploit the considerable limestone deposits of west Durham and also to form a link between the Derwent Iron Company in the north-west of the county and the mouth of the Tees. Although the Derwent enterprise had been founded as recently as 1841, it possessed 14 blast furnaces and 35 coal and iron-stone pits by the end of 1846, making it the largest iron-making concern in England and second only to the Dowlais Company of South Wales in the entire country.[41] Such rapid expansion was made possible by the receipt of large advances from the Northumberland and Durham District Bank, but even without the trade recession of the later 1840s the Derwent Company would have been hard pressed to meet its annual interest commitments. As it was, it was sustained by the provision of extraordinarily liberal credit facilities by its bankers, a policy which kept the concern in existence but one which could not prevent a reduction in the Stockton and Darlington Company's revenues on the Wear Valley line of sufficient severity to threaten the financial solvency of the entire railway. The annual rental for the Middlesbrough and Redcar and Wear Valley lines was well in excess of £48,000 and between 1847 and 1850 the Stockton and Darlington Company was able to meet this commitment only by drawing heavily on its reserve or contingent fund. In October 1847 this had stood at £146,303, but by July 1850 it had fallen to £8,000.[42] In the financial year 1849/50 the net revenue from all three lines amounted to only £28,500 (the total revenue was £169,608) and in these circumstances the Stockton and Darlington board decided to attempt an amalgamation with the leased lines. A Bill was drawn up but it failed to win the support of the Wear Valley shareholders. The lessors did, however, negotiate an arrangement under which they agreed to forgo the full amount of the guaranteed annual rental until commerical conditions improved, with the proviso that if the company's receipts were insufficient to meet the lower rental (between 4 and 5 per cent) the lessors were entitled to the whole of the net revenue of all three lines.[43]

Throughout the period of crisis in the affairs of the Stockton and Darlington Company the Pease family was under considerable financial strain. As early as June 1846 Edward Pease noted in his diary that 'from the family business of the Coal Trade, Collieries and in the Woollen Mills there is no income' and in his reflections on the year 1847 he concluded that 'in no preceding year have I passed through such a depth of conflict and trial owing to the extended trading and mining concerns of [my sons]'.[44] In that year both Joseph and his younger brother Henry received financial assistance from their brother-in-law Francis Gibson and Henry Birkbeck, and following the failure of the Union Bank of Newcastle in October 1847 Edward reluctantly agreed to sustain Joseph's credit as treasurer to the Stockton and Darlington Company by giving him an unlimited financial guarantee.[45] At the end of 1849 Edward's railway shares had depreciated in value by 'not less than thirty to forty thousand pounds' and in the aftermath of the company's revised leasing arrangements of 1850 he commented that 'S. and D. shares once deemed worth £360 have been sold at £30, so that property once deemed worth £60,000 now worth £3,000'.[46] As for Joseph, the perpetual fear of bankruptcy began to affect his health; throughout the latter half of 1847 he was suffering from insomnia and depression, and by the early months of 1849 the first symptoms of glaucoma which was to lead to total blindness later in life had appeared.[47] There were, however, two sources of relief which eased Joseph's financial plight. In 1846 he had joined his father as a partner in Robert Stephenson and Co. and in 1849 his share of the profits amounted to £7,000 – the product of contract prices for locomotives which had been negotiated before the onset of the recession.[48] Furthermore, the coal trade began to revive towards the end of 1848 as the industry adjusted to the termination of the Limitation of the Vend in May 1845, an event which was the logical outcome of the surplus capacity generated by the speculative boom in the Great Northern Coalfield in the period 1836–43. Although there was a marked decline in investment in new colliery winnings after 1844 (there were approximately 29 in the period 1844–50 compared with 61 between 1836 and 1843) as the coastal and local trades stagnated, colliery owners were considerably aided by the growing demand for coke for ironworks and railways.[49] The effect of this was to increase the demand for 'inferior' small coal so that by the end of the decade coke ovens were an increasingly common sight in the north-east, not least at the Peases' own collieries in the Auckland coalfield where there may have been as many as 500 coke ovens by 1850.[50]

The weakness of the Stockton and Darlington Company in the late 1840s lay in the way in which it had developed – as a mineral railway with limited interest in the carriage of merchandise freight and passengers. This meant that in times of trade recession, with falling demand for basic raw materials, it did not have the staying power of the larger, if less profitable, trunk lines whose revenues were sustained by their greater concentration on passenger traffic. The company was therefore dependent for its survival on the good will of its bankers and, in particular, the extensive Quaker financial connections of Edward and Joseph Pease. Impressive though these were, the financial situation confronting the company in 1848 was so serious that the Stockton and Darlington management committee had been prepared to lease their entire line to George Hudson's York, Newcastle and Berwick Railway with a view to an eventual amalgamation. This arrangement failed to come to fruition only because of Hudson's spectacular bankruptcy in the following year.[51] Since the Stockton and Darlington Company had paid a dividend of 13 per cent as recently as 1847 and was well known as the most profitable of railway enterprises, its experiences in the later 1840s provide a striking insight into the nature of British economic development in the mid-nineteenth century. Whilst Samuel Smiles – himself an employee of the South Eastern Railway – proclaimed in 1856 that 'Anybody who devotes himself to making money, body and soul, can scarcely fail to make himself rich, very little, very little brains will do',[52] the reality of the middle decades of the nineteenth century was very different. They were, in fact, marked by 'relentless competitive pressure' on businessmen as they sought to deal as best they could with the squeeze on profitability following the major investment booms which were such a prominent feature of the British industrial economy after 1830.[53] As Joseph Pease stated in evidence before the Parliamentary Committee on Commercial Distress in 1848:

> I know that for the last 10 or 12 years anything like the regular pursuit of business in manufactures has, in nine cases out of ten, been entirely profitless, from the great fluctuations of capital and the value of articles; in fact the man who has made money has thriven by watching the rise and fall of his stock in trade; but the profits of industry have been perfectly nominal.[54]

It is not surprising, therefore, that by the end of 1850 Joseph was anxiously awaiting an increase in the Stockton and Darlington Company's trade and dues from the carriage of its traditional goods – coal, ironstone and limestone – and this was dependent upon a revival in prosperity for the heavy industries of north-east England in general and the Tees and Wear valleys in particular.[55]

What happened to the economy of Teesside after 1850 hardly counted as a revival in prosperity: it was regional economic growth of an altogether different pace and magnitude. The stimulus for expansion was provided by John Vaughan's discovery in June 1850 of major ironstone deposits at Eston on the north-facing side of the Cleveland Hills near to Middlesbrough. It had been known for many years that iron ore was present in north-east Yorkshire. Bolckow and Vaughan were themselves importing ironstone from Whitby to the south of Cleveland and from the mid-eighteenth century small quantities of ironstone had been quarried from coastal outcrops or collected from beaches.[56] The significance of Vaughan's discovery was that he had identified the main seam at a point where the ironstone was at its thickest and near to good transport facilities.[57] Bolckow and Vaughan acted immediately to secure favourable leases for the mineral and by the end of 1850, with the aid of a temporary tramway (which was soon replaced by a branch line to the Middlesbrough and Redcar Railway), they had sent 4,000 tons of ironstone to their Witton Park furnaces. In the following year 188,000 tons of ironstone were produced at Bolckow and Vaughan's

Eston royalty whilst the Derwent Iron Company, which was also hand-icapped by inadequate local ore supplies, had begun to exploit the main seam on the Earl of Zetland's royalty at Upleatham.[58]

The effect of Vaughan's discovery on the finances of the Stockton and Darlington Company was dramatic. By the end of 1851 it was able to resume the payment of the guaranteed rental to the Middlesbrough and Redcar and Wear Valley Railways and also to discharge all of the arrears.[59] Although the revenues accruing from the Witton Park traffic were reduced by the decision of Bolckow and Vaughan to construct three blast furnaces at the Middlesbrough Ironworks, with a further six coming into operation at new works at Eston in 1853, the link with the Derwent Iron Company was especially lucrative. Since the Cleveland ore contained a high proportion of silica, large quantities of limestone were required for fluxing and this also generated additional mineral traffic on the Stockton and Darlington line.[60] As the historian of the North Eastern Railway Company pointed out:

> The Stockton and Darlington Railway Company had reason to congratulate themselves on the quite fortuitous circumstance that their system at one point touched the very edge of the ironstone field and at another, 54 miles away, was in contact with the princi-pal ironworks of Co. Durham . . . It practically put £10,000 a year into the hands of the fortunate company. Dividends rose from 4 to 10 per cent and the holders of Stockton and Darlington stock became, as at an earlier period in the history of the Company, the most envied of all railway proprietors.[61]

On visiting Teesside in 1861 Gladstone observed that Middlesbrough was 'the youngest child of England's enterprise . . . it is an infant, but an infant Hercules'.[62] It was an apt description of a booming industrial town which had begun to outgrow the commercial limitations set by dependance on the coal-shipping trade. In 1851 the population had only edged up to 7,431 after the initial spurt in the 1830s. In 1861 it had reached 19,416 and in 1871, 39,563. By the latter date the town posses-sed those civic institutions which William Fallows had foreseen on the occasion of the visit of the Duke of Sussex in 1838. In 1853, when the principal civic dignitary in Darlington was the Chief Bailiff appointed by the Bishop of Durham, the town was incorporated as a borough with Henry Bolckow as the first mayor, and following the Reform Act of 1867 it became a single-member parliamentary constituency with Bolc-kow again serving as the first member. In 1857 Joseph Pease recorded in his diary, with evident astonishment, that in 1851 the Stockton and Darlington Company had booked 61,319 passengers at Middlesbrough; in 1854 the figure had risen to 89,679 and in 1857 it had reached 109,577.[63] The basis of this expansion was the iron trade in all its

branches. Between 1851 and 1857, as existing capacity was expanded
and new works established, the production of pig iron on Teesside
increased tenfold. In addition to Bolckow and Vaughan, the firm of
Bernhard Samuelson at South Bank and Gilkes, Wilson, Leatham and
Company at Cargo Fleet were engaged in the construction of major
blast furnace capacity on the line of the Middlesbrough and Redcar
Railway. Other important pioneering firms were the Tees-side Iron
Works of William Hopkins and Thomas Snowdon, the Ormesby Ironworks of Alexander Brodie Cochrane, and on the north bank of the
Tees the Bell Brothers' Port Clarence works headed by the highly
talented metallurgist Isaac Lowthian Bell. Further west at Darlington,
the South Durham Ironworks completed the construction of two blast
furnaces in 1855 and thus inaugurated the first major industrial
development in the old market town which had provided much of the
impetus for the Stockton and Darlington Railway.[64] A number of these
firms were, in a sense, protégés of the Pease family. Bolckow and
Vaughan is an obvious case, but of the proprietors of the firm of Gilkes,
Wilson, Leatham and Company the Quaker Isaac Wilson had been
induced to settle in Middlesbrough in the 1840s by Joseph Pease (see
above, p. 28) and was himself father-in-law of the latter's cousin,
Joseph Beaumont Pease, whilst Charles Leatham was Joseph's own
son-in-law, having married Rachel, the elder of his two surviving
daughters, in 1851. The link with the South Durham Ironworks was
even more direct: the firm was chaired by Henry Pease and contained
among its directors a number of well-known Stockton and Darlington
shareholders. Similarly, William Hopkins and Thomas Snowdon were
closely associated with the Stockton and Darlington Railway.[65] What
was emerging in the 1850s, therefore, was not only a new and
geographically compact metallurgical district with excellent transport
facilities along the 'fuel artery' of the Stockton and Darlington Railway
and its related concerns, but also a group of firms which were tied
together by Quaker finance and the inevitable ties of kinship which
were such a prominent feature of the Society of Friends.

In the year of Gladstone's visit, $\frac{1}{2}$ million tons of pig iron was
produced on Teesside and by 1867 nearly 1 million tons. In 1873, with
the iron trade booming, over 2 million tons was produced, nearly
one-third of the total British output. In 1856 the output of Cleveland
ironstone had already reached $1\frac{1}{4}$ million tons; in 1873 it exceeded $5\frac{1}{2}$
million tons.[66] By the latter year Teesside possessed more than 90 blast
furnaces and was the most important pig-iron-producing district in the
world. It was also in the forefront of technological advance and this had
been a necessary prerequisite for the expansion of the north-eastern
malleable iron trade during a period when the prices of the products –
principally rails and ship plates – in which the region specialised, were
low and fairly stable until the early 1870s. It is true that local

ironmasters had the advantage of excellent communications enjoying easy access to the high-quality blast furnace coke of south Durham, but it is important to note that the Cleveland ironstone, although available in prodigious quantity, was of poor quality in terms of iron content. To overcome this problem a series of innovations which came to be known as 'Cleveland practice' was introduced in the mid–1860s. These included blast furnaces which were much larger than elsewhere, direct-acting blowing engines of high efficiency, and regenerative hot-blast stoves. Together, these innovations maintained the domestic and international competitiveness of the Teesside iron industry until well into the 1870s.[67]

At the beginning of 1851, after a number of gloomy references in his diary to the depreciation of railway property, Edward Pease began to take note of 'The discovery of rich extensive veins of ironstone under Eston Nab' and the advantages that this would confer on the Stockton and Darlington Railway. In July he observed with some satisfaction the construction of the Derwent Iron Company's private branch railway from the Middlesbrough and Redcar line to the Zetland ironstone royalty at Upleatham. By the end of the year, however, he had begun to indulge in ruminations on the dangers of his family being caught up in yet another series of business speculations whose 'consequences are to be dreaded'.[68] In the same month he recorded the following diary entry:

> I see in the paper a Notice for a railway near Guisboro'; the prompting cause is the abounding of Ironstone in the vicinity. The prospective scheme introduces my mind into many doubts as to the inviting of my family.[69]

On this occasion Edward was right to be worried. The Middlesbrough and Guisborough Railway, with two branches to the Cleveland Hills, was promoted by Joseph Pease and his oldest son Joseph Whitwell in November 1851. In concept the projected railway differed little from the mineral lines which had been promoted by groups of Stockton and Darlington directors in the 1840s, but it failed to attract any significant interest from within the Stockton and Darlington board. It was, of course, launched at a time when the company was regaining its composure after the severe financial difficulties of the late 1840s when Joseph's own credit had been pressed to the limit, and the joint promoters were not helped by the comment of John Vaughan, the discoverer of the Cleveland main seam, that because of the uncertain commercial value of the ironstone the scheme was 'almost chimerical'.[70] The Peases, however, pressed on with their project and demonstrated their faith in the future of Cleveland ironstone by subscribing £5,000 to the project and also by taking a lease on the Cod Hill royalty at Hutton Lowcross, near Guisborough. The subscription list filled up slowly and in June 1852 the Act for the Middlesbrough and Guisborough Railway received the royal assent. After parliamentary sanction to build their line had been obtained, the directors immediately encountered difficulties in raising the necessary finance. Although Joseph had been able to persuade his fellow Stockton and Darlington directors to subscribe £16,750 out of a total investment of £56,075, the problem was solved only by the offer of a guaranteed dividend by the Peases, rising from 4 per cent in the first year of operation to 6 per cent in the fifth and subsequent years.[71] In view of the Stockton and Darlington Company's recent experience of guaranteed rentals and the promoters' own ignorance of metallurgy it is difficult to resist the conclusion that the Middlesbrough and Guisborough line was an ambitious, if not reckless speculation. It was fortunate for the Peases that John Vaughan's doubts were unfounded. From the start the new railway, which opened for mineral traffic in November 1853, was a commercial success and was soon absorbed by the Stockton and Darlington Company in 1858 on terms of a guaranteed income of 6 per cent on a capital of £96,000.[72]

Less risky, but far more controversial, was the proposal for a rail link between Darlington and Barnard Castle, a small market town 16 miles further to the west up the Tees valley. Joseph Pease had authorised surveys for a possible line as early at 1833[73] but it was not until 1844, when the carpet and shoe lace manufacturers of Barnard Castle joined forces with the Stockton and Darlington Company, that the project became a live issue. The stage was set for a repetition of the events of 1819 since the main objector to the proposed line was Henry Vane, the second Duke of Cleveland who, like his father, was intent on protecting his 'private comforts' in the face of the onslaught of the obnoxious railway and all its works.[74] After an uncomfortable interview, during which the Duke had pointed to the excellence of the turnpike road, Joseph remarked to the Barnard Castle representatives, 'You see the man with whom you have to deal; beyond his own private interests and comforts he has not a feeling. All argument with him is in vain.'[75] Perhaps hoping that the passage of time and the evident benefits of railways would mellow the Duke's opposition the Barnard Castle interest waited until 1852 before reviving the scheme. With Joseph's backing agreement was reached with the Stockton and Darlington Company that it should work the line on completion and charge only half the costs of maintenance and haulage until the Darlington and Barnard Castle dividend reached 4 per cent. Joseph also agreed to ensure the subscription of £22,000 to the project.[76] A Bill of incorporation was drawn up and was considered by a Commons committee in May 1853. The Duke of Cleveland, however, was still implacable in his opposition, having convinced himself that the line was 'the device of a scheming and Artful Individual to deceive the people of Barnard Castle for his own benefit' since it would reduce the cost of transporting coal along the Tees valley from the Peases' Auckland collieries.[77] Although Joseph argued before the Commons committee that an alternative route, north-east from Barnard Castle to Bishop Auckland, would be of equal advantage to his interest, the bill was rejected in June.[78] Ironically, when the promoters renewed their application in the autumn they were confronted by a rival scheme based upon the Barnard Castle–Bishop Auckland route as part of a grandiose strategy for linking the ports of Liverpool and Sunderland. This was the Barnard Castle and Bishop Auckland Junction Railway and it was the product of an alliance between two Barnard Castle solicitors and the West Hartlepool interests led by Ralph Ward Jackson, who alleged that the aim of Joseph Pease was 'to control autocratically the entire district'.[79] This kind of criticism was reminiscent of that of Christopher Tennant and it is *prima facie* evidence of the fact that, despite his reputation for sincerity and purity of motive, to some sections of commercial (and aristocratic) opinion in the north-east of England Joseph was no more than a self-seeking speculator. In this particular case it was also an obvious indication of Ward Jackson's determination to break the Stockton and Darlington Company's stranglehold over the greater part of the mineral traffic emanating from the Auckland coalfield. By the autumn of 1853 the Duke of Cleveland was in the grip of an attack of 'Pease-phobia'[80] which could only have been intensified when a Commons committee approved the Darlington and Barnard Castle line in May 1854 on the grounds that it offered few engineering problems and was strongly supported in Barnard Castle. The line was eventually opened in July 1856, when the Duke of Cleveland attended the customary ceremony. The Duke expressed the hope that all past differences between himself and the Pease family would be speedily forgotten, but cynics no doubt noted that he was to be permitted to nominate a director for life.[81]

In the developing network of rail communications in the mid-nineteenth century the successful completion of one line often led to an agitation for further extensions. Such was the case with the Darlington and Barnard Castle Railway. It has already been noted that Cleveland ironstone, with its significant silica content, was not of the highest quality and by the mid-1850s the Derwent Iron Company was mixing Cleveland ore with richer hematite ores obtained from the Whitehaven district of Cumberland via the Newcastle and Carlisle Railway.[82] Not unnaturally the Teesside ironmakers wished to adopt the same practice, but in order to do so they had to import hematite ore from Ulverston in south Cumberland by a tortuous route to the south via Normanton and Leeds. Now, the completion of the Darlington and Barnard Castle Railway had made it a practicable proposition to link the Stockton and Darlington network with Lancashire and Cumberland by traversing the Pennines over a more direct route into Westmorland.[83] The result was a proposal in August 1856 for the launching of the South Durham and Lancashire Union Railway project to form a link between Barnard Castle and the Lancaster and Carlisle Railway at Tebay. The chief promoter was Henry Pease in collaboration with banking interests in Kendal and five other members of the Stockton and Darlington management committee. The line was estimated to cost £375,000 to construct and the Pease family alone subscribed £15,000 to the project.[84]

The South Durham and Lancashire Union Railway Act received the royal assent in July 1857 and the resulting line, which was completed in 1861, was one of the triumphs of mid-Victorian railway engineering.[85] The Stainmoor summit was 1,374 feet above sea level and Robert Stephenson and Co. were invited to design a new and more powerful locomotive to cope with the severe gradients.[86] Thomas Bouch of Shildon, the designer of the ill fated Tay Bridge, was the engineer of the line, which possessed some of the most spectacular railway viaducts in Britain, the three largest being constructed of wrought-iron girders from ironworks on Teesside.[87] In 1856, at the inception of the project, Joseph Pease had commented to his brother that if 'the busy, bustling, whistling railway ever traverse Stainmoor's wintry wastes, or the inhabitants beyond be supplied with cheapened and excellent fuel . . . they that profit thereby, and rejoice therein, will doubtless have much to thank thee for in thy exertions and perseverance'.[88] No doubt the romantic sentiments were sincere, but the new railway was a hard-headed commercial proposition. In 1858, in the same year that the Wear Valley, Middlesbrough and Redcar, and Middlesbrough and Guisborough Railways were absorbed, the Stockton and Darlington Company also took over the Darlington and Barnard Castle Railway, thus reconfirming its critically important position in the mineral traffic of south Durham and north Yorkshire and preparing the way for a valuable link with the iron-smelting district of Low Furness in south Cumberland. Indeed, the South Durham and Lancashire Union line was worked by the Stockton and Darlington Company and was itself absorbed in 1862. When the new line opened for mineral traffic on 4 July 1861, six trains hauling 600 tons of Durham coal and coke left the Auckland coalfield for Tebay, whilst 150 tons of hematite ore reached Barnard Castle from the west. A new pattern of mineral traffic was about to be established in the north of England and the principal sufferer was the North Eastern Railway Company (NER). The South Durham and Lancashire Union Railway virtually obliterated the NER's trans-Pennine mineral traffic, not least from the Peases' own collieries where the amount of coal and coke destined for the Morecambe and Ulverston districts fell from 20,000 tons in the last six months of 1860 to only 959 tons in the corresponding period of 1861.[89]

The NER had been formed in 1854 during the era of large-scale amalgamations in the British railway system. It was the product of the merger of the York and North Midland and the Leeds Northern Railway Companies with the York, Newcastle and Berwick Railway.[90] The NER controlled 720 route miles covering Northumberland, Durham and much of north Yorkshire and was at that time Britain's largest railway company, a fact which had not escaped the notice of a select committee of the House of Commons appointed in 1852 under the chairmanship of Edward Cardwell to consider the likely commercial effects of railway amalgamations. The Cardwell Committee took a hostile view of amalgamations in principle, but its suspension of the NER merger was overridden in Parliament. The company was formed, moreover, when the Cleveland ore field was in the early stages of exploitation and the new concern naturally wished to procure a portion of the mineral traffic as well as to consolidate its position in the carriage of coal and freight in Durham and Northumberland. It might be thought, therefore, that the NER would have enjoyed a contentious relationship with the Stockton and Darlington Company, but almost from the date of the merger the two companies worked together harmoniously. One factor encouraging this from the Stockton and Darlington perspective was the removal of George Hudson from the affairs of the amalgamated companies; he had been a notable *bête noire* of Joseph Pease in the years before his downfall. Merger discussions actually took place shortly after the formation of the NER but they were premature and ultimately proved abortive. Nevertheless, under an agreement of January 1853 the two companies agreed to avoid mineral competition as far as possible and to co-operate for their mutual benefit.[91] In 1855, for example, the Act for the incorporation of the Deerness Valley Railway, which had been promoted by Joseph Pease and Joseph Whitwell Pease to serve their new colliery on the royalty of Viscount Boyne at Waterhouses to the west of Durham, provided for the working of the line by the NER, some of whose directors had taken shares to the value of £15,000.[92] A more important indication of the close relationship between the two companies was provided by the collapse of the Derwent Iron Company in 1857 as a result of the failure of the Northumberland and Durham District Bank. This was one of a rush of mid-Victorian banking calamities which were the direct consequence of overlending to industrial concerns. They were to reach a climax with the failure of the City of Glasgow Bank in 1878, an event which marked the withdrawal of the banking system from the long-term financing of industry.[93] The Derwent Iron Company had grown too rapidly for a banking concern which had been imprudent enough to lend £1 million on the security of £250,000 of promissory notes and a mortgage of £100,000 on the company's plant.[94]

The problem posed by the collapse of the Derwent Company was that it generated a considerable mineral traffic in the north-east of England with a value in excess of £60,000 per annum on the Stockton and Darlington line alone and with so much capital sunk in local transport facilities there were pressing commercial reasons for preventing the break-up of such a large concern.[95] In 1858 the company was kept afloat by parties already connected with it and was also considerably aided by the joint action of the Stockton and Darlington Company and the NER, who, as major trade creditors, agreed to the suspension of traffic dues for a period of two years up to a combined total for both companies of £200,000.[96] The firm which eventually emerged in 1864 after a protracted process of reconstruction[97] was the Consett Iron Company, which, in marked contrast to its predecessor, proved to be technically efficient and ultimately highly profitable.[98] Throughout this period members of the Pease family, in particular Joseph Whitwell, were actively involved in financing the reconstruction[99] and it was due to Pease influence that their nominee, David Dale, was introduced to the management of the company. In 1846 Dale had begun his business career as a clerk in the Wear Valley Railway Company's office and in 1854 Joseph Pease had appointed him secretary to the Middlesbrough and Guisborough Railway. After the reconstruction of the Consett Iron Company, Dale was appointed joint managing director (with Jonathan Priestman), and on account of his intimate personal links with the Darlington Quaker community the maintenance of close commercial ties between the expanding Pease industrial empire and the reconstructed iron company was assured.[100]

Other factors impelling the Stockton and Darlington Company and the NER to greater co-operation were the threat to the former posed by the ambitious Ralph Ward Jackson and to the latter by attempted encroachments on its north-eastern traffic by other large railway companies. In Ward Jackson's case the successful merger in 1853 of his Hartlepool West Harbour and Dock Company with the Stockton and Hartlepool Railway (which had extended its operations by taking a perpetual lease of the Clarence Railway in 1851) inaugurated 'The Struggle for the Cleveland Ironstone District'.[101] Ward Jackson was intent upon securing access to the ironstone royalties leased by the Bell brothers at Normanby and Skelton. His major and obvious problem was how to link the ore field with a communications network centred on the north bank of the Tees. This he proposed to overcome in 1859 by projecting the Durham and Cleveland Union Railway with trains crossing the Tees on a steam ferry. The Stockton and Darlington response was aggressive in the extreme. As well as proposing to extend the Middlesbrough and Redcar Railway to Saltburn to increase mineral traffic from the Upleatham and Skelton ironstone royalties, the company proposed to connect the Middlesbrough and Guisborough Railway with Ward Jackson's own West Hartlepool system by means of a swing-bridge across the Tees.[102] After an intense parliamentary struggle fought with 'consummate skill and self-possession' by Ward Jackson and Joseph Pease the former was permitted to construct a railway from

Guisborough to ironstone mines at Skinningrove; there was to be no link to the Tees, thus placing the new line, to be known as the Cleveland Railway, at the mercy of the Stockton and Darlington Company. On the other hand, the latter was not permitted to bridge the Tees, although the Saltþurn extension was sanctioned. As Tomlinson observed it was something of a drawn battle.[103] Eventually, after further parliamentary struggles and much local obstruction emanating from the Pease-dominated Tees Conservancy Commission, Ward Jackson achieved his objective. In 1861 he received parliamentary sanction to extend the Cleveland Railway to a jetty on the Normanby estate from which loaded waggons of ironstone were to be transported across the Tees in open barges.[104] The price paid, however, was a high one: Ward Jackson was financially overstretched and in 1865 his West Hartlepool Company was taken over by the NER.[105]

These events in Cleveland must be viewed in relation to the wider interests of the Stockton and Darlington Company. On the one hand competition for the Cleveland mineral traffic was intensifying and on the other the point had been reached by the end of the 1850s when a choice would have to be made between greater co-operation with the NER or involvement in unwelcome competition with the larger company in west and south Durham. The choice that was made – for an amalgamation with the NER – was precipitated by an attempt launched in 1860 by the London and North Western Railway Company to link the Newcastle and Carlisle Railway with the Stockton and Darlington line via the projected Newcastle and Derwent Railway. This would have been the final link in a line of communication from Liverpool to Newcastle and would have enabled the extraordinarily predatory London and North Western Company to penetrate the heart of the NER system with the possibility of a further link northwards to Edinburgh.[106] In the event, after strong pressure from members of the Pease family, the Stockton and Darlington Company refused to co-operate with the former and the Newcastle and Derwent scheme therefore collapsed. By the time the London and North Western Company had devised a further scheme of invasion involving the construction of a new line of considerable length with running powers over part of the South Durham and Lancashire Union Railway, negotiations between the Stockton and Darlington Company and the NER for an amalgamation were all but complete.[107]

The negotiations began in December 1859 at the York headquarters of the NER.[108] From the outset they went smoothly. The Stockton and Darlington delegation, led by John Pease, Joseph's older brother, and Joseph Whitwell Pease, had as its main objective the establishment of full local control over the old Stockton and Darlington network, preferably by retaining the Darlington-based management committee intact for a period of twenty years. In view of the way in which the line had evolved – as a mineral railway serving local mines and quarries – this was not an unreasonable request, especially when considered from the standpoint of the Pease family with its extensive interests in coal, coke, limestone and ironstone. The NER response was that it would be simpler for certain members of the Stockton and Darlington management committee to join the NER board and that 'to them should be assigned for the specified period the management of Stockton and Darlington traffic'. Mutual good will was evident in the inevitable compromise; following the amalgamation a 'Darlington Committee' would be established which would exist for ten years with a possible extension of two years; two NER directors would sit on the committee whilst three members of the Stockton and Darlington management committee would join the NER board. By March 1860 agreement had been reached in principle and in July 1863 the amalgamation Bill received the royal assent after a remarkably smooth passage through Parliament. In 1862 the NER had absorbed the Newcastle and Carlisle Railway and, as noted above, the Ward Jackson empire succumbed in 1865. By these three amalgamations the NER came to be acknowledged as 'the most complete monopoly in the United Kingdom'.[109]

Although failing health prevented Joseph Pease from taking an active part in the negotiations, it is clear that the Stockton and Darlington delegation acted in accordance with his wishes. Following the agreement of March 1860 Joseph noted in his diary that the decision in favour had been a unanimous one on the Stockton and Darlington board 'save my brother Henry who thinks we merge our usefulness and lose Caste'.[110] It may be assumed that Henry was appeased not only by his appointment as chairman of the Darlington Committee in 1863, an office which he held until the winding up of the committee in 1879, but also by the liberal financial arrangements whereby it was agreed that the Stockton and Darlington section of the shareholders should receive $15\frac{1}{4}$ per cent of the joint receipts as well as the sum of £225 for every £100 of stock.[111]

The death of Joseph Pease in 1872 marks a suitable point to survey the extent of the Peases' industrial and commercial interests and to evaluate the family's contribution to the development of the economy of north-east England. In the former case the most important elements were the mineral interests. Here, the Peases had established two separate firms in the 1850s. Joseph Pease and Partners was concerned with the colliery business and the associated activities of coke ovens and the manufacture of fire-bricks. This firm, which dominated the Auckland and west Durham coalfields, included the Adelaide and St Helens collieries near Bishop Auckland, the Tindale, Sunniside, Peases' West, Bowden Close, Stanley and Wooley collieries near Crook, the Esh Winning, Waterhouses, Ushaw Moor and Brandon collieries to the north and east of Crook, and the Windlestone colliery near Ferryhill. In 1870 their combined output was in excess of 1 million tons and almost one-third of this was converted into coke for smelting purposes on Teesside and the Furness district of Cumberland.[112] By contemporary standards Joseph Pease and Partners was a very large concern indeed, and it certainly provided the senior partner with the highest proportion of his income. In 1859, for example, out of a total income of £54,500 Joseph Pease's colliery interests accounted for £14,500. In 1860 the equivalent figures were £74,000 and £30,000 respectively. In both years his share in Robert Stephenson and Co. was the second most lucrative of his investments (£10,000 in 1859 and £18,000 in 1860).[113] The other mineral concern was J. W. Pease and Co., which had been founded in 1852 as an outlet for the energies of Joseph Whitwell Pease in his desire to exploit the Cleveland ironstone and also to take over the family's existing interests in limestone. The enterprise began in a modest way by developing a small royalty at Hutton Lowcross (see above, p. 35) near Guisborough, but in 1857 the concern rose to prominence in Cleveland as a result of its acquisition of the Upleatham royalty – part of the spoils from the wreckage of the Derwent Iron Company. In 1866 the firm extended its operations to Loftus and Skinningrove on the Yorkshire coast and in the early 1870s, under the stimulus of boom conditions in the Tees iron trade, opened up the Craggs Hall (Brotton) and Lingdale (Moorsholm) mines.[114] By the mid-1870s J. W. Pease and Co. was the largest producer of ironstone in Cleveland with an output of approximately 1 million tons per annum (total Cleveland production in 1872 was 6.3 million tons) and a wage bill in this department alone of well in excess of £100,000 per annum.[115] The limestone interests of the firm were centred on Frosterley and Broadwood in Weardale and an extensive trade was carried on with the Consett Iron Company and the numerous iron-making concerns on Teesside. In the mid-1870s output was in excess of 250,000 tons per annum.[116] The other major industrial interests within the Pease family were the original Darlington woollen mills which were carried on under the style of Henry Pease and Co. and the locomotive-building firm of Robert Stephenson and Co. at Newcastle upon Tyne.[117] Although the latter concern was remarkably profitable in the years up to 1870, despite intense competition in the locomotive business, Henry Pease and Co. seems to have languished for want of adequate management. A completely new mill complex was constructed in 1856, but the impression created is of a firm which in the period after 1860 was overshadowed by other Pease interests and was maintained in existence partly out of sentiment and possibly also for reasons of political expediency (see below, pp. 80, 87). Finally, there was the private banking firm of J. and J. W. Pease, as well as the original Middlesbrough Estate. The latter became the sole property of the Pease family in 1858 and it had come to provide the nucleus of a booming industrial town with a population in excess of 39,000 in 1871; it is well

known that Joseph Pease was able to attract men of the calibre of
Bolckow and Vaughan to an untried industrial location by the offer of
favourable leases and a commitment to build up the social overhead
capital of the Estate in particular and Middlesbrough in general.[118] The
firm of J. and J. W. Pease was the successor to the defunct Pease
Partners Bank of the eighteenth century. Originally referred to as 'the
Treasurers' Department' after Joseph had accepted responsibility for
the financial affairs of the Stockton and Darlington Railway in 1833, it
was reconstituted on a more formal basis as a family partnership in 1853
following the introduction to independent management of Joseph
Whitwell Pease. J. and J. W. Pease was, in reality, the counting house
for the various Pease enterprises – including the Stockton and Darlington Company – which had emerged by the end of the 1850s. After
1863 it also became local banker to the NER and the Consett Iron
Company.[119]

This résumé of the Peases' industrial and commercial interests by
itself assures for the family an important place in the economic history
of north-east England. But it is important to note that, with the exception of Henry Pease and Co., this extensive industrial empire, employing 6,000 people in 1870, owed its origins to the Stockton and Darlington Railway. Whilst it would be absurd to claim that the railway inaugurated the industrial era in the north-east of England as a whole, it is
certainly the case that it played a vitally important role in the economic
and urban development of south and west Durham. Two phases can be
distinguished. The first, from 1825 to 1850, was marked by the opening
up of a new coalfield in south Durham with significant inland sales
augmented by a rapidly developing coastal trade via the Tees. Contrary
to the expectations of its original Pease and Backhouse promoters the
Stockton and Darlington Railway generated new traffic. As Joseph
Pease quickly realised, the railway resolved the problem of wayleaves,
and in establishing an efficient system of bulk transport it cheapened
the cost of entry for new firms into the colliery business. It was these
factors in combination which gave to the Auckland coalfield a competitive edge over its Tyne and Wear rivals in the coastal trade. In this
phase Joseph was at his most active. He became a significant colliery
proprietor and as treasurer and chairman of the Stockton and Darlington management committee drove forward with a policy of expanding
the company's network. He was also the leading figure in the development of Middlesbrough's coal-shipping facilities and laid the foundations for the town's future prosperity as an important metallurgical
centre. By the end of the 1840s the initial impulse to economic growth
in south Durham and north Yorkshire had largely run its course; as
indicated already, the commercial crisis of the later 1840s served only to
highlight this fact, especially in view of the growth of intense rail and
port competition on the north bank of the Tees. The second phase of

development began in 1850 and lasted until the early 1870s. Until quite recently, these years were described by economic historians as constituting 'the mid-Victorian boom' when the British economy aspired to the status of 'the workshop of the world'. Whilst these crude designations have come under increasingly critical scrutiny of late,[120] it is difficult to deny their appropriateness when applied to the economy of Teesside after 1850. Economic growth at this time was extremely rapid, stimulated by the commercial discovery of Cleveland ironstone and the consequent attractiveness of Teesside, and Middlesbrough in particular, as a location for iron making. Although the district benefited from the ease of access to Durham coking coal via the Stockton and Darlington line, it was the close availability of cheap and plentiful ore which provided the mainspring for expansion.[121] Nevertheless, the contribution of the Peases to the construction of new mineral lines on the south bank of the Tees after 1853 should not be discounted and this applies also to the trans-Pennine rail link projected by Henry Pease. It may well be that the contribution of railways to the growth of the economy as a whole was not quantitatively impressive before 1870 but their impact on the development of a well-defined regional economy with an abundance of raw material supplies and excellent port facilities was profound, especially in the years after 1850 when the industrialisation of Britain had reached a mature and more complex stage.[122]

Joseph Pease died a very wealthy man. A conservative estimate of the value of his estate would be £320,000, approximately three times the average estate valuation for Victorian businessmen.[123] This was the fruit of his untiring enterprise, both as railway promoter and mine owner, in opening up the mineral wealth of south Durham and north Yorkshire. His funeral, on 10 February 1872, was marked by the closure of virtually all commercial premises in the centre of Darlington and the flying of flags at half-mast on the Darlington section of the NER. Eulogies were preached from many local pulpits in succeeding weeks, the most fulsome tribute coming from the Reverend Henry Kendall of the Congregational Church who went as far as to paraphrase the Book of Job in his description of Joseph as one whose 'substance was mines and merchandise, and roads and horses of iron, and very extensive possessions; so that this man was the greatest of all the men of the North-East of England'.[124] Kendall's sentiments would have appealed to Samuel Smiles, and in an earlier generation to Dr Andrew Ure,[125] with their rhapsodic faith in the benefits bestowed upon society by technological change, and also to a middle and upper class that was only just beginning to question the moral and spiritual implications of unbridled industrialism. There can be little doubt too that Joseph himself would have appreciated such judgements. As his remarks on the founding of Middlesbrough (see above, p. 22) so eloquently revealed, the man of business was in the vanguard of progress, the architect of change who was laying the foundations for 'a great leap forward' in the well-being of mankind by the creation of enlightened institutions. If Joseph had inherited the Quaker entrepreneurial ethic of the eighteenth century, as embodied in his father, he was also an apostle of a new economic order where, in the words of Richard Cobden, 'Commerce is the grand panacea which like a beneficent medical discovery [serves] to inoculate with the healthy and saving taste for Civilization all the nations of the world'.[126]

To his sons, Joseph Whitwell, Edward, Arthur, Gurney and Charles, Joseph left a rich and diverse legacy. His hopes for the future were founded on his eldest son, who, like himself and his own father before him, had begun his business career in a lowly position. In 1845, at the age of seventeen, Joseph Whitwell had entered the family counting house as a clerk to learn the rudiments of book-keeping.[127] After the merger of 1863 he was one of three members of the Stockton and Darlington management committee to join the York board of the NER. The subsequent fortunes of the Pease family were, in large measure, to lie in his hands.

3

Conformity to the World

The year 1875 marked the fiftieth anniversary of the opening of the Stockton and Darlington Railway. Henry Pease, who was at that time chairman of the Darlington Section of the NER and vice-chairman of the York board, pressed his fellow directors to commemorate the jubilee in a manner which would draw public attention to the fact that the Stockton and Darlington Company 'had the unique distinction of being the starting point of the vast network of lines which covered a considerable portion of the globe'.[1] Henry's intention, therefore, was to celebrate the 'Jubilee of the Railway' itself. Accordingly, the sum of £5,000 was placed at the disposal of a Railway Jubilee Committee charged with the task of devising a suitable form of celebration. It was inevitable that Darlington should be chosen as the location for the festivities and the town council, conscious perhaps that the opening of the railway was the one event which gave Darlington a place in history, voted a sum of £1,000 to the mayor, Henry Fell Pease, 'to be expended in decorating and illuminating the town'.[2]

The jubilee celebrations took place on 27 September 1875 and were an outstanding success. The town was adorned with flags, banners and bunting and the 100,000 visitors were not only able to avail themselves of excursions to places as far away as Saltburn but were also treated to an exhibition of locomotives, old and new, and an impressive display of illuminations and fireworks. The highlights of the day, however, were the unveiling by Harry Vane, the fourth Duke of Cleveland, of a bronze statue of Joseph Pease in the town centre and a sumptuous banquet in the evening attended by representatives of the leading British and foreign railway companies, the local aristocracy and gentry, the Lord Mayor of London and, representing the government, Sir Charles Adderley in his capacity as President of the Board of Trade. After being serenaded by the band of the Grenadier Guards, the diners were subjected to a number of toasts and speeches ranging from 'The Railways of the World' to 'The Army, Navy and Volunteers' and 'The Bishop and Clergy of all denominations'.[3]

At one level the Railway Jubilee can be viewed as an orgy of self-congratulation on the part of the railway companies in general and the NER in particular. By the 1870s they wielded immense influence over the nation's commerce: they were the largest corporate enterprises in the country with a vast army of employees and with powerful support in

the form of 'the railway interest' at Westminster. At another level the
jubilee can be regarded as a celebration by the Peases of the achievements of their own family. Indeed, apart from the Duke of Cleveland,
the most important participants in the day's events were Henry Pease,
his son Henry Fell, and Joseph Whitwell Pease. In this light the jubilee
bears eloquent testimony to the changes which had taken place in the
outlook and lifestyle of the Pease family since the early nineteenth
century; it also provides an insight into the changing world of Quakerism. It may be assumed, for example, that Edward Pease would have
been horrified by the day's proceedings. The presence of military bands
and toasts to the armed forces and clergy at a celebration organised by
one of his sons would in all likelihood have produced in him a state of
pained incredulity. For a man who refused to have his portrait painted
and resisted being photographed almost to the end of his life, the idea of
a statue was anathema.[4] In 1857 the most that he had been prepared to
accept in recognition of his services to the Stockton and Darlington
Railway was a rather effusive address (see above, p. 16) which was read
to him, to the embarrassment of the self-conscious delegation of local
dignitaries, in the living-room of his own home.

In her study of Victorian Quakers Elizabeth Isichei has described
how 'conformity to the world' developed within the Society of Friends
during the nineteenth century.[5] It is significant that the major decisions
affecting Quaker 'peculiarities' were taken in the 1850s. At the beginning of the decade the prohibition against erecting gravestones was
removed and after the Yearly Meeting of 1860 it was declared that
peculiarities in speech and dress were henceforth to be optional. Far
more important, however, was the decision taken in 1859 to permit
Quakers to marry out. None of these changes was introduced without
serious controversy and the *status quo* was defended vehemently 'in
terms of utility, tradition, or asceticism'.[6] That the advocates of change
were victorious was due primarily to an increasing awareness within the
Society of the decline in membership. It was argued, for example, that
the distinctive Quaker dress was hardly calculated to encourage
recruitment and may even have served to alienate younger Quakers.
But the most serious cause of decline was the rule which disowned those
who 'married out': it was argued that this not only led to a direct loss of
members but also, in reducing the pool of potential marriage partners
within the Society, prevented some Friends from marrying at all.[7] The
Pease family itself provides a good example of the kind of unfortunate
loss that the Society could experience as a result of the disownment
rule. In 1853 Edward Pease's niece Elizabeth married a Scottish Pres-
byterian, John Pringle Nichol, Professor of Astronomy at the University of Glasgow. The couple had met in the previous year as a result of
their mutual devotion to the anti-slavery movement. Elizabeth herself
was a prominent radical campaigner and advocate of the views of the

distinguished American abolitionist William Lloyd Garrison, with whom she corresponded regularly.[8] Her father, moreover, had been a devout Quaker and founder member of the British India Society, a body formed in 1839 with the aim of securing an expansion of Indian agricultural exports by means of land reform in order to undermine the slave economies of the west.[9] Immediately before her marriage to Nichol, Elizabeth was disowned by the Darlington Monthly Meeting and there is some evidence to suggest that the obvious injustice of the rule as applied in this particular case strengthened the hands of the reformers.[10]

Although changes in Quaker discipline were primarily a result of increasing concern over membership they were also, in a fundamental sense, a reflection of more general forces of economic and social change. Quakerism had always concerned itself with material as well as spiritual matters and by the mid-nineteenth century the Society of Friends contained within its ranks a large number of successful industrialists and financiers. The process of industrialisation was proving to be a powerful solvent of the original conception of a 'peculiar people'. How could the affluent Quaker businessman in an increasingly urbanised society, often in daily contact with colleagues who did not share his religious faith or scruples, maintain his Quaker aloofness intact? The pressure to conform could be intense and many Friends had the requisite means to do so – often in spectacular fashion.

As far as the Peases' Quakerism was concerned, a double standard of conduct was maintained within the family after 1850. Until Joseph's death in 1872 his sons always addressed him in plain speech 'and in many [other] ways submitted to the Quaker traditions and paternal discipline of [their] father'.[11] In public, however, their behaviour was less exemplary. This is illustrated particularly well by the diaries of Francis Mewburn. Although he was an Anglican Mewburn was a shrewd and at times caustic observer of the 'unquakerly' antics of the Peases and seems to have shared much of Edward Pease's dislike of the decline of 'Friendly discipline' within the family. In 1861, for example, he was disturbed to learn of Joseph's sons' involvement in a carol service and in the same year he observed with astonishment that Joseph Whitwell had won a prize at the Cleveland Show for the best hunter – 'A Quaker turned Hunter!'[12]

But it was not only the younger generation of Quakers who had begun to abandon the simple and modest lifestyle espoused by Edward Pease. Joseph and Henry openly declared their faith as Quakers throughout their adult lives, the former serving as Clerk to the Durham Quarterly Meeting in the 1830s and eventually attaining the position of recorded minister.[13] Henry too was destined to become an elder and in 1854 suffered much public ridicule as a result of his participation in a Quaker peace mission to Russia in the vain hope of averting the Cri-

mean War by addressing a personal appeal to the Tsar.[14] Yet, despite
their evident religious convictions, both sons incurred their father's
sustained disapproval for departing from 'the purity of our principles'.
Edward's diaries are replete with reference to his sons' business speculations and his desire for restraint on their part. This was not simply a
product of his fear of financial embarrassment and the absolute necessity for avoiding bankruptcy; it was also an indication of his dislike of
their increasingly ostentatious lifestyles. Criticism of Joseph began
when he spent a considerable sum of money in building Cliffe House at
Marske-by-the-Sea during the 1840s. The fact that it was meant to
serve as a summer residence for Joseph's family when Darlington was
hardly noted for its sanitary arrangements did not appease Edward in
the slightest. To him the house 'was not desirable on any account', the
more so because 'the mansion' was adorned internally with extravagant
fittings.[15] For Edward it was more than sufficient that his oldest son
should possess Southend, Joseph's Darlington home, which had been
acquired from a member of the Backhouse family in 1826, the year of
his marriage. Originally a plain brick house, over the years it was
enlarged and embellished so that even here Edward came to feel that
'the pure simplicity of Jesus . . . is in degree departed from'.[16] By 1860
Southend was surrounded by 27 acres of well cultivated grounds with
'summer houses, temples and ponds' linked by asphalt paths impressed
with 'amethysts and white spar from Weardale'.[17] But it was Henry who
offended his father most deeply by his acquisition in 1845 of Pierremont, an ornate stone-built gothic house constructed in the early 1830s
by John Botcherby, a local builder. Set in 22 acres of ground overlook-
ing the Cocker Beck, the 'showy mansion', as Edward described it, was
destined to become known as 'the Buckingham Palace of Darlington'
and its occupant 'the Laird of Pierremont'.[18] In the late 1870s the
Edinburgh correspondent of the *Gardeners' Chronicle* visited the
recently extended estate and marvelled at the artificial lake and water-
fall – the former lit by gas lamps in winter for skaters – the ornate
fountain and extensive tree plantations, rose arbour and flower-beds.
With its impressive clock-tower embellished with the Pease crest – a
dove of peace with a pea-pod in its beak – Pierremont was indeed 'the
crowning achievement' among the numerous Pease residences in Darlington.[19] Conspicuous consumption on this scale was unprecedented in
the local Quaker community and it did not go unnoticed by contemporaries. In 1854, for example, the antiquary Hylton Dyer Longstaffe
proclaimed with more than a hint of cynicism that 'The leading families
of the Friends have made their fortunes with their own right hands, and
have settled down in all the best and snuggest mansions near the town
. . . there is an air of the quintessence of comfort in their grounds.'[20]
Twenty years later, in 1876, the anonymous author of *Kings of British
Commerce* in an obvious reference to the Peases described the 'Westward

and southward ever-advancing lines of villas' belonging to the middle class 'Here and there interrupted by the spacious lines and handsome residences of some wealthy Quaker'.[21]

Even in their religious observance the wealth of the Peases, with that of their Backhouse, Leatham and Hodgkin 'cousins', was unmistakable, not least because of 'the 12 to 15 carriages and pairs drawn up at the meeting house for the morning meetings on first days' – all equipped with the necessary coachman and footman. The meetings themselves were unexceptional by Quaker standards, being dominated by the brothers John and Joseph Pease, the former 'preaching with his left hand thrust into his black silk waistcoat and with great solemnity and eloquence' as befitted 'the Silver Trumpet of the North'.[22] Until well into the 1870s all the male ministers wore correct Quaker dress and broad-brim hats, while in the women ministers' gallery there was 'a long row of Quaker bonnets and all had in winter great sable muffs'. For Alfred the elder son of Joseph Whitwell, who was fifteen at the time of his grandfather's death, these meetings were interminable, the more so because the women Friends insisted on addressing the meeting in 'an old nasal sing-song' which Alfred clearly found repugnant.[23] In the years before Joseph Pease's death the meeting was followed by 'a great family gathering at Southend of sons, daughters, granddaughters and grandsons'. As Alfred reminisced of the 1860s:

The children after getting their grub (milk, cake, buns and biscuits at 12.00 p.m.) and having run round the wonderful conservatory flowers which opened out of the drawing room and a look at the enormous cage full of canaries, perhaps 40 birds, mostly singing, would spend an hour or so playing in the garden . . . the favourite toy being a sort of wagon carriage which ran splendidly on the asphalt paths . . . At ten minutes to two the butler rang the big bell in the house and at 2 o'clock to the tick we were at dinner. On Sundays we grandchildren each had a red glass Dresden mug. My father and grandfather alone drank claret in dark green glasses. . . . On Sundays there were four courses of sweets and after roast beef, stilton or Cotherstone cheese and cream cheese. . . . Instead of dessert on Sundays the white cloth was alone drawn by a footman, footmen leaving the red cloth with a black vine-leaf pattern all over it, and in front of the son who sat at the bottom of the table was placed a greater copper canister full of toffee. On weekdays dessert was a great affair, pineapples, peaches, nectarines, grapes, figs, melons, all grown on the place and there would always be about six large dishes of such things and four dishes of fruits, gingers, raisins, dried fruits and a dish or two of biscuits and wafers. I remember the first bit of chocolate I ever tasted was at Southend.[24]

Domestic bliss also had its external counterpart and this is well illustrated by the celebration of birthdays and marriages within the Pease
family. In a diary entry for 22 June 1849 Edward Pease expressed his
anxiety 'about tomorrow as a day to be kept as my Grandson J. Whitwell Pease's birthday; everything that has in it a celebration is inconsis-
tent with Christian gravity and simplicity [and] stands in my mind as
condemned, and as unbecoming our profession of the truth, and is a
trespass against it. May all my endeavours be to have the day spent
becomingly.'[25] Edward's failure in this latter respect is recorded in
Francis Mewburn's diary entry for the following day:

> About 6 o'clock a.m. a band of music played divers airs at the
> north gate of Southend and the church bells rang a merry peal in
> honour of the occasion! Music and church bell ringing did seem to
> me singular for a Quaker celebration. On Mon[day] (26th) all the
> pitmen in the employ of Joseph Pease were entertained in a field
> adjoining the Adelaide Colliery; 1,600 sat down. Mr and Mrs
> Joseph Pease and all their eleven children sat down also. After
> dinner there were speeches, but what was so curious – they had
> bands of music; and yet these Quakers will not allow music at our
> horticultural shows and other gatherings! The dinner consisted of
> bread, beef, and ale – 13 cwt each of the bread and beef and 32 half
> barrels of ale. There were 500 mugs, of which only 70 remained
> whole . . . the pitmen amused themselves in shying the mugs at
> each other.[26]

Such boisterousness could perhaps be forgiven on the occasion of the
coming of age of the oldest son of their employer, but it is significant
that Edward's diary entry on the dinner expressed relief at the colliers'
celebrations having been 'peacefully conducted'.[27] The old man's feelings were no doubt spared by censored accounts of the day's proceedings. In fact, the birthday celebrations did not end until 28 June when
about 150 of the Pease family servants were given tea at Southend and
300 women and girls from the worsted mill similarly were entertained at
Darlington's Central Hall.[28]

No less impressive were the Peases' nuptial celebrations. When
Rachel Pease married Charles Leatham of Wakefield in 1851, Mewburn
offered his customary acerbic observations:

> This day (March 6) Rachel, the third daughter of my friend Joseph
> Pease was married to Charles Albert Leatham at the Friends'
> Meeting House in this town. The Meeting House was crammed
> with the wedding party and the respectable people in the town. A
> band of music paraded the streets and welcomed the bridal party at
> South End, and – what may be regarded as curious – the bells of St

Cuthbert's rang a peal and guns and cannon were fired! At the various stations on the Stockton and Darlington Railway eastwards there are flags flying.[29]

Even more ostentatious were the marriage celebrations of the second cousins Henry Fell and Elizabeth Pease in 1862. Thirty carriages left the bride's home, North Lodge, for the Meeting House and on their return the guests were treated to a magnificent *déjeuner* of 'asparagus soup, oyster soup à la reine, soup á la juillien, turkeys, raised ham and veal pies, pigeon pies, boar's head, and ducklings of lamb; spring chickens and boiled fowls, lobster salads, pressed beef and guinea fowls, aspic of eels, of salmon and of shrimps; prawns; and sweets to follow included six kinds of creams, five sorts of jellies, pastries, meringues, hedge hog, hen's nest, cakes, fruit and ices, with nonalcoholic drinks, including temperance champagne'.[30] Such indulgence was rare even by the standards that were coming to be accepted as the norm within the Pease family. After the wedding tour of France, where the couple visited Paris, Tours, Bordeaux, Bayonne and Biarritz, they returned to their newly built mansion – Brinkburn – constructed of Joseph Pease and Partners' celebrated buff-coloured brick and set in extensive grounds adjacent to Pierremont, the home of the bridegroom's father. As with other celebrations the family's employees were not forgotten. On the day of the wedding the 700 workers at Henry Pease and Co.'s mills enjoyed a railway excursion to Redcar where they were entertained by an accompanying sax horn band.[31]

It is easy to be critical of a lifestyle which contained within it an increasing element of moral ambivalence, but it is a point worth reiterating that by the 1860s the Peases were part of that 'glittering superstructure of great industrialists and financiers' who were inevitably coming to be assimilated within the nationwide upper class as they acquired their ornate mansions and landed estates.[32] It can hardly be denied that wealth destroys simplicity but, as indicated already, for the Quaker elite their growing 'conformity to the world' was both a cause and a consequence of the relaxation of discipline within the Society of Friends itself. Up to 1870, moreover, the Peases were not exceptional in their failure to maintain religious discipline. In Lancashire, for example, the same process of growing laxity can be observed in the family of Henry Ashworth, a wealthy Quaker cotton manufacturer and contemporary of Joseph Pease. Even before 1850 Ashworth permitted his sons and daughters to attend private dances 'occasionally on two or three nights a week' with homecomings at 4 a.m. His sons smoked cigars, went horse racing and, unlike the Peases, visited theatres. Ashworth himself maintained a large wine cellar and again, unlike Joseph, was an avid field-sportsman, especially after 1850 when with increasing prosperity he began to hire shooting-lodges and estates in Scotland.[33]

Whilst Edward and even Joseph and Henry Pease continued to reside until their deaths in their marital homes, this cannot be said of Joseph Whitwell Pease. Indeed, in the latter case the lifestyle that had been achieved by the mid-1890s was akin to that of a landed magnate. As Joseph's oldest son, Joseph Whitwell was heir to the greater part of the Pease industrial empire and without anticipating future events it is sufficient to point out that in 1894, after having served as traffic manager and vice-chairman, Joseph Whitwell had risen to the prestigious position of chairman of the NER. In 1854 he contracted a traditional Quaker marriage after successfully courting Mary, one of the daughters of Alfred Fox, a well-known Quaker shipping agent of Falmouth, whose family had amassed a small fortune during the Napoleonic wars due to the favourable anchorage facilities offered by the Helford river.[34] The Whitwell Peases' first residence was Woodlands, another substantial Botcherby house set in its own grounds to the east of Pierremont. They lived there until 1867 when, with their seven children, they moved to Hutton Hall near Guisborough. This was only the second 'purpose-built' Pease residence and it was on an altogether different scale from anything then existing in the family. The estate itself, extending to 2,912 acres, covered some of the most attractive countryside on the north-eastern face of the Cleveland Hills near Roseberry Topping. The Hall, with its 6 reception rooms and 38 bed- and dressing-rooms and stabling for 24 horses was constructed of hard red brick in gothic style. It was built by the eminent architect, Alfred Waterhouse, the designer of the Manchester Town Hall and the Natural History Museum in London. The cost of the buildings alone was £88,000. Twenty gardeners were employed and approximately the same number of house servants.[35] The visitor to Hutton Hall, having alighted at the Peases' personal railway halt on the local branch line of the NER, could not fail to be impressed by the wealth and standing of its owner, epitomised by the large stone-carved coat of arms, underlined by the motto *Pax et Spes* – 'Peace and Hope' – and surmounted by the familiar dove of peace, which stood at the end of the lengthy driveway. Life at Hutton was grand. The Whitwell Peases 'lived off the fat of the land . . . sausages imported from Cornwall to be sure of the best; fish by train from York; a variety of fruit, e.g. nectarines, peaches, apricots, melons, grapes etc., and York hams'.[36] The menu never varied from week to week through summer and winter. The impact of Hutton on the visitor can be illustrated by the reminiscences of A. J. C. Hare, a peripatetic country house guest. In the late 1870s, after staying at Raby Castle as a guest of the Duke of Cleveland, he proceeded to Hutton Hall, arriving at night. On waking the following morning Hare was astonished to find that he was not 'amid the Middlesbro' smoke' but was in a house surrounded by 'high moorland fells beyond the terraced garden':

I laugh when I think how the Duchess of Cleveland rejoiced in giving Mrs Pease such a pleasant change [at] Raby, to see this intensely luxurious house, by Waterhouse, filled with delightful collections of books, pictures and carved furniture and its almost Arabian-night-like conservatories.[37]

It was at Hutton that Joseph Whitwell was able to indulge his passion for country life and field sports – shooting, hunting and coursing. In 1875 he bought Kerris Vean, a comfortable house near Falmouth, for the benefit of his wife, and annual summer visits were enlivened for the children by trips on the *Roseberry*, the family's steam yacht. Other excursions took place to Scotland, where Joseph Whitwell was regularly entertained by his shooting and sailing companion, Sir Donald Currie, and himself acted as host at Corndavon Lodge, Crathie, which he rented for the shooting season from the Royal Invercauld Estates.[38]

In 1882 Joseph Whitwell was offered a baronetcy by Gladstone. After a brief discussion with his family, especially his elder son Alfred, who expressed his indifference on the matter, the offer was accepted – almost half-heartedly if diary entries are to be taken at face value. As Joseph Whitwell commented:

> We have most numerous letters and most kind congratulations on the honour proposed to be conferred upon us. To us it seems to make but little difference – but it is pleasant to think that quiet labours have been appreciated, that the work of those who have gone before me has in me at least met a public recognition.[39]

This was the first occasion on which a Quaker had accepted an honour from the Crown, and it served to confirm Sir Joseph Whitwell Pease in his position as the most influential industrialist in south Durham and north Yorkshire. But the baronetcy was not merely a recognition of industrial success for, as Sir Joseph appreciated, it was primarily a political honour bestowed on an important Dissenting family which had, for many years, rendered admirable service in defending 'the Liberal Citadel of South Durham'.[40] Sir Joseph may have been the first Quaker to be created a baronet, but his father had been the first Quaker Member of Parliament, having been elected to the reformed House of Commons as the Radical member for South Durham as long ago as 1832. By the time Sir Joseph received his baronetcy his uncle Henry had served as Liberal member for the same constituency from 1857 to 1865 and on the latter's retirement Sir Joseph had inherited the seat. In 1868 his relative and close friend Edmund Backhouse had been elected as Liberal member for Darlington and on Backhouse's retirement in 1880 the seat had passed to Theodore Fry, the husband of Sir Joseph's cousin Sophia.[41] In the same year his brother Arthur was elected as the

3   Sir Joseph Whitwell Pease, Bt. (1828–1903) in old age, *c*. 1898.

Liberal member for Whitby and only a few years later, in 1885, his cousin Henry Fell Pease was elected Liberal member for the Cleveland division of North Yorkshire and his own son Alfred as the senior member for the City of York, also in the Liberal interest. In 1892 Sir Joseph's younger son Jack entered Parliament as the Liberal member for Tyneside and finally, in 1898, his nephew, Herbert Pike Pease, won a by-election in Darlington as a Liberal Unionist.

Altogether thirty-three Quakers entered Parliament during the reign of Victoria and almost one-third of them can be identified with the Pease interest.[42] The focal point of the family's political involvement was south Durham and north-east Yorkshire, and within thirty years of Joseph Pease's election the Quakers and their allies had constructed a formidable political machine. As one observer has commented, by the late 1860s 'A Pease could be returned at any time he chose because he combined the politics of influence with the politics of individualism'.[43] The platform on which Joseph had stood in 1832 was clear-cut and unambiguous – to ease the burdens on Dissenters, to secure the abolition of slavery and to give to the electors of South Durham an opportunity to vote for a candidate who would represent the newly enfranchised urban industrial and commercial interest in the face of traditional aristocratic landed influence, as represented by the Duke of Cleveland and the Marquess of Londonderry.[44] Although Joseph retired from parliamentary politics in 1841[45] his brother Henry encountered no difficulties in reasserting the family's claim to the seat in 1857. Indeed, by that time there was an electoral understanding between the Pease and Cleveland interests based upon the mutual respect of two powerful political patrons. The patronage was in the ascendant for the former and it derived its strength from 'the extensive quaker and dissenting community of the Tees Valley, reinforced by the vast commercial network built up in coal and iron between 1820 and 1860 in Auckland, Darlington, Middlesbrough and Stockton'.[46] Yet although the representation of Quakers increased in Parliament after 1832, reaching a peak in the mid-1880s, no Quaker MP, with the exception of John Bright, achieved any great distinction at Westminster before 1900. In the case of Joseph Pease this was understandable. His candidature was bitterly opposed within his family, especially by his mother-in-law, Jane Gurney, and it was only after Edward Pease had been assured of 'the absolute purity and sincerity' of his son's motives that he offered no further resistance.[47] As Joseph realised, his religious beliefs precluded political advancement and his short parliamentary career was undistinguished. With his handsome Quaker dress of collarless coat, knee breeches, silk stockings and buckled shoes, he may have been 'the best dressed man in St Stephen's looking for all the world as if he had just come from a Court levee' but 'Mr Pease . . . one of the most useful, though not one of the most shining members of the House' was noted only as a propo-

nent of the anti-slavery cause, for his unorthodox views on the desirabil-
ity of agricultural protection and for his trenchant opposition to statutory restrictions on the hours of work of factory children.[48] Half a century later, Sir Joseph Whitwell Pease's ambitions extended only to the
Privy Council and a desire to serve as Chancellor of the Duchy of
Lancaster,[49] an office dismissed by Bright as 'that useless place'.[50]

Whilst it was well known that the Peases were potentially a powerful
and influential group in the Commons, their claims for political
advancement were reduced by their refusal to vote as a bloc.[51] This was
exemplified by the dissension within the family caused by Gladstone's
policy of Home Rule for Ireland. In 1864 Sir Joseph's brother, Arthur,
had married Mary Lecky, the daughter of Ebenezer Pike of Bess-
borough in Co. Cork. The Pikes were an old Quaker family and their
opposition to a separate Irish legislature was extreme.[52] Ebenezer's son
had fought two unsuccessful parliamentary elections against Charles
Stewart Parnell and in deference to 'the Orange petticoats of his wife'
Arthur veered towards Unionism.[53] In 1886, when he declared his support for H. O. Arnold Foster, the Liberal Unionist candidate for Darlington, political loyalties within the family were sorely strained as Sir
Joseph and his sons remained committed to Gladstone's policy and
were therefore obliged to support Theodore Fry's candidature in the
face of one who had 'entered with zest into an opposition against a
blood relation'.[54] In 1892 Arthur unsuccessfully contested the Darlington seat himself and eventually defeated Fry in 1895.

In fact, like most Quakers in Parliament, the Peases directed their
energies to campaigning for philanthropic movements and 'faddist'
reforming agitations. The office of President of the Peace Society was
practically hereditary in the family, being held successively by Joseph,
Henry, Joseph Whitwell and Jack Pease. As noted already, Joseph
Pease was an anti-slavery agitator in the 1830s and was also an early and
courageous advocate of animal welfare,[55] whilst Joseph Whitwell's
philanthropic zeal embraced the campaign against capital punishment
(an interest inherited from his father) and the presidency of the Anti-
Opium Society. At a more mundane level he was a leading spokesman
for the 'railway interest' at Westminster.[56] Whilst representing Whitby,
Arthur Pease was parliamentary spokesman for the British and Foreign
Anti-Slavery Society and was also deeply committed to the temperance
movement, holding at one time the positions of President of the North
of England Temperance League and Vice-President of the United
Kingdom Alliance.[57]

It is difficult to resist the conclusion that the Peases were the anti-
thesis of career politicians: the espousal of a multitude of philanthropic
causes was not the route to high office and in any case their major
interests lay elsewhere. There is some evidence to suggest that Sir
Joseph was offered a minor ministerial appointment by Gladstone after

1880 but it was refused[58] and there may well be some truth in Richard Cobden's observation on Quaker industrialists in general that as 'a rich capitalist' his only interest in national politics was the enhanced social position that he enjoyed in the north-east of England.[59] On the other hand, it is perhaps to Sir Joseph's credit that when he was offered a peerage in 1894 he expressed his indifference, leaving the decision to Alfred, who allowed the matter to lapse.[60]

It was only with the third generation of parliamentary representation in the Pease family that political ambitions began to emerge. As the senior member for York in the later 1880s Alfred attracted the attention of Lord Rosebery as a highly informed spokesman on Irish affairs. Alfred was a convinced Home Ruler and after his defeat in the general election of 1892 Rosebery offered him the position of extra-parliamentary private secretary until he could find another seat.[61] Unfortunately, his wife suffered a sudden breakdown in health which entailed removal to a warmer climate and Alfred was unable to return to the House of Commons until 1897, when he succeeded Henry Fell Pease as the member for Cleveland. By then, however, his political aspirations had been blunted: contemporaries, in particular his friend Edward Grey (later Viscount Grey of Falloden) had overtaken him, and in any case he had no wish to compete with his brother who had recently been appointed a Liberal whip.[62] Both Alfred and Jack were the first Peases to receive a Cambridge education and it is no coincidence that they married non-Quakers. In 1880 Alfred had married Helen, the daughter of Sir Robert Nicholas Fowler, a former Quaker turned Anglican, and Tory member for the City of London.[63] In 1886 Jack confirmed his social status in south Durham in spectacular fashion by marrying Ethel, the only daughter of General Sir Henry Havelock-Allan, the Liberal Unionist member for the south-east division of the county and one of the outstanding military heroes of the Indian Mutiny.[64]

Whilst it may have been true that gaining social prestige was a contributory motive for the Peases' parliamentary activities, it would be unjust to dismiss their commitment to local politics and government as being prompted by similar ambitions. By the mid-nineteenth century the Peases, in their capacity as leading employers and landowners, were major ratepayers in Darlington, and even if they had wished otherwise their involvement in the administration of the town was unavoidable. It was therefore appropriate that it was at local rather than national level that the Peases should exert their own considerable patronage and power. Ironically, it was here, at the very centre of their influence, that they were subjected to a campaign of vilification and abuse whose outcome, although favourable to the Peases, provides a fascinating case study of popular opposition to a form of urban oligarchical control which was as rigid and all-pervasive as anything exerted by the landed interest. In fact, the Peases' involvement in the public affairs of Darlington between 1850 and 1874 was 'conformity to the world' with a vengeance.

In the period before 1850 when Darlington was still a relatively small market town it was governed by a multiplicity of authorities, the most important of which were the office of Chief Bailiff, a position in the patronage of the Bishop of Durham, and the improvement commission appointed under the Local Paving Act of 1823. There was no resident magistracy and in 1837 the creation of the poor law union under the auspices of a county administration meant that the town was deprived of some of its powers in this important area.[65] The office of Chief Bailiff became an anachronism after the abolition of the Bishop of Durham's palatinate powers in 1836, and following the passage of the Public Health Act of 1848 a campaign was launched from within the improvement commission – dominated by Peases and Backhouses – for the establishment of a local board of health which would concern itself with much-needed sanitary reforms and would also give an impetus to a more unified administration of local government in place of the plethora of parochial authorities. But, as one observer has pointed out, the petitioners to the General Board of Health for an inquiry to ascertain whether the town merited the appointment of a local board under the terms of the Act (an annual death rate in excess of 23 per 1,000 inhabitants) formed an interested party.[66] In May 1849 the Darlington Gas and Water Company had been incorporated, with John Pease, the principal officer of the improvement commission's sanitary committee, as chairman. Henry Pease was one of the managing directors and Joseph a leading shareholder. The three Pease brothers were ardent and genuine advocates of a pure water supply and Henry in particular was to invest heavily in water companies and the manufacture of drainage pipes. His most important venture was the Weardale and Shildon Water Company founded in 1865 to serve the Peases' colliery villages in south-west Durham.[67] The liquid forthcoming may have had 'the colour of India Pale Ale and a slight taste of pond', but it was unpolluted and made a significant contribution to the reduction of water-borne disease.[68] In the context of the times investment in such companies was therefore praiseworthy but the suspicions of those who were critical of the Peases' interest in sanitary reform and the sale of water were in no way allayed when it was announced that the solicitor to the Gas and Water Company was to be responsible for the petition to the General Board. Even at this early stage a 'dirty party' had emerged in Darlington, and long-standing antagonisms surfaced in September 1849 when the opponents of sanitary reform urged the return of the Chief Bailiff, Francis Mewburn, from holiday in Derbyshire to prevent a Quaker from presenting an address to the Queen, who was due to pass through the town *en route* for Scotland. Mewburn obliged and thereby dealt an open reprimand to what his son later described as 'That grasping ambition, and overweening vanity which . . . have been so frequently displayed in arrogant attempts to ignore the position [and] usurp the functions . . . of the venerated and respectable gentleman holding the appointment of Chief Bailiff'.[69]

In October 1849 William Ranger, superintending inspector of the General Board of Health, began his inquiry and in June 1850 his report, recommending the establishment of a local board of health for Darlington, was published. A provisional order was made on 1 August 1850 and subsequently confirmed by Act of Parliament. The Act provided for the creation of a local board of eighteen members to be elected on the basis of a property franchise with one-third of the membership retiring each year. The first elections took place on 25 September and of the successful candidates ten were Quakers, including two Backhouses and the three Pease brothers. Only one member of the 'dirty party' was elected.[70]

In the seventeen years of its existence the local board of health made commendable progress in improving Darlington's sanitary arrangements, especially in view of the rapid expansion in population (from 11,587 in 1851 to 27,729 in 1871) which followed the opening up of the Cleveland ironstone district and the beginnings of heavy industrial development in the town.[71] But it was in the area of public administration that the greatest strides were made. By means of private Acts of Parliament in 1854 and 1861 the board succeeded in obtaining far greater authority than allowed for in the Act of 1848. Its borrowing powers were greatly increased, as was the area of its jurisdiction. By the late 1860s, in addition to the normal monthly meetings, there were 'standing committees for general purposes and parks; finance; streets; sewage; drainage and lighting; gas and waterworks and sanitary inspection. They were served by a bureaucratic establishment of secretary, clerk, treasurer, medical officer, surveyor, rate collector, two inspectors of nuisances, market keeper and clerks, costing £1,077 in salaries in 1867'.[72] In this way the board succeeded in establishing some uniformity of local government administration in the town. This was achieved, however, at the cost of mounting opposition to Quaker control of the board and more especially the influence of the Pease family. The factor which produced open resentment was the advice tendered to the local board by its first surveyor, George Mason, that in order to improve the drainage of the town it was imperative that the board should purchase or lease the works of the Gas and Water Company. Alternatively, the board would have to construct a rival plant. The problem was that the company's water charges were too high to enable the board to secure the acceptance of the maximum number of consumers, even under compulsion. To complicate matters the investors in the Gas and Water Company on the local board, led by John Pease, did not wish to be bought out on the grounds that Darlington owed its public-spirited entrepreneurs a profitable reward for their endeavours and that in any case the board was an unsuitable organisation for conducting a business. The bargain that was eventually struck – confirmed by the Darlington Local Board of Health Act of 1854 – was that the board agreed to purchase the Gas and Water Company for the sum of £54,000 with the result that each shareholder received £25 for every £12 10s he had invested in 1849. John Pease announced that the purchase price 'was such a reward as public spirit ought to be satisfied with', but others begged to differ: for years to come the events of 1854 were to expose the Peases to the charge of unbridled profiteering.[73]

Further criticisms of the board centred on its enhanced borrowing powers and the opportunities this gave for favouritism in the offer of contracts. In 1856 the Darlington Ratepayers' Association was formed, composed principally of property owners, pig keepers and ratepayers and led by Nicholas Bragg, former secretary of the Darlington Chartist Association. Although he had been involved in litigation with the Peases in 1850 following allegations of 'ill usage of his father's grand-daughter in one of the mills of Henry Pease and Co.',[74] Bragg disclaimed any personal animosity against the Peases. Nevertheless, he proved to be their tireless critic, notably in accusing individual members of the family of corrupt trading practices. Representatives of the Ratepayers' Association were present at the board's audit in 1856, and Bragg laid detailed charges against Joseph Pease, claiming that in 1854–5 he had sold pipes and coals to the value of £1,430 to the board in contravention of section 19 of the Public Health Act.[75] The amount was trivial and Joseph denied all knowledge of any such transactions, but he immediately issued a warning to his agents not to tender to the board. In 1865, however, Bragg returned to the attack with accusations that over a period of years Joseph had engaged in illegal trading with the board to the value of £80,000.[76] The General Board refused to act on the basis of individual allegations and the charges were allowed to pass. The damage to the local board's reputation, however, was cumulative.[77]

Another source of resentment against the Peases was their seemingly hypocritical concern with moral and spiritual welfare. Their own ambivalence in these matters caused Francis Mewburn to offer some extremely penetrating criticisms of his Quaker associates and this too encouraged opposition to the board of health. By 1870 the Peases were employing 29 salaried teachers, 7 sewing mistresses and about 60 pupil teachers, principally in their Durham and Cleveland mining settlements. Seven permanent missionaries were also employed, visiting colliery villages on a regular basis and distributing Bible tracts, *The British Workman* and *Band of Hope Review*.[78] Joseph and Henry were also in the habit of circulating penny leaflets among their workforce. One of Joseph's texts, for example, stated: 'I pity the publican and his wife. I weep when I see a family taking over a public house. Their history is a fearful catalogue of woes. The charm of the women is defaced and the strong men are hurried to an untimely grave.'[79] The message imparted, therefore, was one of temperance and also opposition to frivolous pursuits such as music-making and attending theatres. This kind of activity aroused little hostility in company mining settlements not just because the communities concerned were entirely dependent upon the Peases (with every brick in every house stamped 'Pease') but also because it was wholly consistent with the outlook and lifestyle of a substantial proportion of the workforce. In the Deerness Valley, for example, where Joseph Pease and Partners owned the Waterhouses, Esh Winning and Ushaw Moor collieries and where Methodism was especially strong, Quaker paternalism embraced flower and agricultural shows, the provision of cricket grounds and aged miners' homes, support for colliery bands and, more significantly, generous responses, both financial and material, for the construction and maintenance of chapels and schools in the belief that this would promote stability and contentment in the workforce.[80] With a trade union organisation dominated by convinced Liberals and Methodists adhering to a *laissez-faire* economic creed emphasising the interdependence of capital and labour there was little likelihood of a major challenge to the political and economic *status quo* emerging before 1900. In all of these respects the situation was potentially rather different in Darlington because of the town's less deferential and more complex community structure. Theatre licence applications were regularly opposed in the Darlington police court by Pease-inspired Quaker delegations to the extent that a division of opinion arose among the ranks of local Liberals. One famous incident occurred in 1860 when a licensing bench composed of Colonel G. J. Scurfield and R. H. Allan – two landed Liberals – and Joseph Whitwell Pease divided two to one on the issue of a theatre application. Scurfield, who had moved Henry Pease's adoption as Liberal candidate for the South Durham constituency in 1857, commented that he had no desire to

> throw dampness and dullness amongst them, for Darlington was quite unlike any other place; certain influences were brought to bear, what that influence was he would not say, but no public movement could go forward without that influence being felt. There is a sort of cloud or pall hanging over the town, which seemed to swamp every sort of amusement.[81]

After these pointed remarks Joseph Whitwell was subjected to a sarcastic response from the superintendent of police, who stated that in his experience departures from Band of Hope temperance meetings were as noisy as those from the theatre.[82] An indication of local resentment in this context was marked in 1859 by the founding of the Darlington Licensed Victuallers' Association headed by John Wrightson, an 'opposition' innkeeper and pig-breeding member of the local board of health. In the following year the town gave birth to its own corps of Rifle Volunteers. This new challenge to Quaker hegemony produced a major confrontation, heightened in Henry's case by the recent and successful conclusion of a long press campaign in favour of the town's acceptance for public display of a Russian cannon captured in the Crimea.[83] At the Volunteers' inaugural meeting in July 1860 the partisan Colonel Scurfield was in the chair with Joseph Pease in attendance in his capacity as president of the Peace Society and intent upon opposing the formation of such a body. After delivering a speech on foreign affairs, Joseph left feeling unwell, but not before his brother John had been silenced by uproarious heckling.[84]

These challenges to the power of the Peases over the local community were little more than pinpricks in the side of the majority party on the board of health, and from the mid-1850s onwards a concerted effort was made to secure the election of anti-Pease candidates to the board. In practice this proved to be extremely difficult to achieve because of the plural voting system enshrined in the 1848 Act. Two examples from the 1862 elections illustrate the position. According to the poll book for the election held in that year Henry Pease was entitled to 12 votes as a householder, 12 as proxy for the Stockton and Middlesbrough Water Company, 12 as proxy for the South Durham Iron Company, 6 for Henry Pease and Co. and 5 in partnership with Robert Thompson, the proprietor of the *Darlington and Stockton Times*. Similarly, Joseph Whitwell Pease was entitled to 10 votes as a householder, 12 as proxy for the Stockton and Darlington Railway, 1 as proxy for the Public Baths and 1 in partnership with his father for property in Whessoe Street. Since registered electors were entitled to choose six candidates for each vote held this meant that Henry and Joseph Whitwell were together entitled to a sum total of 426 votes. In 1862 there were seventeen candidates and the 1,234 electors cast 7,678 votes: of these 648 were accounted for by members of the Pease family alone and all the Peases voted for the same six candidates.[85] To complicate the elections there was a 'bogus' candidate – William Barningham, a local ironmaster and nominee of the Peases – whose candidature was widely regarded as a device to confuse uncommitted voters. In addition, the Peases could count on the 'deference' votes of their own railway and mill employees. In view of these obstacles it was surprising that two 'opposition' candidates were elected, but even here it was claimed that one of them had given private assurances to Joseph Pease that if elected he would desist from opposing the majority interest on the board.[86]

Confronted by the seemingly impossible task of electing opposition members to the board, Nicholas Bragg had earlier launched a campaign for the division of the town into wards which would have had the effect of diminishing the influence of plural voters. This was permitted under the Local Government Act of 1858 and a petition was signed by over 500 people asking for government approval for such a move. Since it was a foregone conclusion that the local board would do all in its power to resist the petition, Bragg and his associates decided to enlist the support of James Farrer, the Tory MP for the dual-member South Durham constituency. Farrer proved sympathetic but illness prevented him from acting, so the matter came into the hands of the senior member for the division – Henry Pease. Needless to say, Henry encountered no difficulty in securing the perpetual deferment of the necessary legislation.[87]

Thwarted continually and scoring only minor successes against the Peases, the aggrieved Licensed Victuallers, Volunteers, beneficed clergy, Tories and dissident Liberals turned their attention to the possibility of obtaining municipal status and a separate parliamentary seat for the town. For the former, at least, they had a good case: towns of a similar size in the north-east of England were incorporated, and it was well known that Joseph Pease had lent his support to Middlesbrough's claim for incorporation in 1853.

The first move in the campaign for municipal status came in October 1865 when an 'opposition' member of the board of health, Richard Benson, gave notice of a resolution 'That in the opinion of the Board, the time has arrived when Darlington ought to become a corporate borough, and that the Clerk be instructed to take immediate steps to obtain such incorporation'.[88] A petition in favour of incorporation signed by 1,139 ratepayers failed to move the board, and Benson's resolution was eventually defeated by thirteen votes to two.[89] Nevertheless, the majority party yielded slightly by acquiescing in a referendum of electors to ascertain their views on the merits of incorporation. At the same time, the chairman of the board of health, Joseph Pease, undertook to consult twenty incorporated towns on their experiences of municipal government. The referendum took place in March 1866. On collecting his voting paper, each elector was presented with an address by Joseph reporting his findings on the issue of incorporation.[90] Unsurprisingly, he was utterly opposed to abolition of the board of health, deploying three arguments in support of his case. In the first instance he emphasised the greater expense that would be incurred by a municipal borough in operating those services, such as the police and magistracy which were already provided by other competent authorities. Secondly, he expressed grave reservations on the issue of contested elections with their 'costly banners, party-coloured favours, range of hired vehicles, bands of music with stirring tunes, party cries, political, religious and local, persuasion, intimidation, coercion, bribery, profligacy, well known within a hundred miles of us, every Voter submitting to all that loss of time, labour, convenience, and remuneration which our simple voting processes are intended effectively to prevent'. Finally, Joseph devoted considerable attention to rights of voting. Municipalisation would increase the number of voters from about 1,600 to between 4,000 and 5,000. Such a large extension of the franchise, combined with the abolition of plural voting via the ward system of election, would ensure that 'the vote of the owner and occupier of property . . . of the value of £20,000 sterling [would] count for no more than that of the artizan, who having lived three years in the same cottage-room, has never paid one sixpence to the rates except through his landlord'. Moreover, 'all Ladies, whether owners or occupiers, are entirely disfranchised in like manner though their rates may be the heaviest in the district'. Apart from the Quakerly concern for the rights of female voters these were remarkably unprogressive views for the year before the introduction of the second Reform Act. Joseph's address was, of course, a blatant appeal for the *status quo* but it is difficult to judge how it affected the result of the referendum. Although 562 votes were in favour of incorporation and 472 against, there were 388 abstentions and 174 voting papers unreturned. The majority party on the board of health felt justified in claiming the result was inconclusive and announced their intention of not proceeding with Benson's resolution.[91]

That the Peases were thwarted in their obstruction was due in large measure to the efforts of Henry King Spark, a self-proclaimed 'independent Liberal'. Spark had been born at Alston in Cumberland in 1825, the son of a Methodist lead miner and a schoolmistress. In 1847 he joined the *Darlington and Stockton Times* as a printing apprentice and only a few years later amassed a small fortune in the coal merchanting business due to luck rather than business acumen. He then acquired colliery interests in Cumberland and in 1863 became the proprietor of the *Darlington and Stockton Times* itself after the bankruptcy of its original owner. As one of the few non-Quaker entrepreneurs of any note in Darlington, with a large estate at Greenbank near the centre of the town, Spark became a leading figure in the local community.[92] He possessed strong links with the opposition party on the board of health, and in May 1866, after a meeting of '10 gentlemen' at Greenbank, a committee of 'dissident liberals and conservatives' was formed with the aim of obtaining incorporation.[93] In November Spark's campaign was launched for a petition to the Crown. The movement was propitious for in the previous September the ailing Joseph Pease had resigned as chairman of the board of health and the majority interest on the board was ill served by an open letter to the inhabitants of Darlington from John Pease which was circulated during the second week of November. The letter was a rather pathetic attempt to undermine Spark's campaign at the outset by pointing to the previous record of the board of health with special prominence being given to the maladministration of the City of New York as a warning on the dangers of civic status.[94]

In September 1867 Darlington received its charter of incorporation as a municipal borough. In the final stages of the campaign the Peases had offered little opposition and had submitted no case against incorporation during the inquiry conducted by the Commission of the Privy Council in March 1867.[95] But if the 'Corporation Party' believed that their triumph in the ensuing elections was assured – the more so because of Joseph Pease's apparent retirement from public affairs – they were sorely mistaken. In fact, all that happened in Darlington in the aftermath of the first municipal elections in November 1867 was that one Pease-dominated body was replaced by another.

Spark himself chose to stand in the strongly working-class east ward of the town where his principal opponent was Henry Fell Pease. Predictably, Spark presented himself as the radical reformer who had destroyed the corrupt board of health and who therefore, if elected, had the strongest possible claim to the mayoralty. Indeed, his handbills bore the exhortation 'For Mayor: King Henry the Ninth'. His reasons for standing in the east ward were set out eloquently in an address delivered to a crowded meeting held in St John's School on 23 November 1867:

> My sympathies are with working men. I have great regard for the class from which I have sprung. I have the highest possible esteem for the independence and character of the working classes of this ward (loud cheers). But there is a further, and to yourselves, a more interesting reason why I am here. I knew that it was intended to make the ward a sort of Pocket Borough. That it was believed that certain influences were so powerful in this ward that you would be made to return any body who might be sent to you for that purpose (loud cheers). I felt then . . . because this seemed to be the battle ground where the principle of Incorporation would have to be most severely fought that the proper place for me was the East Ward.[96]

Spark then referred to the greatest danger confronting his candidacy in this particular ward, which contained the local workshops of the NER. Having accused Henry Fell Pease of exerting 'undue and unfair influence' upon railway employees by canvassing them at their place of work 'in the presence of those in authority over them', Spark concluded by appealing for the rejection of that 'self-elected body or clique' – the Pease-dominated board of health party.

The results of the first municipal elections were a disaster for Spark and his 'Corporation Party'. In the crucial east ward Henry Fell Pease topped the poll and Spark himself avoided defeat by two votes.

Altogether, five Peases and seven of the ten board of health candidates were elected to the new council. Two other members of the Pease family – Joseph Whitwell's brothers Gurney and Arthur – also topped the poll in their respective wards, while Joseph and John Beaumont Pease joined the aldermanic bench. The mayoralty was at first offered to Joseph but he refused it on the grounds of failing health and the honour then passed to Henry.[97] A further indication of the continuation of the old order was the appointment of the former clerk to the board of health, Hugh Dunn, as the first town clerk.[98] As one observer has commented, these results 'served to underline the enormous power of industrial influence in company towns over the electors unprotected by the secret ballot'.[99] To Darlington's rapidly expanding workforce the Sparkite slogan of 'free and good government for the borough' and the appeal to civic pride were less important than the provision of employment. Even in Darlington, therefore, as in the textile towns of Lancashire and the West Riding,[100] the traditions of deference and paternalism were ultimately as powerful in stifling independent radicalism as in the Peases' mining villages. But the fatal weakness in the Sparkite campaign was that it was a loose alliance of dissident Liberals, Conservatives, Anglicans, publicans and trade union leaders who were unable to compete with the disciplined forces at the disposal of the Peases and the majority board of health party. Spark himself, moreover, with his childish designs on the mayoralty, was open to the charge of individual ambition, a weakness which was ruthlessly exploited by his opponents.[101] In the final analysis the Peases and their allies may have been unable to prevent municipal reform, but they were the town's natural rulers – a group of individuals who, in the words of John Pease, were 'upright business men of known standing and character'.[102]

As a result of his failure to secure any significant alteration in the balance of political forces at local level, Spark then turned his attention to the forthcoming parliamentary election consequent upon the enfranchisement of the new borough in June 1867. Once again the Society of Friends mobilised and in June of the following year a 75-man selection committee, which had been brought into being by the borough's Liberal Registration Society, declared – with one dissentient – its choice. The official Liberal candidate was to be Edmund Backhouse, senior partner in Backhouses' Bank, a Quaker and one of the original members (1850–2) of the local board of health. At one stage in the proceedings Henry Fell Pease had considered offering himself as a candidate but in view of the bitterness displayed in the municipal elections he wisely deferred to Backhouse. The latter was, in any case a Quaker 'cousin' and with Joseph Whitwell already in Parliament 'there was nothing to be lost by such a small concession to the sensitivities of moderate middle class opinion'.[103] In July, having received a requisition containing 2,000 signatures and in the aftermath of 'a magnificent and enthusiastic meeting . . . numbering by common consent over 5,000 of the people of Darlington',[104] Spark himself decided to stand as a Radical candidate. An outstanding feature of the election campaign was the remarkable coincidence of views of the two candidates on national issues, and the ensuing poll, in November 1868, was a repeat of the municipal contest with Backhouse receiving 1,789 votes to his opponent's 872.

The extent of Spark's defeat was surprising. On nomination day a show of hands revealed Spark to be the more popular candidate by three to one, and he was adamant that he had received 1,350 firm promises of support.[105] Once again, accusations of 'undue influence' were made and credibility was lent to them by the resignation of several members of Backhouse's campaign committee because of the partisan behaviour of agents and employers, including members of the Pease family, notably Gurney and Henry Fell, who were observed 'accompanying' workmen to the booths on polling day. Although the NER had proclaimed its neutrality in the election it is significant that of twenty-four employees of the company traced in the poll book only the stationmaster at the NER's Bank Top station voted for Spark.[106]

Such allegations, which went as far as a petition against Backhouse's election, received some substantiation in the aftermath of the parliamentary election of 1874. Backhouse and Spark were once again the candidates, together with the Conservative, Thomas Gibson Bowles. Whilst the latter polled only 302 votes, Spark received 1,607 and Backhouse 1,625. This was a dramatic reduction in the Quaker's majority, with a slump in his share of the poll from 67 per cent to 46 per cent – while Spark's rose from 33 per cent to 45 per cent. The best gloss that contemporary opinion could put upon Backhouse's near-defeat was that the intervention of a Conservative candidate had cost him almost 200 votes, that in 1868 Backhouse had received virtually the whole of the Catholic vote but that in 1874 this was transferred *en bloc* to Spark, and that of the 1,000 additional voters on the register only 250 voted for Backhouse. The point was also made that Spark had never stopped electioneering since 1868 and had thrown open the grounds of the Greenbank estate to 'holiday-makers', while Backhouse chose to reside outside the borough so that his 'peculiar claim to support, his intellectual ability, his financial skill, and his invaluable services, were neither known nor appreciated by strangers, who judged men only by their professions upon the platform'.[107] In reality the situation was less complex. There were in fact two major differences between the elections of 1868 and 1874. The first was the introduction of the secret ballot after the Ballot Act of 1872 which in theory, at least, prevented the exertion of 'undue influence'. Secondly, and perhaps of greater importance in view of the Liberal government's anti-labour legislation,[108] the trade-union vote, centring on the local ironworkers' society, was 'immeasur-

ably stronger' than it had been in 1868. Under the leadership of John
Kane, the 500-strong society had advanced in status to a national organisation with 30,000 members by the time of the 1874 election. Despite
an uneasy relationship between Spark and Kane the ironworkers' vote
went to Spark and it was this, in combination with the secret ballot,
which almost secured Backhouse's defeat.[109]

To Darlington's Quaker establishment the 1874 election was a
traumatic event. In an article entitled 'The last of Mr Spark' their press
organ the *Northern Echo*,[110] commented:

> It is a matter for public congratulation that the political career of
> Mr Spark has been so abruptly terminated. He has done nothing
> for the town save monopolising the credit due to others who
> laboured with him and before him for the Charter of Incorpor-
> ation; he has consistently vilified its elected Member; he has mis-
> represented and abused its leading citizens; he has taken no part, or
> next to none, in the efforts which have been made to improve the
> moral, religious and social position of the borough.

Such views were as biased as they were unfair: the Quaker oligarchy
had dragged its feet over the issues of incorporation and parliamentary
representation, and whatever defects there may have been in Spark's
integrity and character – his proclivity for muck-raking, innuendo and
misrepresentation – it cannot be denied that his services to the town
deserved more sympathetic recognition.

The final act in the saga took place in 1880, when Spark again offered
himself as a parliamentary candidate in opposition to the official Liberal
and Quaker industrialist, Theodore Fry. On this occasion the oligarchy
was better equipped to contain the challenge, partly because Spark was
deprived of the support of the *Darlington and Stockton Times*. For a
number of years his financial position had been deteriorating due to a
chronic inability to live within his means and mismanagement of his
colliery business in Cumberland. On the morning of the election the
Darlington and Richmond Herald carried a leading article setting out
'Some Truths about Mr Spark'.[111] It recounted his full life history and
revealed that in 1876 on property valued by Spark at £336,000 the
realisation value had amounted to only £2,350. As the *Herald* ingenu-
ously concluded, its aim had been to 'afford the people of Darlington
some data upon which to judge whether this undischarged debtor and
vainglorious braggart is in very truth "a fit and proper person to represent Darlington in the Commons House of Parliament" '. Despite these
revelations Spark, devoid of canvass support and favourable newspaper
coverage, managed to poll a respectable 1,331 votes to Fry's 2,772. In
June 1880 Spark's bankruptcy was announced and on debts of £100,000

he eventually paid no more than 'one sixth of a penny' in the pound.[112] Thereafter, he disappeared from the political scene.

The period of the Sparkite revolt against Darlington's Quaker elite lasted for little more than a dozen years. The peak of Henry King Spark's influence was reached in 1874 when he came near to winning the parliamentary seat, and yet it was only two years later that John William Steel, a local Quaker apologist, was able to describe Darlington with perfect seriousness as 'the English Philadelphia':

> Till the followers of Fox and Penn settled on Skernside Darlington was a humdrum country town. Since the opening of the first public railway it has extended its ancient mills, formed engineering works the most complete between Glasgow and Doncaster and is yearly adding to the branches of its iron industries. Of all this activity Quakers have been the motive power and naturally they have increased in number. They form, however, but a small portion, not a tenth, of the 34,000 persons dwelling in Darlington but they still largely constitute the purse and the governing bodies of the town. And thus have the people delighted to honour the followers of Fox. Since the enfranchisement of South Durham, nearly one half of the members chosen as representatives have been Darlington Quakers; and naturally enough the representative of the borough itself has also been of the like faith. Darlington became a municipal borough some ten years ago and out of nine mayors seven have been Friends. One third of the Aldermanic bench is of this way of religious thought; a third of the school board members are of the 'meeting house' persuasion; and when a short time ago a new scheme nominated several members by virtue of their offices it was found that these all were Friends.[113]

By 1870 formal membership of the Darlington Society of Friends was just under 400 and although the ranks were swelled by the category of habitual attenders the actual membership thus fell far short of a tenth of the town's population.[114] The power and influence of the Peases therefore depended not so much upon their religious affiliation, but upon their status as leading employers and ratepayers. Similarly, with the Backhouses, their position as bankers and providers of credit gave them a critically important position in the community. Nevertheless, the importance of Quakerism in sustaining the influence of the Peases, especially in the institutions of local government, should not be discounted.[115] The Quakers in general were middle-class. Approximately two-thirds of the membership in the north-east of England consisted of clerks, shopkeepers and other small tradesmen, and the remaining third was dominated by the professional and manufacturing classes. Quakers, therefore, were generally of relatively high social standing, well educated, well disciplined and closely knit by generations of intermarriage. Industrialisation had been accompanied by increasing prosperity and with the growth of 'conformity to the world' the Darlington Friends, who accounted for one quarter of all Quakers in Northumberland and Durham, had provided a powerful challenge to traditional landed influence.[116] There is an irony, therefore, in the fact that the radicalism displayed by Joseph Pease in 1832 had been eradicated in little more than a generation. By 1867 the Society of Friends had supplanted their former antagonists as defenders of a new order of society based upon industry and commerce – the company of the elect dispensing God's patronage in the face of crude opportunism.

4

The Great Depression

In the final quarter of the nineteenth century the industrial economy of north-east England enjoyed considerable expansion. Whilst there was some slackening in the momentum of growth as certain industries, notably lead mining, chemicals, pottery and glassmaking, suffered decline, others forged ahead on the basis of expanding markets both at home and abroad.[1] The principal growth industries in this period were those which had provided the dynamics of expansion in the mid-nineteenth century – coal mining, engineering and the metallurgical industries. Within this growth Teesside consolidated its position as a major centre of heavy industry, rising to prominence after 1880 as a considerable producer of steel.[2] The local wrought-iron industry had been carried forward by an insatiable demand for ferrous metals of all kinds after 1850, but by the mid-1880s it had been eclipsed by its more modern rival. Regular production of acid steel began in the district at the Eston works of Bolckow Vaughan and Co. in 1876, utilising imported hematite ores in a Bessemer converter. But following the successful introduction of the Thomas-Gilchrist process in 1879, substantial quantities of basic steel began to be manufactured from blast-furnace metal derived from the hitherto unusable Cleveland ironstone with its high phosphoric content. Other areas of expansion on Teesside, most of them utilising the new steel technology, included such specialist activities as bridge construction, metal tube and pipe making, railway equipment of all kinds and shipbuilding.[3] Unfortunately, there was a price to be paid for this expansion, and it took the form of intensified cyclical instability as a result of increasing dependence on overseas markets for the products of a relatively small number of major growth sectors. The pattern of industrial activity which was emerging on Teesside after 1850 was to have profound consequences in the inter-war period when mass unemployment in the staple export trades accompanied the progressive collapse of the international economy. But even before 1914, as Lady Florence Bell pointed out in her remarkable study *At the Works*, the great majority of Middlesbrough's industrial workforce was on the borderline between marginal security and 'poverty and want'.[4]

The economic fortunes of north-east England as a whole after 1870 can be illustrated particularly well by the experience of the NER.[5] In the years 1870–3 the overseas demand for British capital goods, especially iron manufacturers, boomed, and the company's gross revenue increased at an annual rate of more than 10 per cent. Although gross revenue continued to increase until 1875, business confidence was being undermined by a combination of overseas financial crises and the mounting difficulties of local iron manufacturers in the face of increasing competition from steel rails. Between 1873 and 1879 the region's iron output fell by more than 50 per cent and this was inevitably reflected in a rising tide of bankruptcies and closures. On Teesside alone 1874 witnessed the failure of the Erimus Iron Works, Swan Coates and the Lackenby Iron Works. In the following year Tom Vaughan and the Britannia Ironworks failed and they were followed in 1879 by the Skerne, Tees Side, Imperial and Ayrton Ironworks and Hopkins Gilkes and Company.[6] For the NER the 'iron smash' led to a severe reduction in the carriage of coal, limestone and ironstone, and between 1876 and 1879 gross revenue fell by 16 per cent with a concomitant fall in dividends. In November 1879, however, there was an upturn in receipts, partly in response to increased demand for steel rails in the USA. Since bulk steel-making was in its infancy in the northeast, the major contribution to recovery came from the need for more shipping space which in turn boosted the fortunes of the shipbuilding industry where steel had yet to oust iron plates. Thus in the early 1880s the NER's mineral traffic boomed and, with a marked expansion in the carriage of freight and passengers, dividends once more approached the levels of the mid-1870s. In 1884 there was a severe reduction in the demand for iron plates and in the face of chronic overproduction Bolckow and Vaughan shut down half of their blast-furnace capacity and were obliged to ask the NER for a reduction in traffic rates for all materials transported to and from their Witton Park works. Once again, therefore, the NER's gross revenue declined sharply and in 1886 the worst dividend since 1868 was declared. Recovery from the recession of the mid-1880s came slowly as the shipbuilding industry began to experience a phase of cyclical expansion. This was augmented by rising coal exports and an increase in the carriage of passengers. The upswing of the late 1880s was, however, of short duration, and by 1890 the shipbuilding industry was once more in recession. In 1892 the fall in revenue for the NER was exacerbated by the Durham coal strike. Ironically, the situation eased slightly in 1893–4 as a result of coal strikes in south Yorkshire and Scotland which gave a modest boost to the north-eastern coalfield. The impetus for recovery after 1895 did not come initially from the export sector but from rising goods traffic receipts in response to a domestic building boom. Thereafter, however, the NER's mineral traffic enjoyed sustained expansion as a result of increased coal exports and imports of iron ore.

As the virtual monopoly supplier of rail transport in the north-east of England, the experiences of the NER mirrored those of the regional economy. Whilst account must be taken of the relative buoyancy of the company's passenger revenue and the implications for dividends of mounting state regulation and labour militancy, what is particularly striking is the well defined pattern of boom and slump in response to external stimuli. Even in those industries which enjoyed impressive market expansion in the decades after 1870 the secular trend of output concealed a considerable degree of cyclical fluctuation. In the coal industry, for example, the boom years of the early 1870s were followed by a long recession which lasted until 1879; further recessions occurred in the mid-1880s and 1890s. Thus, although the two decades after 1875 were characterised by considerable growth in output and employment they were not years of prosperity for the industry, the period from 1890 to 1893 being 'a brief oasis of prosperity in a desert of low returns to both capital and labour'.[7] The response of colliery owners to commercial uncertainty was inhibited by the organisation and structure of their industry as a whole. One solution for low selling prices mooted in the early 1890s was for the establishment of sales cartels and such organisations were formed in Lancashire and Cheshire in 1893 and in the Durham coalfield in 1894. By the end of 1895, however, both cartels were defunct due to underselling by non-member firms and rail and sea competition from other colliery districts. In short, the pronounced regional and intra-regional diversity of the coal industry, with each mining district possessing its own cost structure, combined to produce intense competition in the domestic market which was in turn reinforced by the periodic instability of the export trade. The only effective remedy for coping with depressed selling prices was to reduce wages – a highly attractive policy as the wage bill could amount to 75 per cent of total costs of production. Indeed, in the years after 1873, when prices for most grades of coal collapsed, the wage bargaining mechanism in the industry was formalised on the basis of selling price sliding-scales: wage rates were calculated by reference to the current price of coal in relation to selling prices in an agreed base year. This was achieved with the acquiescence of trade unionists in the belief that if wages were bound to fall in times of recession so they were bound to rise when trade was recovering.[8] Although sliding-scale wage agreements were subsequently abandoned in the Durham coalfield in 1889 in accordance with the trend in other mining districts, it is noteworthy that labour relations remained generally good,[9] at least until the Durham Miners' Association (whose leaders had always stressed the coalfield's vulnerability to fluctuations in the export trade) affiliated with the increasingly militant Miners' Federation of Great Britain in 1908.[10]

As a director of the NER with extensive interests in coal and ironstone mining, Sir Joseph Whitwell Pease was well aware of the vagaries of the trade cycle and its adverse effects on a largely self-sufficient regional economy. He was, of course, not alone in this, and his own concern was matched by that of fellow industrialists in attempting to mitigate the worst effects of trade recession. In 1898, when Sir Joseph was chairman of the NER, his deputy was Sir Isaac Lowthian Bell, the eminent iron and steel magnate, and the rest of the board included Sir David Dale, closely identified with the Pease interest and by that time chairman of the Consett Iron Company, Sir Lindsay Wood, former chairman of the Durham Coalowners' Association, and Sir James Joicey (later Lord Joicey), one of the north-east's leading colliery entrepreneurs. Other directors represented the interests of shipbuilding, shipping and engineering industries, individual ports and agriculture.[11] Yet, despite its status as a near-monopoly, the NER consistently refused to exploit its bargaining position *vis-à-vis* its customers. Even before the Railway and Canal Traffic Act of 1894 which served virtually to freeze railway rates, the company's pricing policy was unusually moderate and this went hand in hand with a relatively progressive attitude towards the conduct of labour relations.[12] At one level it can be argued that the NER's monopolistic powers were constrained by the continuing competition of canal and sea transport and the ever-present dangers of invasion from new or rival companies. But in view of the composition of the directorate – the interrelatedness of their interests and the fact that several members were major traffic senders in their own right – it is equally valid to argue that the NER was 'a sort of holding company for the region as a whole, and to attempt to isolate its pricing policy in terms of the individual firm may not be fully relevant'. As the company's most recent historian has concluded, such a contention is difficult to prove, but there is some evidence to suggest that the NER 'may have been attempting to maximize not just company profits, but to some extent also the profits of local industry'.[13]

The fact remains that the cyclical pattern of economic activity in the years after 1870 had profound implications for the process of decision-making in industry and commerce, and as far as the Peases are concerned it is impossible to provide a full analysis of the special difficulties with which they were confronted without taking account of the distinctive economic environment of late-Victorian Britain. Even before the economic downturn of 1873 which preceded the 'iron smash' of the later 1870s the financial fortunes of the Pease dynasty were betraying signs of weakness. The principal source of difficulty was the private bank, J. and J. W. Pease. Until the death of Joseph Pease in 1872 this concern consisted of a partnership between Joseph and his five sons, Joseph Whitwell, Edward, Arthur, Gurney and Charles. In 1872 Gurney also died and this was followed in 1873 by the death of Charles. The effect of these deaths was to diminish the resources of the remaining brothers in the bank since it was agreed that the interests of Gurney and Charles in the family businesses should be bought out so that their estates could be invested more securely in order to provide a less speculative source of income for the widows and children of the deceased brothers. It was a consequence of their knowledge of how serious it would be for the financing of the family businesses and the private accounts of their surviving relatives in the event of further deaths that Joseph Whitwell, Edward and Arthur inserted provisions in their wills giving the remaining partners power to leave their business investments intact. Such was the case following the death of Edward in 1880 when his interest in J. and J. W. Pease alone was bought out for the sum of £5,818. This was of small comfort, however, to Edward's surviving daughter Beatrice, then aged fourteen. Her father had died with an overdraft of £176,883 in J. and J. W. Pease and the charges arising from this had to be set against the earning power of his industrial assets, much to the embarrassment of Joseph Whitwell and Arthur, the trustees of Edward's estate.[14]

After Edward's death the partners in the bank were Joseph Whitwell with a share of fourteen-twentieths, Arthur with five-twentieths and Alfred, the elder son of the former, with one-twentieth. In January 1881 the number of partners was increased to four when Alfred's brother Jack was given a one-twentieth share by his father when he came of age whilst still an undergraduate at Cambridge. As Jack commented many years later, 'I knew nothing of the liability of the business, but was told that I should get £400 per annum or so additional income'.[15]

The rapidly succeeding deaths in the Pease family had further implications for the conduct of its business affairs. Gurney had been actively involved in managing the ironstone department of J. W. Pease and Co. and even before the death of Charles, whose principal responsibilities lay with the bank, considerable discussion had taken place concerning the overextension of the family's managerial capabilities. Henry Pease was exclusively concerned with the Darlington Section of the NER and his son Henry Fell was almost wholly engaged in the running of the family woollen business. In June 1872 two courses of action were considered in relation to the mining enterprises: one 'to take in fresh blood, the other to sell either to a limited [company] or altogether'.[16] It was eventually decided that David Dale should be invited to become a partner with a one-tenth share in J. W. Pease and Co. and Joseph Pease and Partners. By this time Dale's credentials as a businessman were impressive: in 1869 he had been appointed sole managing director of the now flourishing Consett Iron Company and in 1871 he had accepted a similar appointment with the Darlington Section of the NER. Through his association with the Shildon Locomotive Works he was thoroughly conversant with the management of a successful engineering concern and he already possessed an outstanding reputation as an advocate of arbitration in labour disputes, having accepted the appointment as first president of the Board of Arbitration and Conciliation for the Manufactured Iron Trade of the North of England in 1869.[17] In all of these respects Dale was potentially a highly congenial working colleague. His views on labour relations, for example, were especially attractive to Sir Joseph, whose insistence that trade unions should desist from 'meddling in the market for labour' was matched by an equally firm belief in the concept of partnership between labour and capital.[18] Joseph Pease, moreover, had inaugurated Dale's business career (see above, p. 40) and the attractions of offering him a partnership could only have been enhanced by his status as a leading Darlington Quaker possessing close personal relationships with members of the Pease family. In July 1872, therefore, Dale was offered and accepted a one-tenth partnership in the Pease mining concerns[19] and it was largely due to his influence that in 1882, after the deaths of Edward and Henry, a single private limited liability company was established with a capital of £2.25 million to administer the coal, ironstone and limestone departments.[20] The new concern, Pease and Partners Ltd, was chaired by Sir Joseph Whitwell Pease, whilst Dale was appointed vice-chairman and managing director. The other partners in the enterprise were Arthur, Alfred and Jack, and the cousins Henry Fell and Edwin Lucas Pease.[21]

With Dale as the principal executive manager, Pease and Partners proved to be a moderately profitable concern, at least until 1890, when the company earned a record surplus of £290,000 over working charges.[22] There followed, however, a period of extremely flat trade until 1896 with particularly poor results in 1892, mainly as a result of the extended labour dispute of that year.[23] In fact, from 1892 to 1896 the company paid no dividend, with the result that the average 6½ per cent paid in the 1880s was reduced to an overall rate of 2 per cent for the fourteen years to June 1898.[24] With the exception of the Middlesbrough Estate and railway dividends, it was colliery enterprise which provided the Pease family with its principal source of income after 1880. As imports of Spanish and Algerian ores rose in response to the expansion of steelmaking capacity on Teesside and at Consett the ironstone side of the business went into long-term decline at the same time as the output of coal increased. In the latter respect Pease and Partners was a relatively fortunate concern: unlike many of its north-eastern counterparts it was to some extent shielded from market fluctuations induced by the state of overseas demand. In view of their respective positions and personal business relations, both Sir Joseph and Dale were in a strong position to negotiate long-term sales contracts with the NER, the Consett Iron Company and a number of other Teesside iron and steel firms.

There can be little doubt that the recruitment of David Dale proved highly beneficial to the economic fortunes of the Pease family. An unimaginative man with a rather cold manner, he was 'simply the soundest man of business, the most experienced pilot on the sea of commerce that the north-east of England could produce'.[25] In view of subsequent events it was unfortunate that his business expertise was not employed more extensively in running the remainder of the Pease interests, where a greater degree of objectivity, even ruthlessness, would have been desirable. Dale's business responsibilities, however, were extremely onerous, and this resulted in Sir Joseph being left to deal almost single-handedly with the financial affairs of three companies whose liquidity problems ultimately proved to be intractable. The first of these concerns was Robert Stephenson and Co. Joseph Pease had left a large interest in this firm to his sons but the deed of association left the management entirely to the Stephenson family. Such evidence as exists indicates that at the very time when foreign competition was mounting in the period after 1870 the firm was failing to maintain the contacts built up by Robert Stephenson during extensive overseas travels before his premature death in 1859. Certainly, Sir Joseph's diaries contain many references to the shortage of orders and financial losses.[26] In 1883, after a visit to Newcastle, he noted that 'The management seems all asleep and wants waking up.'[27] Three years later, at Sir Joseph's suggestion, the firm was converted into a private limited company, one main object being to reduce the liability of the estate of the recently deceased Edward Pease to calls on capital account (£5,304) for which he was liable.[28] At the end of 1886 a lease was taken on a shipyard at Hebburn-on-Tyne for the building of marine engines and boilers in order to facilitate a reorganisation of the locomotive construction department at Newcastle. The losses continued to mount, however, and, as the official historian of the company noted, the extensions of 1886 proved to be 'more apparent than real' since they left unanswered the question of whether it was desirable to persist in the operation of plant and equipment at the old Forth Street works which was technically obsolescent and poorly organised.[29] From 1876 to 1899 the cumulative losses of Robert Stephenson and Co. amounted to £580,267. Of this total £197,122 was debited to the private accounts of Sir Joseph and Arthur Pease in J. and J. W. Pease. To this figure could be added the sum of £10,916 – the amount paid by the surviving Pease brothers in purchasing the shares of Gurney and Charles in the company.[30]

Another concern whose affairs preoccupied Sir Joseph was the iron-making firm of Wilsons, Pease and Co. This was the successor to the engine works and iron foundry established at Middlesbrough in 1843 by Edgar Gilkes, Isaac Wilson and Charles Leatham.[31] Joseph Beaumont Pease, the grandson of Joseph Pease of Feethams, was the son-in-law of Wilson and he was admitted to partnership in the concern in 1858 following Leatham's death. After his own death in 1873 Joseph Beaumont's shares passed to Joseph Whitwell, and thereafter the firm was managed by members of the Wilson family. It received cash injections from Sir Joseph to the extent of £28,784 during the recession of 1879–81 and, as in the case of Robert Stephenson and Co., he debited his own account at J. and J. W. Pease with the requisite sum.[32] Even so, by 1901 Wilsons, Pease and Co. had accumulated a heavy overdraft of £151,698 on its own account at the bank.[33] In that year the plant and equipment were antiquated and the management, under the guidance of the ageing Theodore Wilson, virtually moribund.

The third concern, Henry Pease and Co., was the original family woollen business. In the latter half of the nineteenth century it was managed successively by Henry, Edward and Henry Fell Pease, although Sir Joseph was often consulted in the running of the company. This was hardly surprising in view of the fact that he was the senior partner in J. and J. W. Pease and the company required extensive overdraft facilities. Between May 1871 and June 1902 Henry Pease and Co.'s losses totalled £260,477.[34] Its overdraft at J. and J. W. Pease alone amounted to £140,000, whilst Sir Joseph had extended credit at regular intervals from his own account at the bank to the extent of £119,282.[35] The problem confronting the firm can hardly have been technical obsolescence. In the years 1870–3 buildings which were less than twenty years old were refurbished and new equipment to the value of £30,000 installed. In 1873 net profits totalled £15,000, but by the end of the decade, coinciding with the period of Edward's management, the cumulative losses amounted to £100,000, with £40,000 being lost in the single year 1879–80. In May 1880 Sir Joseph wrote to his elder son Alfred stating that 'I am more anxious about this mill business than any other of our concerns simply because I have not that confidence in the daily administration that I have in the others'.[36] According to Sir Joseph, the firm habitually carried excessive stocks which required drastic reduction if the losses were to be stemmed. After the advent of Henry Fell Pease to the management, however, matters did not improve. In 1888 Sir Joseph noted in his diary that the administration of the mills was 'wretched', and in 1892, following the announcement of 'disgusting losses', it was revealed that some employees had been engaged in the fraudulent dating of stock – 'Keeping back invoices and taking credit for the goods they represented!'[37]

Thus, over a period of thirty years Sir Joseph poured £395,000 on his own account into three enterprises which were persistent loss makers. But his generosity had even wider limits. In the later 1870s at the time of the 'iron smash' he extended help on a personal basis to several Middlesbrough ironmasters, notably Tom Vaughan, William Hopkins, James Taylor and William Taylor, and placed £20,000 at the disposal of Isaac Wilson's Middlesbrough Potteries, only to see the concern wound up in September 1890. Together with his brother Arthur, he came to the aid of relatives in financial distress, in particular Henry Fell Pease and members of the Fox and Fowler families. At the death of the former in 1896 his overdraft in J. and J. W. Pease stood at £181,843; advances made to him during his lifetime and the difference between the value of the securities retained by the partners and the overdraft produced a loss of £70,476 to the bank after his death.[38] This was followed in 1897 by a loan of £39,678 to William Fowler, the distinguished chairman of John Fowler and Co., steam plough manufacturers of Leeds. Fowler, who was a brother-in-law of Sir Joseph and Arthur, used the loan for an abortive investment in petroleum exploration, and in December 1902 the total loan with accumulated interest amounted to £51,195.[39] Sir Joseph also absorbed losses of £5,000 made by the *Northern Echo* after 1879 and spent £69,998 over the period 1879–1901 in maintaining the Darlington properties held by the Pease family as a whole, again debiting his personal account for this sum. Finally, he took full responsibility for the immense losses of £222,631 sustained by the family's ironstone and limestone business in the years 1875–80 before its absorption into Pease and Partners Ltd.[40]

In succeeding years, after the onset of trade recession in 1873, the financial position of J. and J. W. Pease was deteriorating. Year by year the bank was becoming increasingly illiquid as it extended almost unlimited credit to loss-making firms. In addition, the private accounts of the principal partners – after 1880 Sir Joseph and Arthur – displayed large and growing overdrafts as they absorbed part of the losses of these firms out of their own incomes. What was especially dangerous in this situation was that the problem of illiquidity endangered the ability of the partners to meet their obligations to those public enterprises – the NER, the Consett Iron Company and the Weardale and Shildon Water Company – which gave a substantial part of their local banking business to J. and J. W. Pease. The strategy adopted by the partners to enable them to continue as bankers was a fourfold one. The first element was the selling and mortgaging of property. Sir Joseph's first two London homes were in Princes Gardens, a fashionable square in Kensington. At some time in the 1870s, probably in the first part of the decade when the coal and iron trades were booming, he purchased a magnificent mansion set in its own grounds in Kensington Palace Gardens. In 1886, however, it was placed on the market and it was sold in 1889 when Sir Joseph bought a more modest but still substantial house in Grosvenor Gardens. In November 1892 the latter was mortgaged and this was followed in 1897 by a mortgage of £127,000 provided by the National Provincial Bank on the Hutton and Pinchinthorpe estate.[41]

The period from 1892 to 1896, which followed especially poor trading conditions, was one of extreme difficulty for Sir Joseph and he began to supplement mortgages by the receipt of bank loans against the security of his shares in Pease and Partners. At this time his personal expenditure was averaging £8,500 per annum and out of this he was obliged to maintain a 3,000-acre estate in north Yorkshire and houses in London and Falmouth, as well as paying the wages of staff, entertaining, and attending to his parliamentary duties. In 1892 he inaugurated a campaign for economy in his household at Hutton (then about 20-strong), attempted to curtail his own expenditure, which he found difficult to do 'and keep up any state' and eventually sought comfort in endeavouring 'to look higher for aid in all these difficulties'. Sir Joseph's prayers were soon answered in the receipt of loans against the security of shares from Prescotts and the National Provincial Bank.[42] In 1894 he attempted to negotiate a loan from the National Temperance Society, but finding their terms too onerous he obtained accommodation to the extent of £40,000 from the National Discount Company against the security of his Pease and Partners shares. In the same year Sir Joseph again had recourse to the National Provincial Bank for an advance of £5,500 against the security of the family property at Marske in order to help Arthur who was experiencing financial difficulties in the running of the Normanby Ironworks, a firm in which he and his sons had a large interest.[43] No more graphic an illustration of Sir Joseph's financial plight can be provided than his grateful acceptance in 1895 of a loan of £25,000 from his Scottish host and shooting companion, Sir Donald Currie, after the receipt of 'letters troublesome' urging his return to Darlington. The relevant diary entry is revealing:

> I told [Sir Donald] that we were making little profit in the coal trade and having had to advance to Stephensons . . . we were working with too little margin . . . we were over our limit in London but our bankers were very good to us . . . he offered to lend me £25,000 for 12 months to be renewed 6 months after if I wanted. Anything more generous I never knew – it nearly knocked the wind out of me.[44]

Finally, in February 1896 Sir Joseph entered into discussions with the National Provincial Bank on 'a general scheme to end some of our overdraws'; the result was not a loan but the mortgaging of the Hutton and Pinchinthorpe estate.[45]

The mortgaging of property and the negotiation of loans were augmented from 1893 by the receipt of regular financial aid from a number of banks to enable J. and J. W. Pease to meet the biannual dividend payments of the NER, the Consett Iron Company and the Weardale and Shildon Water Company. In August of any year overdraft facilities to the extent of £120,000 were extended to J. and J. W. Pease by the York City and County Bank, Prescotts Bank and the National Provincial Bank. These were supplemented by secured loans from Messrs Gurneys' Bank in Norwich and following the great amalgamation of 1896 (see below, p. 101) from Messrs Barclay and Co. after they had absorbed the Gurney and Backhouse banking interests. The arrangement with Norwich provided for two loans in February and August of any year totalling £50,000, rising to £60,000 after February

1898. Since the use of their shares in Pease and Partners was precluded by the requirements of other loan arrangements Sir Joseph and Arthur were obliged to offer as security a portion of their shares in the Middlesbrough Estate.[46] This had been incorporated as recently as July 1886, probably with the intention on Sir Joseph's part of overcoming the reluctance of bankers to offer loans on the security of heritable property.[47]

The final direct expedient that Sir Joseph resorted to was the reorganisation and reconstruction of the three firms which were a major burden on his own finances and those of the bank. After the death of Henry Fell Pease the mills of Henry Pease and Co. were reconstituted under new management and in 1898, when Sir Joseph became the sole surviving partner, they began to make modest profits.[48] For Robert Stephenson and Co. a more drastic plan was implemented. In 1897 steps were taken to wind up the business with Sir Joseph sacrificing his legal claim to the priority of the debenture stock which he held to the extent of £108,848.[49] Two years later, in co-operation with Sir Christopher Furness (later Baron Furness of Grantley), Sir William Armstrong and Sir Raylton Dixon – all of them national figures in the shipping and shipbuilding industries – Sir Joseph floated a new public company which immediately set about the task of dismantling the old Forth Street works and constructing a new locomotive-building plant on a 54-acre site at Darlington as well as the largest dry dock in the north-east of England at the company's Hebburn shipyard.[50] This was followed in 1901 by a similar exercise for Wilsons, Pease and Co. which became a public concern under new management charged with the task of modernising the plant and equipment.[51]

Before proceeding to an assessment of Sir Joseph's commercial policies after 1873 there is one further aspect of his business activities which merits attention since it has some bearing on his own financial position and also that of the wider Pease industrial empire. This concerns his attitude towards the conduct of labour relations in the heavy industries of north-east England. As one of the most important employers of labour active in Liberal politics, Sir Joseph appears as a representative of those proponents of enlightened capitalism, such as A. J. Mundella and Samuel Morley, who believed that one of the basic principles of Liberalism was that there should be a partnership between capital and labour in the belief that the interests of working men and their employers were identical. The well-being of industry benefited all alike: the prosperity of capitalists would ensure the prosperity of working men and their families and this could be achieved only by the maintenance of industrial peace.[52] These principles of 'a liberal capitalism and capitalist Liberalism' found expression in arbitration and conciliation in industry after 1870, a period which witnessed the consolidation of 'Lib-Labism' when respectable labour leaders, more often than not Nonconformists, tended to be associated politically with the Liberal Party.[53] It has already been noted that Sir Joseph proclaimed himself to be in accord with the views of David Dale in these respects (see above, p. 78) and their agreement was reflected in Dale's use of Sir Joseph as an arbitrator in the northern manufactured-iron trade on several occasions after 1875. The relevance of this in the present context is that as a proponent of orthodox political economy, and in the midst of the long-term price fall after 1873, Sir Joseph felt bound to make arbitration awards which, in reflecting the 'general state of trade', invariably resulted in wage reductions. In 1882, for example, the operative vice-president of the Board of Arbitration and Conciliation for the Manufactured Iron Trade of the North of England refused to propose a vote of thanks to Sir Joseph as a result of his adverse award to the union and in 1892, at the time of the great dispute in the Durham coalfield, he is reputed to have adopted an extremely harsh stance on the claims of the Durham Miners' Association.[54] In view of the mounting financial difficulties with which he was confronted it would be tempting to conclude that Sir Joseph's advocacy of wage reductions during the 'Great Depression' was determined by purely selfish commercial considerations – that in reality the alliance between capital and labour was a sham and that his paternalism as an employer (see above, p. 63) was at best ambiguous and at worst hypocritical. Whilst it cannot be denied that Sir Joseph's invocation of the laws of political economy weighted the scales of industrial partnership heavily in favour of capital, it would be misleading to conclude that his actions in the sphere of labour relations were motivated by personal, let alone class interests. This is confirmed by the fact that at the peak of the 'iron smash' in 1879 Sir Joseph publicly denounced his fellow colliery owners in Co. Durham for attempting to overturn the existing sliding-scale agreement for the coalfield unilaterally and in the dispute of 1892 he took a courageous stand as the only leading colliery owner in the country who was prepared, from the outset, to accept an arbitrated settlement.[55] Sir Joseph was a firm advocate of the view that the level of selling prices should be the principal determinant of wages and to that extent his own economic interests were undoubtedly safeguarded, especially in periods of trade recession. But in the context of the times his commitment to political Liberalism and its industrial counterpart – arbitration – was based upon the concept of 'the spirit of a unified industrial capitalist system in which labour and capital were organically interrelated and interdependent'.[56] It is legitimate to conclude, therefore, that the strength of 'Lib-Lab:sm' and the acceptance of orthodox political economy by trade union leaders in the mining communities of north-east England played their part in sustaining the Peases' financial position – however unconsciously, or unselfishly, on Sir Joseph's part.

In appraising Sir Joseph's strategy as an entrepreneur over the thirty-year period from 1870 to 1900 it is difficult to refute the verdict that in marked contrast to his forebears he was lacking in business acumen. If the hallmark of entrepreneurial success is the maximisation of profits by the exploitation of favourable investment opportunities then it is equally valid to argue that the truly competent entrepreneur should know when to liquidate or reconstruct an unsuccessful business. This argument applies with particular force to Sir Joseph in view of the persistent losses sustained by Henry Pease and Co., Robert Stephenson and Co., and Wilsons, Pease after 1875 and the obvious dangers that this entailed for the stability of J. and J. W. Pease, a private banking concern with unlimited liability on the partners. In all three cases reconstruction was delayed for at least a decade beyond what could be considered reasonable in view of their commercial records during the previous fifteen years. The dangers of illiquidity, moreover, were pointed out to Sir Joseph by members of his own family. Alfred especially was concerned to bring to his father's attention the deteriorating position of the bank.

Alfred began his business career in J. and J. W. Pease in 1880 and when Pease and Partners was created in 1882 he advocated the formation of a public company and in the same year argued forcefully for the winding up of Henry Pease and Co. – 'This dreadful sink [which] swallows up an overdraft of £7,000 a year'.[57] In 1886 he called for the formation of a limited liability company for the loss-making *Northern Echo* and in June 1888, after a particularly worrying period in the bank, recorded the following entry:

> The last fortnight has been an anxious one, in fact for a year past I have felt that the clouds of the future have been gathering. Anxieties in business matters that cannot be put on paper are harassing enough especially when you feel that serious events may take place for which you are not in the least responsible. The advice I have given when asked for it, has only found support from Jack; for years my forebodings and opinions on the way certain private persons were managing their concerns have been received as the views of a pessimist and a croaker and now these persons led away by sanguine temperaments and inability to realise *facts* find themselves in queer street.[58]

With the exception of the *Northern Echo*, which was disposed of in September 1889,[59] Alfred's views went unheeded and within four years of this outburst he had resigned as private secretary to Lord Rosebery and abandoned his position (but not his partnership) in the bank in order to accompany his wife, who was suffering from a lung infection, to Algeria. Until her death in 1910 Helen Pease was periodically very ill, but rather than find a companion for her from within the ranks of maiden aunts and cousins within the wider Pease family, Alfred chose to accompany his wife abroad himself. He spent the greater part of the period from 1892 to 1895 in Algeria with Helen and in the following three years earned for himself a reputation as a hunter of big game in Somaliland with a series of publications on African and British wildlife.[60] The devotion to his wife was admirable but, as his first son Edward later pointed out, a really ambitious man, whether in business or politics, would have remained at home.[61] Although it is a matter for conjecture, it is possible that after a decade of seeing his advice on critical issues ignored Alfred, the heir apparent to the Pease dynasty, used his wife's ill health to escape from a situation which he found increasingly intolerable. He complained on more than one occasion that his father's chief confidant in J. and J. W. Pease was his factotum, Charles Fry, a first-class accountant, but totally overawed by Sir Joseph and, according to Alfred, 'without any notion of policy or plans' and 'unable to budge on any of his preconceived ideas and methods'.[62]

In defence of Sir Joseph's actions a number of arguments can be offered; some of them are conjectural, but others are based upon firm evidence of his intentions and policy. In the first instance, if it is valid to claim that entrepreneurs in the staple industries, with their experience of extremely buoyant trading conditions in the decade before 1914, encountered understandable difficulties in revising their business expectations in the fundamentally different commercial conditions of the 1920s, then a similar argument can be deployed in defence of Sir Joseph. His formative years as an entrepreneur coincided with the opening up of the Cleveland ironstone district, the iron boom on Teesside and the large profits earned by the Stockton and Darlington Railway and the other family businesses in coal, coke, limestone and ironstone. The peak of prosperity was reached in 1873 when Joseph Pease and Partners alone made record profits of £140,000 and Wilsons, Pease and Co. £60,000.[63] The mid-Victorian decades were not without business fluctuations, but for Sir Joseph and his fellow north-east industrialists the rising *trend* of prosperity implanted standards of what was normal and correct in the commercial world, standards which remained substantially intact after 1873, despite the downturn in prices. Sir Joseph therefore regarded the 'ups and downs' of trade as inevitable, and if previous experience was to be trusted trade revival was bound to come – as indeed it did on several occasions after 1873, albeit on a modest scale. Given this optimistic outlook based upon the accumulated knowledge of years of business experience, there are grounds for understanding in part at least why Sir Joseph persisted in advancing credit and absorbing the losses of unprofitable concerns. This gives rise to a further point. The industrial interests of the Pease family were spread over a number of businesses by the third quarter of the nineteenth century and this in itself greatly complicated the process of decision-making because each business possessed its own cost structure and record of profitability. There was a steady if unspectacular income from the Middlesbrough Estate whilst Pease and Partners' colliery department was the mainstay of Sir Joseph's income. But even the loss-making firms had their good years and this again may have served to prolong unrealistic expectations. A third factor which should be borne in mind is that until the mid-1890s there is no evidence to suggest that Sir Joseph encountered any difficulties in securing accommodation from his bankers. It was the provision of loans at frequent intervals that enabled J. and J. W. Pease to survive. It is possible, therefore, that any serious attempt by Sir Joseph to curtail his own expenditure, let alone the liquidation of concerns with which he was closely associated, would have injured his credit. Again, it must remain a matter for conjecture, but in so far as Sir Joseph was endowed with a strong sense of public duty and an awareness of his status as one of the most influential industrialists in the north-east of England, he was not prepared to disregard the damage to confidence in the regional economy if, say, Wilsons, Pease or Robert Stephenson and Co. had been wound up in the 1880s. It is also possible that Sir Joseph was consciously influenced by the example of his father who had extended generous financial aid to Teesside industrialists from the 1840s onwards. As for Henry Pease and Co., the same arguments apply, but in this case there are additional dimensions. It is important to remember that this firm was the original family business and, Alfred's strictures notwithstanding, it was looked upon with feelings of sentiment and affection. Furthermore, it was located in Darlington, the centre of the Peases' business activities. To have closed Henry Pease and Co. would have resulted in 800 people being thrown out of work in the local community and this Sir Joseph was not prepared to tolerate in view of the distress that would be caused to a significant proportion of the town's inhabitants.[64] It is likely that these humanitarian considerations were the product of a Quaker conscience, but a more cynical view would be to suggest that in the aftermath of the Ballot Act of 1872 the closure of the woollen mills might have been accompanied by the re-emergence of electoral difficulties for the 'company of the elect'.[65] In short, Sir Joseph's acceptance of the losses of Wilsons, Pease, Robert Stephenson and Co. and Henry Pease and Co. should not be judged solely in terms of 'rational' entrepreneurial behaviour.[66]

As for Sir Joseph's dismissive attitude towards his elder son, this can be better understood when it is realised that Alfred bitterly resented his father's decision to place him in J. and J. W. Pease rather than in the colliery department at the outset of his business career. As he stated in retrospect:

I begged to go into the mining or colliery office but no, I was to go

4 Sir Alfred Edward Pease, Bt. (1857–1939), *c*. 1898.

into the place [my father] selected, with Charles Fry. So to the Counting House I went by early train 5 or 6 days a week for some five years. There was nothing for me to do. I took up each clerk's work in turn, from the bottom to the top, and everyone of these poor fellows had a more monstrous and soul-killing occupation than the other, from the bottle washer who had to address envelopes, lick stamps and enter the addresses in a book . . . to the keeper of the ledger who all his life totted up columns of figures and called over at 3 o'clock. For 22 years I was supposed to do . . . this useless job in a back room and never had a day or an hour's responsibility. . . . It is a wicked thing to put a young man into work for which he has no inclination and to prevent him from having any word in the path he is to take through life.[67]

If Alfred's feelings are readily understandable – born into relative afflu- ence, Cambridge-educated and eager for a position of responsibility – then so are his father's. At the insistence of *his* father Sir Joseph too had begun his career 'at the bottom' and the counting house would provide his own son with the firm grounding in business that he had received. In this light Alfred's well-founded pessimism was dismissed as the peevish 'croaking' of a man who, intentionally or not, gave the impres- sion that he disliked the whole notion of a business career – at least as defined by his father. In analysing these personal relationships it should also be borne in mind that Sir Joseph Whitwell Pease was extremely conscious of his status as Joseph Pease's eldest son: he had inherited the position of his father and was therefore the chief custodian of the fam- ily's financial interests. As Alfred remarked:

To the end of his life my father . . . never could be dispossessed of the old-fashioned notion of the family's common stock and com- mon interest: his labour, and as long as he had it, his wealth, was at the disposal of his family.[68]

Within a period of two years in the early 1870s Sir Joseph's father and two of his brothers had died and only a few years later another brother and his uncle Henry. He was then left to run the family's business affairs with his remaining brother Arthur, his cousin Henry Fell and his own sons, ably assisted by David Dale. But Henry Fell had 'no head for business' and Arthur, whilst he had 'excellent judgement', lacked application.[69] His sons, moreover, were youthful and inexperienced, with the additional disadvantage in Alfred's case of a state of health which appeared almost as uncertain as that of his wife.[70] All of these factors no doubt combined to accentuate whatever feelings of pat- riarchal responsibility Sir Joseph possessed and probably encouraged him to keep the affairs of J. and J. W. Pease almost exclusively to himself. For students of entrepreneurship, therefore, the experience of the Pease family serves as a warning to those who would wish to assess entrepreneurial performance either by qualitative generalisations or the 'rational' assumptions inherent in counterfactual hypotheses. The activities of Sir Joseph Whitwell Pease provide an excellent illustration of the need for historians to take account of unique circumstances, often of the most personal kind. Businessmen in the late Victorian era, as in other times, were not paragons of objectivity reacting coldly and rationally to a given set of economic conditions. A myriad influences were at work, some of them objective, but others highly subjective.[71]

In conclusion, it must be conceded that although Sir Joseph was always optimistic as to the prospects of commercial revival his diaries for almost twenty years after 1879 provide a depressing record of perpetual and occasionally intense anxiety over business affairs. The term may now be unfashionable among economic historians, but Sir Joseph would have agreed vehemently with the prevailing contemporary opinion that the period from 1873 to 1896 was one of 'Great Depression' in trade and industry. Nevertheless, despite his worries concerning overdrafts and loans he was always confident that his financial position, although precarious at times, was fundamentally sound. Ultimately, he was convinced that his assets, together with those of Arthur, would outweigh any conceivable liabilities. That he was to be proved wrong in this was the true measure of Sir Joseph's tragedy. One of the most critical factors, so far unmentioned, in destroying his credit and driving his family towards bankruptcy is the subject of the next chapter.

5

The Portsmouth Affair

Joseph Pease's second son, Edward, began his working life in the woollen mills under the supervision of his uncle Henry. He was never robust in health and by the time of his marriage to the devout Quaker, Sarah Sturge, in 1862, Edward had virtually withdrawn from active involvement in the business. Thereafter, 'his life was spent partly in good works doing kind things, but mostly in travelling on the Continent, fishing in Scotland, walking a great deal and in the social life of his relations'.[1] At some time in the 1860s he bought an estate near Bewdley where he experimented in forestry and acquired a fascination for the breeding of mules with a view to proving their value in agriculture. He was devoted to his elder brother and after his father's death it was Sir Joseph who attended to Edward's financial requirements and also the business interests bequeathed to him. Judging by the results, Sir Joseph's supervision must have been lax since at the time of Edward's death in 1880 his affairs were in an embarrassed condition due to lavish expenditure at Bewdley and it is doubtful if his estate would have proved solvent on a realisation of the assets.[2]

Sarah Pease died in 1877, and after Edward's death their only child, Beatrice, then aged fourteen, was placed under the guardianship of Sir Joseph and Lady Pease and brought up as their daughter at Hutton Hall. By Edward's will, dated in 1876, he entrusted all his property to his remaining brothers, endowing them with very large discretionary powers. Beatrice was to become the sole residual legatee on attaining the age of twenty-one or marrying under that age, and after the creation of Pease and Partners in 1882 the interest held by Sir Joseph and Arthur on Beatrice's behalf as trustees of her father's estate was 3,098 £100 shares with £80 paid and 5 per cent stock to the value of £41,500, redeemable by the company at 5 per cent premium. The trustees also held as part of the estate 7,560 shares of £10 each (£8 paid) in the Middlesbrough Estate and 312 shares of £100 each with £83 paid together with debentures to the value of £15,606 in Robert Stephenson and Co.[3] Although the estate was subject to heavy charges for which the trustees had made themselves personally liable, there can be no doubt that Edward Pease had bequeathed to his only daughter a substantial fortune with the major asset of the trust being the interest in Pease and Partners.

When Beatrice became Sir Joseph's ward, his younger son Jack had only recently left Cambridge and, with his reputation as a field-sportsman established,[4] his extrovert personality and *bonhomie* attracted to Hutton Hall a wide circle of friends and acquaintances sharing his interests in shooting and hunting. It is an indication of the rising social status of the Pease family that one of Jack's house guests in the early 1880s was Newton Wallop, Viscount Lymington, the heir to the Earldom of Portsmouth. It seems that at first Lymington was attracted to Sir Joseph's third daughter, Blanche, but having been informed by Jack that she was not 'the heiress' he rapidly developed an interest in Beatrice.[5] The couple were engaged in November 1884 and Sir Joseph recorded his approbation of the event with the following diary entry:

> I quite hope the right thing has been done. All we hear about [Lymington] and his [family] seems right in the best sense of the word. Lady Portsmouth especially took my judgement as an excellent woman fearing God and bringing up her 12 children well.[6]

Less than two weeks later the tone of Sir Joseph's diary entries changed dramatically after he had received a note from his solicitor, Arthur Lucas, informing him that the newly engaged couple were 'at their proposal' coming to see Lucas to discuss Beatrice's financial future.[7] The result of this information was a lengthy lecture delivered to the couple by Sir Joseph, who attempted to explain the complicated state of Edward Pease's affairs and also no doubt drew attention to the uncertain income to be derived from the trust estate due to fluctuations in the coal trade. In December Sir Joseph had further interviews with Beatrice and Lymington 'on their or rather her affairs' with the result that he became increasingly suspicious that Lymington had 'a decided notion about the *main* chance'.[8] Sir Joseph's final diary entry for the year concluded with the cryptic observation that 'Lymington's engagement to Beatrice seems all right though not what any expected'.[9]

Thus, within a few weeks of Beatrice's engagement Sir Joseph's enthusiasm for the prospective marriage of his ward had cooled considerably. His firm belief that Lymington was a mere 'fortune hunter' was to intensify in the years after the couple's marriage in 1885, when hardly a month passed by without Sir Joseph receiving an inquiry either from Beatrice or her husband as to the prospects for a colliery dividend. By November 1888 he was berating Beatrice for 'her want of confidence in us and her unreasonable grumblings for money – it is getting unbearable' and in November 1891 he expressed his astonishment at her desire to sell all colliery shares in the trust in order to have 'a stated income'.[10] In February 1893 Beatrice (now Countess of Portsmouth) and her husband put forward proposals for the realisation of the trust estate which were rejected by Sir Joseph on the grounds that the depressed state of the coal trade rendered the sale of the colliery property impossible. As Sir Joseph remarked, 'They always seem to think that someone will buy when there is no income'.[11] By this time Sir Joseph was thoroughly irritated with the Portsmouths and no doubt they with him. Their relationship reached a new low, however, in October 1893 when Sir Joseph was informed by Beatrice that she intended to consult Sir Richard Nicholson, a prestigious London solicitor, with a view to the realisation of the trust estate.[12] Sir Joseph's immediate reaction was to dismiss the Portsmouths as 'two spoilt children', but because of Nicholson's intervention he concluded wisely that 'I must try and show that all has been honestly conducted and for their benefit'.[13] There then commenced a voluminous correspondence between Nicholson and Sir Joseph with occasional interventions from the Portsmouths. Sir Joseph's position, from which he never departed, was set out in a letter addressed to Nicholson in January 1895. After drawing attention to the sustained fall in the price of Durham coal since 1890 he concluded:

In our interview of 21st November I endeavoured to show you how inadvisable it would be to try and sell the ordinary colliery shares with a dividend (and that uncertain) of 2 per cent., when a much larger rate has been paid and may be hoped for in a better state of commercial affairs. Such an investment should pay from $7\frac{1}{2}$ to 10 per cent. on the average of years. In order to secure a purchaser at this rate (but even allowing for future contingencies of more) Lady Portsmouth's trust shares could not realise more than half par value. You have only to look at the mining and ironworks share lists to convince you; therefore a sale would mean a sacrifice of one half their par value. In what position would you then leave the margin between assets and liabilities? Whilst so far as relates to future income you would have sold £247,840, which paid you last year 2 per cent., to reinvest £123,920 at £2. 15s. per cent. which is about all the prescribed investments would yield, and you have cut off your future hopes. You speak of getting up a 'syndicate' to purchase these shares. A syndicate only gives less than an ordinary purchaser. It purchases at a risk to get a corresponding profit! I have already said that we decidedly object to the sale *now* as most detrimental to the estate.[14]

For Nicholson's part, his view, also consistently expressed, was that a purchaser for the colliery shares could and should be found, if not a syndicate then individual members or friends of the Pease family. This was, of course, the nub of the matter. Sir Joseph was quite entitled to draw attention to the recession in the coal trade after 1890, which meant that the sale of the colliery property was inadvisable because of the possibility of a recovery in prices. In this respect he was being as consistent in his conduct of Beatrice's affairs as he was of his own. The logic of Sir Joseph's position, therefore, was that the only possible purchasers at a reasonable price were the existing partners in the colliery business – in effect himself and Arthur. What Sir Joseph could not tell Nicholson was that his financial position was increasingly precarious due to the mounting overdrafts of the partners in J. and J. W. Pease and also of the loss-making businesses alluded to in the last chapter. To the Portsmouths and Nicholson, therefore, Sir Joseph's policy on the trust estate was at best difficult to understand and at worst dictatorial and unreasonable.

Confirmation of the Portsmouths' deep frustration was provided by the dispatch to Sir Joseph's solicitor in August 1896 of a long and detailed letter from Nicholson in which he drew attention to the length of time his clients had been urging realisation, that for the three years 1892–5 Beatrice had received no income from the trust estate (valued in June 1895 at £290,388), and finally that 'it is contrary alike to the spirit and intention of the settlement that the Trustees and Executors of Mr Edward Pease should continue indefinitely to retain Lady Portsmouth's fortune in . . . concerns . . . subject to all the vicissitudes of the large trading interests with which it is mixed up'.[15] It was Nicholson's intention, therefore, to issue a writ against the trustees and executors of Edward Pease alleging that they were 'not justified in continuous and indefinite postponement and that they are not warranted in thus retaining Lady Portsmouth's fortune in its present state of investment, in a concern in the management of which she is absolutely powerless to interfere, against her wishes and interests'.[16]

Confronted by Nicholson's hostile intent, Sir Joseph, on his return from holiday in Scotland, decided to accede to the Portsmouths' wishes. A conditional agreement was entered into in March 1898 and this was confirmed by Mr Justice Sterling in the Chancery Division of the High Court of Justice on 7 July. It provided for the purchase by Sir Joseph, Arthur, Alfred and Jack of the whole of the commercial assets in Edward Pease's estate for the sum of £273,555. The purchase price of the shares in Pease and Partners Ltd – £166,053 – was put at 33 per cent discount and those in Robert Stephenson and Co. at nil. In his affirmation before the court Sir Joseph stated that 'the sum payable by the purchasers is fair and reasonable, the purchase and compromise having been entered into with a view to prevent any forced and improvident realization of assets'.[17] Although Mr Justice Sterling had before him the views and wishes of the Portsmouths and the advice of their accountants based upon an examination of Pease and Partners' balance sheets down to June 1896, it is highly likely that Sir Joseph's affirmation was the critical factor for the judge. He was, after all, an acknowledged expert on the coal trade with long and intimate experience of the affairs of Pease and Partners. He was, in effect, giving to the court his knowledge and experience not just as a trustee but as a person of great stature in commerce and industry who had also shown considerable affection and kindness to Lady Portsmouth in the past. For these reasons Mr Justice Sterling was no doubt persuaded that the sale of the trust shares in Pease and Partners at a 33 per cent discount was, in Sir Joseph's words, 'fair and reasonable'.

In order to meet the court's ruling the trustees were obliged to make an immediate cash payment to Lady Portsmouth of £222,833 (including £166,053 for the shares in Pease and Partners) with the further sum of £50,722 to be paid to the trustees of her marriage settlement by the end of November 1903.[18] For the impoverished partners in J. and J. W. Pease these were considerable sums and as early as October 1897 Alfred, Jack and Sir Joseph had agreed that in the event of a settlement with the Portsmouths 'the alternatives are to sell out or buy in £400,000 ordinary shares' in Pease and Partners.[19] Further discussions on the matter of 'rearranging our capital' in Pease and Partners took place in February 1898[20] and by May it had been agreed, with the acquiescence of Arthur and Sir David Dale, that one way of meeting the financial obligations arising from the impending settlement would be to part with two-thirds (the proportion required by the Stock Exchange) of the colliery and ironstone business by a public flotation of Pease and Partners.[21]

The Peases were forced to consider a scheme for flotation because they were unable to meet the Portsmouths' wishes by calling on their own financial resources. In this respect their predicament was also a product of the evolution of British banking practice in the final quarter of the nineteenth century. Whilst Sir Joseph encountered little difficulty in obtaining short-term financial accommodation from a number of banks, this was clearly an inappropriate means of raising the funds for such a large transaction even if they had been available and, as noted already, from the late 1870s the banking system had effectively withdrawn from the business of long-term capital formation in the industrial sector of the economy. The later 1890s, moreover, were an opportune period for a public flotation in view of the current popularity of domestic issues of capital in the aftermath of the Baring crisis of 1890, the Wall Street panic of 1893 and the ending of the Australian land boom, all of which served to undermine the confidence of investors in foreign securities in the latter half of the decade.[22] Sir Joseph's original intention was to issue preference shares and redeem the debenture interest in the old company, but after discussions with sharebrokers in London it was decided that a new Pease and Partners should be formed with a suggested capital of £1,350,000, a sum which was arrived at on the basis of the average profits of the old company for the three years to June 1898. This figure amounted to £115,000 on a rising trend.[23]

By July 1898 the draft prospectus for a new company had been prepared and it was issued in the following September, two months after the settlement with the Portsmouth. In the weeks leading up to the flotation Sir Joseph seems to have been worried about taking such an irrevocable step and the final details were not agreed upon until 14 September – four days before the actual sale to the public. Nevertheless, at the end of the day of flotation Sir Joseph recorded 'a very exciting day' in his diary – 'a regular run for our shares. Telegrams coming and going all day'.[24] In fact, the oversubscription was considerable – eightfold for the ordinary shares and twelvefold for debentures. Sir Joseph's euphoria was, however, short-lived, for within weeks of the flotation of Pease and Partners Ltd Sir Richard Nicholson, at the insistence of the Portsmouths, had declared his intention of applying to the court for the agreement of July 1898 to be set aside.

The case of the *Earl of Portsmouth v. Pease* was heard before Mr Justice Farwell once more in the Chancery Division of the High Court in November and December 1900. Since the resulting judgment raised serious doubts about Sir Joseph's personal integrity, and had profound and far-reaching effects on the financial position of the Pease family, it is necessary to examine the case in some depth.[25]

The main thrust of the Portsmouths' case was that a full disclosure of facts was not made before Mr Justice Sterling. He had been asked to allow the trustees to purchase Edward Pease's holding in Pease and Partners at 33 per cent discount on the grounds that the price was reasonable in view of Lady Portsmouth's desire for a stated income and that this was the only way in which a 'forced and improvident' realisation of assets could be avoided. Yet at the very time when an agreement was in the final stages of negotiation the trustees, by their own admission, were in receipt of expert advice that they could successfully launch a new company which would give them more than par for the shares on offer. Confronted by this point of the non-disclosure of a material fact, Mr Justice Farwell found in favour of the Portsmouths:

> The defendants' Counsel tried to argue the case as though the trustees had done nothing to determine in their own minds the course they would adopt if they got the property, and I do not say that a trustee desiring to buy is bound to disclose his intended mode of using the property if he gets it. But the non-disclosure here is of a fact, that is, the advice given by the experts, and although it is true that the company might have been a failure or might never have been brought out, yet those considerations do not affect the duty to disclose.

To make matters worse the Court was shown correspondence conducted between Sir Joseph and Sir David Dale during June 1898 when the latter attempted to satisfy himself that no material facts concerning the formation of a new company were being kept back from the Portsmouths. More especially, were they aware of 'the improved and improving nature of the mining property'? Sir Joseph's response was to reassure Dale that the Portsmouths were fully acquainted with the situation and this does receive some corroboration from the Portsmouths' affidavit placed before Mr Justice Sterling in which they stated their willingness to accept a settlement 'whether or not the securities to be sold are or are not likely to increase in value, because in any event they must be considered of a highly speculative character'. There can be little doubt that Sir Joseph emphasised the vagaries of the coal trade as much to Sir Richard Nicholson as he had done to the Portsmouths ever since their engagement, but in the final analysis Farwell was bound to side with the Portsmouths in this respect. It may have been a mere point of law and despite the consultations with sharebrokers the scheme for a public flotation may have been tentative,[26] but on the evidence before him Farwell's adverse judgment, however unfair to the Peases, was inevitable.

The judge did not, however, refrain from making further damaging observations, mainly at Sir Joseph's expense, to the effect that the order confirming the original agreement was predicated on three false statements which rendered Sir Joseph 'an unsatisfactory witness'. The first of these concerned the value to be placed on the old company. Once again the evidence here was unequivocal. The Portsmouths' accountant based his advice on a valuation of assets as at June 1896 – approximately £870,000. In June 1897, however, revaluation took place and the figure was raised to £1,200,000. The Portsmouths were kept in ignorance of this and Sir Joseph failed to inform the court of the alteration. Farwell's second point concerned Sir Joseph's assertion that the existence of commercial and industrial depression was a factor which affected the value to be placed on the trust estate assets. In his summing up on this point Farwell had before him the prospectus of the new company which drew attention to the rising prosperity of Pease and Partners, as reflected in the record of profits since 1896. These had risen from £40,000 in the half-year to December 1896 to £75,000 in the half-year to June 1899. On the basis of these figures the judge understandably thought that it was stretching the point to absurdity to claim that the old company was in a state of depression. Finally, and perhaps most damaging of all, the judge questioned Sir Joseph's affirmation that the sum paid to the Portsmouths was 'fair and reasonable'. On this point it is worth quoting at some length from his summing up:

> When the order of 17 July [1898] was made the last balance sheet showed that the old company had a capital paid up of £1,100,000 and £500,000 debentures. It had assets which the directors had been advised to be sold to a new company for £1,350,000, and it

had besides a cash balance at the bank of £618,366, and it had a
half year's profit available for distribution of over £70,000. Sir
David Dale was a liquidator of the old company and he told me
that each member of the old company had received for each £100
share with £80 paid up in the company £62. 7s 6d cash, £16. 19s 4d
in ordinary shares and £21. 16s 4d in deferred shares in the new
company, and in addition to this £33,000 was divided as dividend.
Putting the shares in the new company at par, and I was told they
were at a premium, each shareholder got in round figures 25 shillings in the pound while the trustees of Lady Portsmouth got 13s
4d in the pound only. In the face of these facts and figures I am at a
loss to understand how Sir Joseph Pease could affirm that the price
was fair and reasonable.

A leader in *The Times* immediately after the case concentrated attention
on Sir Joseph's evidence before the court and 'the grave charges affecting a name held in esteem'. The judge, concluded *The Times*, had not
'minced matters' and in doing so had produced 'remarkable findings
which, if permitted to stand, may have consequences beyond the setting aside of the sale of Lady Portsmouth's shares'.[27] As events were to
prove this was a gross underestimate of the effect of the judgment.

In simple terms Farwell's decision to set aside the agreement of July
1898 resulted in the Pease family having to transfer to the Portsmouths
5,257 ordinary shares and 6,760 deferred shares in Pease and Partners
Ltd. This was equivalent to the proportion of shares held by the trust
estate in the old company and the value placed upon them at the time of
the transfer was £241,000. In addition, the Peases were required to
make a cash payment to the Portsmouths of £61,000 and to meet their
legal costs, amounting to £10,000. It is an irony, however, that these
immense losses were overshadowed by the profits forgone as a result of
the public flotation of Pease and Partners. In the two years from June
1899 to 1901 the new company's gross profits totalled £721,894 and in
July 1900 a dividend of 20 per cent was declared to be followed a year
later by one of 17½ per cent.[28] To the extent that the bulk of these
dividends went to the public both the Portsmouths and the Peases (who
collectively had held 12,732 of the 13,750 shares in the old company)
paid a very high price indeed for the litigation.

To the Peases the outcome of the Portsmouth affair was tantamount
to robbery. Alfred's verdict on the judgment was that Mr Justice Farwell was motivated either by 'personal or political animus' or his desire
'to advertise himself by doing something startling in the first *cause
célèbre* that came before him'.[29] As for Jack, he felt that his family had
been made 'victims of circumstances by a man who had acted as no
other man would have in intimidating his wife into coercing her uncles
to buy her property'.[30] These are understandable reactions on the part

of two people who had been only marginally involved in the development of the affair since the death of Edward Pease. Far more revealing were Sir Joseph's reflections as he recorded them in his diary at the end of 1901:

> We wound up the law suit with Lord and Lady Portsmouth in which we all felt we were most iniquitously robbed . . . after having found her a home till her marriage . . . after having held on to her colliery property and done all I could through all the bad times of [the] coal trade – having bought at a full price all their mining shares under threats of an action – having got up a company and so sold our own mining property to pay for theirs. They charged us with fraud [and] a boom having come on in the coal trade . . . Arthur's estate and mine were defrauded . . . – such is gratitude and love.[31]

To understand Sir Joseph's reaction it is only necessary to point out that at a very early stage in Beatrice's engagement he had come to regard Lord Portsmouth as a fortune hunter. This in itself was bad enough, but it had deeper implications for Sir Joseph's conception of himself as the guardian of the family's 'common stock', and Beatrice as his ward and niece was very much a part of that stock.[32] Hence Sir Joseph was unwilling to realise the trust estate assets until literally forced to do so by the threat of litigation. His view, constantly reiterated throughout the later 1880s and 1890s, that there was depression in the coal trade, whilst accurate in itself, was probably of secondary importance in resisting realisation: the matter was far too personal to be considered solely in relation to the price of coal. But the question remains – once the decision had been made to accede to the Portsmouths' wishes in 1896 were Sir Joseph's subsequent actions those of a competent man of business? In the light of the Farwell judgment the answer must be no, especially in respect of the failure to inform Sir Richard Nicholson of the possibility of a public flotation. That the flotation was an outstanding success was without doubt the factor which encouraged the Portsmouths to apply to have the original agreement set aside. Indeed, when the possibility of an appeal was being considered the Peases were informed that their case for a reversal of the Farwell judgment was weak precisely because 'the advice . . . received in May 1898 was sufficiently definite as to the future flotation, to justify a court considering the fact ought to have been disclosed'.[33] The most that could be hoped for was that a higher court might remove the dishonest motives attributed to Sir Joseph. In the event no appeal was made, with the result that Sir Joseph's integrity – and by implication that of other members of the family – remained at issue.

A retrospective view of the Portsmouth affair, however, suggests that

Sir Joseph was hardly a villain intent upon defrauding a ward in chancery by the exercise of crooked cunning. In 1898 he was seventy years of age, a tired old man harassed by solicitors and increasingly distracted by the deteriorating position of J. and J W. Pease. In August 1898 Arthur, his principal partner in the bank, died and his sons, Arthur Francis and Herbert Pike, declined to take up their father's shares, thus impairing the credit of the bank still further.[34] If there had been any doubts in Sir Joseph's mind about the wisdom of a public flotation it was his brother's death at a critical point which made a sale to the public imperative.[35] His technical error as a trustee in failing to disclose his possible intentions received harsh judgement which derived much of its validity from the exercise of great retrospective wisdom by Mr Justice Farwell. Since the Portsmouths possessed an overwhelming determination to secure realisation – as indicated by their acceptance of the possibility that the trust property, once sold, might increase in value – the public flotation arguably represented a *forced* sale of assets with the sole object of meeting the conditions of the 1898 agreement. It was simply unfortunate for Sir Joseph that in the weeks leading up to the flotation the price of coal was rising more rapidly than at any time since the early 1870s. The great turn-around in trade which he had always anticipated was occurring. From Sir Joseph's point of view its timing could not have been worse.

6
Collapse

One of the most impressive features of English banking development in the nineteenth century was the growth of joint stock banks at the expense of their private counterparts. After a hesitant beginning following their legalisation in 1826, the former, with their standardised commercial procedures and greater resources of capital, were able to acquire the major part of the new banking business created by the ongoing process of industrial and commercial expansion in the middle decades of the century. Their growing dominance was further enhanced by legislation in 1858 and 1862 which extended the facility of limited liability to joint stock banks. The combined effect of the new legal form and greater capital resources was to attract new investors and depositors, thereby generating increased financial resources for further expansion. The Baring crisis of 1890 adversely affected the reputation of private banks and after the attack by G. J. Goschen (later Viscount Goschen) on the inadequacy of their cash reserves the stage was set for a drive towards amalgamation in the banking system, with the larger joint stock companies absorbing their smaller rivals and also significant numbers of private banks.[1] A peak of merger activity was reached in 1896 and it was marked by the founding of a substantial joint stock bank with headquarters in London – Barclay and Company of Lombard Street – destined to become one of the 'Big Five' after the First World War. The new bank was the product of an amalgamation between Gurneys of Norwich, Backhouse of Darlington and Barclays of London, three long-established Quaker banking partnerships, and during the next few years it embarked upon a policy of expansion by absorbing several private banks, principally those which had enjoyed close commercial ties with the founding concerns or personal relationships with their respective partners.[2] In view of the intimate connections between the Gurney, Backhouse and Pease families, it was not surprising that in 1898 Francis Augustus Bevan, the first chairman of Barclays, should attempt to open private negotiations with Sir Joseph Whitwell Pease for a takeover of J. and J. W. Pease. From Barclays' standpoint this was a most desirable merger. Although J. and J. W. Pease had never carried on as commercial bankers in competition with other recognised public banks, they were responsible for a number of lucrative business accounts, ranging from the NER to the Consett Iron Company. But, because of his preoccupation with the Portsmouth settlement and the public flotation of Pease and Partners, Sir Joseph judged the moment for an amalgamation to be inopportune. The partnership arrangements in J. and J. W. Pease, moreover, had been rendered uncertain by the declared wishes of his nephews, Arthur Francis and Herbert Pike, not to take up their late father's shares in the bank.[3] The matter was therefore allowed to rest for several years until April 1902, when Sir Jonathan Backhouse, the local director of Barclays, suggested to Sir Joseph that it would be far more convenient if the regular advances obtained by J. and J. W. Pease from the Norwich branch of Barclays (formerly Gurneys) should be arranged at Darlington.[4] Backhouse's proposal was a logical one and it provided Alfred and Jack with the long-awaited opportunity to relieve Sir Joseph of the burden of running the bank's affairs. It was soon enhanced by a definite offer from Barclays to take over the business of J. and J. W. Pease, either wholly or in part. With the help of additional pressure from Sir David Dale, Sir Joseph succumbed to his sons' wishes and by the middle of July 1902 negotiations had begun in earnest for an amalgamation with Barclays.[5] Since the events which followed were to be the cause of much bitterness in the Pease family it is necessary to describe in some detail the course of the negotiations, for in a very real sense their outcome was tantamount to a condemnation of Sir Joseph's entrepreneurial capabilities and judgement during the previous thirty years.

The initial discussions were concerned exclusively with the proposed new arrangements for financial accommodation from the Darlington branch of Barclays. These were conducted on terms of the utmost friendliness between Backhouse and Sir Joseph with the former proposing that there should be an unsecured loan of £50,000, instead of the usual £30,000 from Norwich backed by shares in the Middlesbrough Estate. At the beginning of August, however, when negotiations had begun for the takeover of J. and J. W. Pease itself, Sir Joseph was informed by Backhouse that his London board had decided that the sum to be advanced later in the month should be secured. Sir Joseph raised no objections to this and assumed that the condition had been imposed because of 'the non-liquid state of our assets'.[6] This was the position when the first critically important meeting to discuss a possible takeover took place in Darlington on 8 August 1902. It was attended by Sir Joseph, Alfred, Dale and Backhouse, with Henry Birkbeck, a personal friend of Sir Joseph, representing Barclays' London board. Since Birkbeck had been a partner in Gurneys of Norwich before the great amalgamation, it is reasonable to assume that he was well acquainted with J. and J. W. Peases' financial requirements. But despite the close personal relationships between the various parties the negotiations did not go entirely smoothly. Birkbeck confirmed that his board was worried about Sir Joseph's financial position and insisted on knowing the precise details of how J. and J. W. Pease proposed to meet the impending dividend payments of the NER and the Consett Iron Company on or around 23 August. The Peases' reaction was to point to the existing arrangements with their London and York bankers (Prescotts, the National Provincial and York City and County Banks) which were still intact and also to stress that the transfer of their business to Barclays within a few weeks of the receipt of accommodation from these sources was hardly satisfactory. Sir Joseph therefore suggested that it was only fair that the necessary accommodation should be forthcoming from Barclays. After some discussion Birkbeck and Backhouse undertook to ask their fellow directors to advance £150,000 (inclusive of the original £50,000) on securities agreed upon for three months and that all further negotiations for the transfer of the business should be postponed until the autumn when members of Barclays' board would have returned from their holidays.[7]

The total loan agreed upon at the meeting of 8 August was £154,784, of which £100,000 was secured by 10,000 Pease and Partners deferred shares and the remainder by 6,848 shares in the Middlesbrough Estate. On 11 August Barclays' board sanctioned this arrangement but insisted that the partners in J. and J. W. Pease should offer the additional security of the whole of their private estates. It was also agreed that in order to pay off the loan more rapidly J. and J. W. Pease would transfer to Barclays all surplus cash coming into their hands on the NER and Consett Iron Company accounts. Since the monthly receipts from these sources averaged £50,000, it is clear that Barclays had ample security for their advance.[8]

At this stage in the negotiations the Peases began to be increasingly concerned about Barclays' demands for additional security. Clearly, Birkbeck and Backhouse, having been shown summary statements of the bank's position, were themselves becoming more and more embarrassed at the extent of the liabilities. As Alfred recorded in his journal:

> Near the end of this awful week of worry and anxiety I really cannot recollect the incidents of each day. I have nothing to remember but masses of figures and puzzles and the reams of paper consumed in working out financial problems at Darlington and Hutton. There is nothing to affect our character and integrity but with things at their present prices the problem of finding cover for all our accounts is terribly difficult to solve and if the negotiations with Barclays fail we shall have to call our bankers together and do the best we can . . . Poverty does not alarm me but the process of reaching it is the hard part.[9]

In the event Barclays were to absorb J. and J. W. Pease but in circumstances that Alfred could not possibly have foreseen.

On 16 August Alfred reached a preliminary agreement with Birkbeck that Barclays would take over the whole of the business of J. and J. W. Pease and that Birkbeck himself would devise a scheme to place Sir Joseph's financial affairs on a sounder footing, possibly involving the formation of a trust to liquidate his assets. The only conditions that Birkbeck sought to impose were that Edward Hutchinson, the local solicitor employed by both parties, should have full authority to examine the accounts of J. and J. W. Pease and that the eminent chartered accountant William Barclay Peat should also be invited to give an opinion on the bank's financial condition. Alfred agreed to the former but in the absence of his fellow partners demurred at Peat's involvement. To this Birkbeck raised no objection, and in response to Alfred's query concerning the family's impending departure for the shooting season in Scotland offered the reassurance that the £150,000 advance had been sanctioned and pointed out that negotiations for a takeover would resume at the earliest opportunity in the autumn.[10]

Thus on 19 August Sir Joseph and Alfred travelled to Scotland, the former to join his nephew, Arthur Francis, for a yachting and shooting holiday at Oban and the latter to Perth to meet Jack before proceeding to the shooting-lodge of their brother-in-law Gerald Buxton.[11] Despite Birkbeck's assurances that all was well, Sir Joseph left Darlington with premonitions of disaster, recording in his diary that a holiday in such circumstances was hardly welcome under the feeling of 'are not the hours of your heart all numbered'.[12] After arriving in Oban, his worst fears seemed to be confirmed for 'On coming in to dress for dinner I was horrified by a telegram from Badcock [manager of J. and J. W. Pease] stating that Sir D. Dale and Edward Hutchinson desired to see me tomorrow'.[13] Alfred and Jack received similar summonses.

Alfred was the first to arrive in Darlington and was angered to learn that contrary to his understanding Peat had been called in to express an opinion on the accounts of J. and J. W. Pease and that during the course of his investigation he had discovered a clause in the articles of association of the Middlesbrough Owners which gave them power to exercise a prior lien and veto on transfers of shares owned by any person in debt to them. Since Sir Joseph was a debtor to the Middlesbrough Estate, Peat had advised Barclays to reject the entire loan arrangement. With the NER dividend amounting to £160,000 payable on 23 August the partners in J. and J. W. Pease were in a desperate position. It was too late to contact Prescotts and the York City and County Bank and, ironically, Sir Joseph himself, on the journey to Oban, had wired the National Provincial Bank that he did not require their financial assistance in view of Birkbeck's assurances.

On 22 August – 'Black Friday' to the Peases – Peat advised the partners in J. and J. W. Pease that they had little option but to sign a document which he had drafted as follows:

1) Messrs Barclay and Co. to purchase Messrs J. and J. W. Peases' assets at fair values which should be as near as possible realisable values.
2) The Goodwill to be paid for in addition at a sum to be agreed upon.
3) The proceeds of 1) and 2) to be utilised for payment to the creditors *pro rata* of J. and J. W. Pease.
4) *All* current banking accounts of J. and J. W. Pease to be closed and re-opened with Barclay and Co. Ltd. who will allow credit to approved customers . . .
5) The assets of J. and J. W. Pease to include the private estates of the Partners, other than Furniture, Horses, Carriages etc . . .
6) A maximum of two years to be allowed for realising the assets, interest on the value till realisation to be charged by Barclay and Co.[14]

Utterly dismayed, and in the absence of Backhouse and Hutchinson, the Peases agreed to these terms in the knowledge that a chartered accountant of the highest standing had informed them that it was his firm opinion that J. and J. W. Pease were insolvent.

To Alfred, Peat's terms were 'dreadful', involving as they did the sacrifice of the partners' fortunes. The only consolation was that their credit was likely to be saved. But even this comforting belief was shattered on 26 August, when Barclays issued a press announcement stating that they had made arrangements for taking over the greater part of the current business of J. and J. W. Pease, but that they were not undertaking the liabilities of the firm.[15] The effect of this notice was disastrous for the Peases on two counts. In the first instance it was effectively a public denial of their credit-worthiness and in the succeeding days they were deluged with writs from business and private creditors. Secondly, and of much greater consequence, it undermined the value of their assets. Their ordinary shares in Pease and Partners Ltd, for example, valued at £274,260 on 21 August, had depreciated by £89,278, or £3 per share, by 8 September 1902. The inevitable result was the widening of the gap between the ascertained liabilities and assets.[16]

At this point it is worthwhile attempting to assess the motives of the various parties to the negotiations in the weeks preceding 'Black Friday'. There is a large body of information setting out the evolving views of the Peases, whereas no records have come to light which explain Barclays' policy to the takeover. In itself this is not unusual since commercial considerations dictated that negotiations for banking takeovers should be strictly confidential and the early discussions in Darlington took place on an informal basis between individuals who were on terms of personal friendship. Nevertheless, it is possible to avoid the dangers of a one-sided analysis by the application of reasonable conjecture based in part upon Barclays' subsequent actions which are well recorded.[17]

In certain respects it was this very fact of the personal and informal nature of the negotiations which led to the events of 22 August. In approaching Sir Joseph on the matter of a possible takeover it can be safely assumed that Sir Jonathan Backhouse was not conversant with the true financial position of J. and J. W. Pease. It is highly likely that this applies with equal measure to Alfred and Jack, who persuaded their father to respond positively to Backhouse's approach. It was only after the intervention of Birkbeck that doubts began to be raised about the stability of the bank, but even then both parties were content to arrange a loan of £150,000 on the basis of long-standing arrangements with the Norwich branch of Barclays and its willingness to accept the Middlesbrough Estate shares as security for financial accommodation. It is difficult to believe that the prior lien on these shares was not discussed at the meeting on 8 August because the secretary to the board of the estate company was in attendance.[18] By this time both Alfred and Jack, having examined the balance sheets of J. and J. W. Pease, possibly for the first time in detail, were themselves deeply anxious about the illiquid nature of their father's assets, but they allowed themselves to be lulled into a false sense of security by Backhouse and Birkbeck in particular. The critical factor, and the one which gave rise to great bitterness on the Peases' part, was the decision of Barclays' board, with the active connivance of Edward Hutchinson, to ask W. B. Peat to examine the arrangements devised by Backhouse and Birkbeck. From that point onwards what had been a rather lax and informal affair was subject to the scrutiny of a first-class accountant of considerable reputation who saw it as his primary duty to protect the interests of Barclays – hence his objection to the Middlesbrough Estate shares and his recommendation that the loan arrangement should be rejected. Since Hutchinson was clearly identifying himself with Peat's position it was especially unfortunate for the Peases that they were deprived of independent legal advice following Peat's revelations of J. and J. W. Peases' insolvency within 23 hours of the payment of the NER dividend. If Peat had been involved earlier, then it is possible that a crisis would have been averted with the Peases obtaining their usual accommodation from other bankers. The position of J. and J. W. Pease would not have been improved, but it would have bought time and this was the commodity which Alfred and Jack, with their heightened awareness of their father's financial plight, required above all else. A further source of bitterness for the Peases was the press announcement concerning Barclays' repudiation of the liabilities of J. and J. W. Pease. In retrospect it is difficult to defend this statement because in depreciating the partners' assets it harmed all parties – Barclays themselves and J. and J. W.

Pease's debtors and creditors. The only rational and perhaps fair explanation is that the announcement reflected the fact that the informal local negotiations were at an end and the whole matter was now being conducted from Barclays' head office in Lombard Street according to the strict letter of the law.

The following days and weeks were extremely anxious ones for Sir Joseph and his sons as Peat proceeded with his valuations which would decide whether they were to be declared bankrupt or if the business of J. and J. W. Pease was to be voluntarily wound up. A startling but wholly welcome development occurred at the end of August when Sir Christopher Furness, Jack's shooting companion in Scotland but hardly a close friend of the family, initiated a movement for the formation of a guarantee fund for Peat's use to keep the partners out of bankruptcy.[19] Furness was prepared to contribute £40,000 and over the succeeding days the total swelled to £160,000. In recognition of their father's role as a leading partner in the bank until his death, Arthur Francis and Herbert Pike contributed £20,000 and other members of the family a further £21,000. Guarantees were also forthcoming from Sir David Dale (£5,000), Sir Isaac Lowthian Bell (£10,000), A. J. Dorman (£5,000) and Sir Bernhard Samuelson (£5,000).[20] It was abundantly clear, therefore, that several of the leading industrialists of the north-east of England, both as a result of sentiment and considerations of commercial stability in the region, were not prepared to permit the partners in J. and J. W. Pease to be declared bankrupt. Even members of Barclays' board were prepared to contribute to the fund – Henry Birkbeck (£5,000), Robert Barclay (£2,500) and Samuel Gurney Buxton (£2,000). In addition to the guarantee fund, Peat's task was also eased by the willingness of members of the Pease family, including innumerable widows and maiden aunts, to abandon or postpone their claims to the extent of £70,000.

By the middle of September Peat had completed his detailed examination of the accounts of J. and J. W. Pease. The gross liabilities amounted to £1,268,031 and the gross assets were estimated at £1,017,816. After deducting the value of securities held by the major creditors the former figure was reduced to £705,828 with net assets at £455,613.[21] The largest unsecured creditors were as follows:

Consett Iron Company	£ 99,115
North Eastern Railway Company	£231,995
Pease and Partners Ltd	£119,766
Weardale and Shildon Water Co.	£ 17,295
	£468,171[22]

The partners, according to Peat, were technically bankrupt, but in view of the Furness guarantee fund and the willingness of family creditors to forgo their claims he was able to present the following scheme for a voluntary liquidation to Barclays' board and the major creditors:

1) Mr Peat is to be appointed assignie of all the Estates and effects of Messrs. J. and J. W. Pease and the partners' private Estates, excluding furniture and personal effects.

2) The creditors (other than family creditors who are to agree to postponement of their claims) are to consent to accept such cash Dividend as the Trustee can pay and to forego all hostile proceedings whatsoever.

3) The guarantors of £160,000 are to consent to an immediate payment in cash of £50,000.

4) All the Estates and effects so vested in the Trustee, Mr Peat, are to be handed over to a limited company of which the ordinary capital is to be distributed amongst the creditors and there is to be a first mortgage debenture charge of £270,000.

5) Barclay and Company Ltd. are to advance to the Trustee the sum of £270,000 at 4 per cent. interest against the above mentioned mortgage debenture and also against £60,000 of the above mentioned guarantees . . .

6) The sum of £50,000 is to be paid by Barclay and Company Ltd. for the goodwill of the business.[23]

These proposals were accepted in principle by Barclays' board, except for the advance of £270,000, which was reduced to £148,000. It was also agreed that all the smaller creditors should receive full compensation in order to reduce the possibility of a receiving order in bankruptcy being made against J. and J. W. Pease. In the event of such an order being made before the expiration of three months of the confirmation of the deed of conveyance and assignment then all creditors would have the right to claim the unpaid balances of their debts. The essence of Peat's scheme, therefore, was that since the Peases' assets could not be realised immediately it was necessary for Barclays to make a loan – in effect a mortgage against the collateral security of the disposable assets with additional security being provided by the Furness guarantee fund.

For Barclays Peat's scheme had several attractions. It safeguarded the interests of the smaller creditors and was designed to appeal to the major unsecured creditors since it would yield as much by way of dividends on realisation as could be obtained by proceedings in bankruptcy. In this respect the guarantee fund was of vital importance for, as the solicitor to the NER pointed out, in so far as the guarantees were conditional upon a voluntary liquidation the company's losses could well exceed his estimate of £125,000 should the partners be declared bankrupt.[74] Similar views were no doubt expressed to the boards of the

Consett Iron Company and Pease and Partners, with the result that by the end of 1902 Peat's scheme had been accepted by all the major creditors. Finally, the scheme minimised the embarrassment for a large banking concern with substantial Quaker representation on the board of directors of a public disclosure of J. and J. W. Peases' affairs. Throughout the nineteenth century many private banks had failed or been taken over in dubious circumstances and although J. and J. W. Pease was a relatively small concern its senior partner was a distinguished public figure and, the Portsmouth case notwithstanding, with a hitherto unimpeachable reputation for upholding the principles of the Society of Friends. No doubt there were other members of Barclays' board, in addition to those who subscribed to the guarantee fund, who shared an emotional revulsion at the prospect of such a man being stigmatised by formal proceedings in bankruptcy.

Sir Joseph, Alfred and Jack signed Peat's deed of conveyance and assignment in December 1902 and by the following March they were free from the threat of bankruptcy. Over the next three years the realisation committee, composed of Peat and representatives of the major creditors, proceeded to liquidate the assets of J. and J. W. Pease. By February 1906, when the committee ceased its work, the total dividend paid to the unsecured creditors had amounted to 8s 6d in the pound, a sum which was a reflection of the low valuations placed by Peat on the assets in September 1902 and the public knowledge of an enforced sale following the announcement of the deed of assignment.[25] The Peases' holdings in Robert Stephenson and Co. and Henry Pease and Co. were disposed of at break-up value, those in Wilsons, Pease and Co. for £50,000 (on a 1901 valuation of £200,000) and the ordinary shares in Pease and Partners sacrificed at par value and the debentures at £5. The National Provincial Bank was unable to sell the Hutton estate until 1906, when it was disposed of for the sum of £69,000 on a valuation in August 1902 of £117,000.[26] These figures provide some substance for the Peases' assertion that the value of their assets was unfairly depreciated by Barclays' public repudiation of J. and J. W. Pease's liabilities.

Sir Joseph and his sons had good reason to be grateful to their relatives and Sir Christopher Furness in particular, but the understandable relief which followed the avoidance of formal bankruptcy was obliterated by the public and private humiliations directly attributable to the failure of J. and J. W. Pease. The most hurtful public consequences for Sir Joseph were the obligatory resignations as chairman and director of the NER and Pease and Partners. On 25 September 1902, having resigned as chairman of the NER, he travelled to York to attend a board meeting but was refused entry. On the following day Dale, acting for the board, had the distasteful task of asking for his resignation as a director and also for the surrender of his NER travel documents.[27] These were subsequently returned in February 1903, but in the same month, after a stormy shareholders' meeting of the NER when losses of £120,000 attributable to the failure of J. and J. W. Pease were announced, even the normally taciturn Peat was moved to write personally to Sir Joseph expressing his deep regret that 'your cup of bitterness has indeed been quaffed to its last dregs'.[28] Other wounding consequences of the bank failure were Sir Joseph's enforced resignation as a Tees Conservancy Commissioner in January 1903 after forty years of service, his resignation as vice-president of the National Society for the Prevention of Cruelty to Children and as president of the Society for the Suppression of the Opium Trade, and finally his decision, as a result of penury, not to seek re-election to the House of Commons.[29] Most pitiful of all, however, were the private indignities imposed upon Sir Joseph and his family. These were the result of the private liabilities of the partners in the bank amounting to £24,000.

Whilst Peat's draft deed of assignment permitted the partners to retain the whole of their personal effects, this was on the understanding that their value would be set against the private liabilities. Thus, throughout the autumn of 1902 the Peases were forced to sell off their carriages, horses, farm livestock and equipment. By the beginning of November, however, it was obvious that the sale of the effects would fall short by a considerable margin of the sum required to meet the private liabilities. The creditors therefore agreed that the balance of the private liquidation account should be met from the guarantee fund and general assets of J. and J. W. Pease – but at the expense of severely curtailing the value of the furniture and other private effects to be retained by the partners.[30] The strain of these events on Alfred and Sir Joseph in particular was almost unbearable, the more so since they were under continuous pressure from the National Provincial Bank, the first mortgagees of the Hutton and Pinchinthorpe estate, to arrange for the sale of their homes. At one time Sir Joseph entertained hopes of being able to raise sufficient capital from relatives to redeem the Hutton mortgage, but he was advised against this by friends on the NER board and his solicitor on the grounds that it would endanger the acceptance of the deed of assignment and encourage one or more aggrieved creditors to press for bankruptcy.[31] Relationships within the family were hardly eased by Jack's lavish expenditure on the renovation of Nunthorpe Hall, a dilapidated seventeenth-century mansion close to the outskirts of Middlesbrough which he had purchased in 1900.[32] During the next two years £16,000 was spent on the house and according to Sir Joseph's solicitor it was the outstanding bills and fees on this property in August 1902 which caused the creditors to adopt a harsher attitude to the partners' private effects than would otherwise have been the case.[33]

Sir Joseph's sons suffered greatly as a result of the failure of J. and J. W. Pease. The worst affected was Alfred: the humiliation of having to borrow money from servants and living on the charity of relatives had an adverse effect on his health and in October 1902 he resigned his parliamentary seat. When the deed of assignment was completed, the heir to the Pease dynasty possessed £2,300 worth of furniture and personal effects, £788 cash in the bank, 40 shares in Pease and Partners and half of his post-nuptial settlement of 2,000 Pease and Partners shares held in trust to provide an income for life. Deprived of director-ships he estimated his total annual income at £500. As he recorded in his journal:

Jack's and my position is very hard as we are ruined to pay our father's and uncle Arthur's losses. Of the whole of our two private estates together about £150,000 has gone into the liquidation of J. and J. W. Pease. Out of J. and J. W. Pease Jack and I have had in the last 10 years just £15,000 . . . and not more than twice that in our lives and this without deducting income tax and bad debts which we have been debited with.[34]

In the new year, however, two events occurred which helped to lift Alfred's gloom. In March 1903 the Colonial Office offered him a resi-dent magistracy in the Transvaal with a salary of £1,000 per annum. During the Boer War Alfred had lent his support to the war effort, but in speeches and pamphlets had called for a policy of reconciliation with the Boers after their defeat. With his knowledge of African affairs he was clearly an appropriate choice for a judicial post which would enable him to 'conciliate the conflicting interests and animosities caused by the war'.[35] Despite his loathing of South Africa's 'sordid population and barren landscape', Alfred accepted the offer and took up residence at Barberton in the eastern Transvaal in the summer of 1903. In the meantime he was able to rescue the one thing that was dearest to him from the wreckage of the realisation. In April 1903 the National Pro-vincial Bank, having failed to sell the Pinchinthorpe estate, offered it to Alfred for the sum of £14,000. With financial aid from close relatives he was able to purchase the property.[36] His original intention was that Sir Joseph, after relinquishing Hutton Hall, would reside at Pinchin-thorpe, but in the event the estate was leased by Herbert Samuel (later Viscount Samuel), Alfred's successor as Liberal MP for Cleveland.

For Jack the failure of the bank was not as traumatic as for his elder brother. His emotional commitment to the Nunthorpe property could hardly have matched that of Alfred for Pinchinthorpe and he had the additional advantage of being able to retain his London home in Mayfair since the lease was in the name of his mother-in-law. Within two years of the failure he was once more a member of the board of Pease and Partners and his political career was very much intact. Sev-eral factors account for this. In the first instance he was saved from the consequences of his own impetuosity in wishing to launch a public defence of his father's handling of the affairs of J. and J. W. Pease. His friend and parliamentary colleague J. B. Paulton, the Liberal member for Bishop Auckland, was in large measure responsible for restraining Jack from openly denouncing the actions of Barclays. As Paulton pointed out:

> People don't blame *you* for [the failure] but the reason why they don't is because they believe you were most unwillingly forced to acquiesce in the continuance of unsound conditions against your own judgement. Therefore endeavours to prove that your dear father was justified either in running the risks or in causing you to share them, only tend to involve you in personal responsibility . . . to put it plainly or brutally, you *cannot* induce anyone to accept the view that things were on a sound and solvent footing. Consequently the more you minimise the blame on one pair of shoulders, the more will be put on others . . .[37]

Wisely, Jack decided to follow Paulton's advice. He also acceded to the wishes of his parliamentary leader, Sir Henry Campbell-Bannerman, and the Liberal Chief Whip, Herbert Gladstone, that he should 'disappear' from Westminster until public discussion of the bank's affairs had begun to wane.[38] The opportunity to do this was provided by an invitation from David Denbigh, a director of Pease and Partners, to accompany him in the autumn of 1903 on a visit to Mexico to assess the prospects for the exploitation of copper ore deposits. Such a visit, suggested Denbigh, would give Jack 'a fair claim to go on the board of Pease and Partners'.[39] Denbigh's judgement was correct and Jack was re-elected to the board in August 1904 after his return from Mexico. His name was generously proposed by Sir David Dale, the new chairman of the company, and seconded by Sir Jonathan Backhouse.[40]

Finally, what of Sir Joseph? On leaving Hutton Hall he took up residence at his Falmouth home, Kerris Vean, where he was looked after by his unmarried daughter, Maud. There he led 'a dismal existence', doing 'nothing but brood over figures'.[41] His health had suffered badly as a result of the destruction of his public reputation and he died of heart failure on 23 June 1903, the day of his seventy-fifth birthday. It was a tragic and lonely end to the life of a man who at the height of his powers had occupied a uniquely important position in the political and economic life of north-east England. In retrospect it is difficult not to be sympathetic to Sir Joseph's plight in the final years of his life. The Portsmouth affair culminating in the Farwell judgment and the death of his remaining brother Arthur all took their toll, and it is clear that by the summer of 1902 he was no longer capable of exercising effective control over his business affairs. It is certainly true that contemporary opinion, in so far as it was able to judge the matter, inclined to the view

5   Joseph Albert ('Jack') Pease (1860–1943), first Baron Gainford of Headlam,
    c. 1895.

that he had been harshly treated. The press comment which followed the announcement of the deed of assignment was overwhelming in its praises of his commercial and industrial activities and attributed the failure of the bank to his policy over many years of giving extensive financial aid to businesses in danger of bankruptcy themselves.[42] Such opinions were only reinforced by the attendance at Sir Joseph's funeral of representatives of the board of Barclays and also the principal directors of the NER, the Consett Iron Company and Pease and Partners.[43]

At the same time it would be wrong to adopt the stance of an unqualified apologist in assessing Sir Joseph's career. In dealing with the Portsmouth affair, for example, he permitted personal prejudice and petty animosities to cloud his judgement on the realisation of the trust estate. He was well acquainted with Lord Portsmouth's intentions and it can only be judged reprehensible on his part to have treated the Portsmouths, and latterly Sir Richard Nicholson, with sustained contempt. In the running of J. and J. W. Pease it may have been understandable, even laudable, to extend hundreds of thousands of pounds' worth of financial aid to loss-making enterprises, but this policy, exacerbated by the result of the Portsmouth case, was to bear fruit in the events of August 1902. It was simply naive of Sir Joseph to maintain that the bank was solvent when the value of at least two-thirds of the partners' assets were dependent upon prevailing commercial conditions, especially in the highly volatile coal and metallurgical trades. It is also clear from the surviving mass of papers, correspondence and diary entries that when they were judged to be insolvent Alfred and Jack were in a lamentable state of ignorance about the bank's affairs both in regard to the issues of unlimited liability and the unliquid nature and uncertain value of their father's assets. No doubt the brothers shared part of the blame for their ignorance, but the ultimate indictment of Sir Joseph is that whilst retaining exclusive control of J. and J. W. Pease he endangered his sons' inheritance by exposing them to the threat of bankruptcy.

These are hard judgements. There are, however, mitigating circumstances, both objective and subjective. When Joseph Pease died in 1872, the Peases' industrial fortunes were heavily dependent upon the manufactured iron trade and when this sector of the economy of north-east England went into precipitate decline in the late 1870s it was inevitable that Sir Joseph's financial position should begin to deteriorate. His response was twofold. As an entrepreneur it was to await a rise in the price of industrial raw materials whilst drawing on accumulated reserves, an entirely reasonable strategy in extractive industries. A coal mine, for example, has little abandonment value since the scrap value of assets is negligible and to shut down a mine and then reopen it at a later date is a costly process due to the deterioration of roadways and water damage. In these circumstances the objective conditions of the industry meant that Pease and Partners in particular and colliery owners in general had little alternative but to maintain their mines in production: although selling prices in the late-nineteenth-century coal industry were generally depressed there was always the hope of commercial revival.[44] As the guardian of the Peases' 'common stock', Sir Joseph was also motivated by far more subjective considerations. The problem confronting him in attempting to maintain the family's industrial interests intact was that the price decline which began in the 1870s was persistent, extending over more than two decades. This would have been difficult to deal with under any circumstances, but for Sir Joseph the situation was complicated by the Peases' holdings in loss-making concerns in the manufacturing sector of the economy. There can be little doubt that Robert Stephenson and Co. and Henry Pease and Co. were sustained in part for non-entrepreneurial reasons (see above, pp. 87, 90), and the resources to facilitate this policy were derived from J. and J. W. Pease supplemented by the receipt of short-term credit from other bankers and the mortgaging of property. It is worth re-emphasising that Sir Joseph was solely responsible for this policy; no other members of the family were permitted to interfere in the running of J. and J. W. Pease. This was regrettable because it prevented any rational discussion of the future conduct of the family businesses. Alfred felt this keenly and even Dale, whom Sir Joseph respected greatly, found his occasional strictures on the bank's financial state dismissed as of little consequence. For thirty years after the death of Joseph Pease the bank's affairs were therefore masked from private and public view. In this context the experience of the Peases is illustrative of one of the themes identified by Professor Perkin in his analysis of entrepreneurial society in the nineteenth century. The emergence of great family businesses and joint stock enterprise was a logical consequence of the increasing scale of business organisation and it encouraged entrepreneurs to remain at the head of their firms, attracted by the prospect of greater wealth and power. As a result, 'the old cycle of business life, by which the successful moved out to the land to be replaced by newcomers from below, was in an increasing number of cases broken'.[45] Although Perkin is referring primarily to the adverse consequences of the rise of the joint stock company for social mobility his concept can be applied to the Peases. The death of his brothers, the indolence of Henry Fell and Arthur, together with the inexperience of Alfred and Jack, encouraged Sir Joseph to regard himself as indispensable and so he was to the extent that he possessed an overwhelming desire to maintain the various family businesses intact. It may be a simple observation on Perkin's part but it is highly illuminating: it was the railway which made it possible for entrepreneurs to reside on country estates and postpone the decision to retire from active business involvement. How could this intensely patriarchal man have combined the roles of landowner, politician and businessman in the absence of the railway? The irony was that whilst the NER was vitally necessary to the running of the Peases' mineral enterprise it played its part in facilitating the downfall of the Pease dynasty by enabling Sir Joseph to retain exclusive control of J. and J. W. Pease whilst continuing to enjoy the rural delights of Hutton Hall, the London season and the ritual sporting excursions to Scotland.

A final poignant comment on the failure of J. and J. W. Pease relates to the actions of Lady Portsmouth. In June 1903 she wrote to Sir Joseph's son-in-law, Gerald Buxton, enclosing a cheque to the value of £2,500 to enable Alfred 'to start a new home' and declared her wish to present his younger son with a silver watch formerly in the possession of George Stephenson.[46] She also asked Buxton to act as an intermediary in effecting a reconciliation with her uncle. Although he rejected the offer of the watch Alfred did accept the gift of money but left instructions before he departed for South Africa that it should be used to help any individual creditor of J. and J. W. Pease at Buxton's discretion. Sir Joseph's response was even more predictable: there could be no reconciliation unless Beatrice acknowledged that he had acted honourably in the administration and realisation of her trust estate.[47] Unhappily, Sir Joseph died before Lady Portsmouth could respond.

7
Aftermath

On returning to England in 1907 Alfred could not fail to be reminded of the changes in family precedence and status brought about by the events of 1902. Although his brother had been re-elected to the board of Pease and Partners in 1904, it was the fortunes of their cousin, Arthur Francis, which were in the ascendancy. Indeed, to the discomfiture of Alfred and Jack, Arthur had served as the company's representative on Peat's realisation committee and in 1906, following the death of Sir David Dale, he had become chairman and managing director. At first Alfred considered re-entering Parliament but, as he later recalled, 'Mr Asquith was out for the "Labour" vote and the Liberal Whips were preferring left-wing candidates'.[1] In 1909 he resigned from the Liberal Party in protest at Lloyd George's 'Socialist' budget and Asquith's compromising 'neo-Liberalism', both of which stood in marked contrast to the principles espoused by the old Gladstonian party. As for the world of business, it too held few attractions. Of all the Peases, Alfred comes closest to the stereotype image of the gentrified industrialist imbued with an ever-deepening revulsion against the impoverished spiritual and moral values bequeathed by the Victorian industrial age.[2] As early as 1881 – the year after he began his business career – he commented of Middlesbrough's jubilee celebrations that 'my grandfather and his contemporaries managed to lay the foundations of a huge hideous town, a den of misery, dirt and debauchery planted by the once green fields on the banks of the Tees'.[3] Alfred's autobiographical reminiscences, sketched out during the First World War, resurrected these strictures and revealed him as a man out of sympathy with the age, disillusioned by the rise of corporate enterprise and looking back to an earlier period of patriarchal relations between masters and men. He would have agreed wholeheartedly with the views of his friend, Sir Edward Grey, that an industrial epoch that had spawned 'telephones and cinematographs and large cities and the *Daily Mail*' had made 'the country hideous and life impossible'.[4]

Despite a detestation of 'ash heaps and chimneys', Alfred retained his interest in the Middlesbrough Estate, becoming managing director after the First World War. But the remaining years of his life, until his death in 1939, were dominated by life at Pinchinthorpe. From here he attended to the affairs of the Middlesbrough property and to his civic duties as a deputy lieutenant, magistrate and county alderman for the

North Riding. He published several works on field sports and natural history and finally, in 1932, a volume of political memoirs notable for its vigorous but critical defence of Gladstone's Irish policy.[5] Occasionally, as in the case of the centenary celebrations for the Stockton and Darlington Railway in 1925 when he felt that there was insufficient recognition of the services of his father to the development of the railway system, Alfred's bitter recollections of his near-bankruptcy would re-emerge.[6] In general, however, the final years of his life were extremely happy, mainly as a result of a greatly enriched family life which followed his third marriage in 1922 and the birth of a daughter and two sons during the succeeding five years.

Whilst Alfred was content to retire to the rural anonymity of Pinchinthorpe, the same cannot be said of Jack. Reduced in financial circumstances, he concentrated on his political career. He was already serving as a junior whip for the Liberal Party at the time of the bank failure and on the formation of the Campbell-Bannerman government in 1905 he was made a junior lord of the Treasury. In 1908 Asquith appointed him Chief Whip, a critically important office when the Liberal government was attempting to sustain some form of electoral compromise with the newly emergent Labour Party.[7] In 1910 he entered the Cabinet as Chancellor of the Duchy of Lancaster and in the following year was promoted to the office of President of the Board of Education. He held this post until May 1915 and received his final ministerial appointment (outside the Cabinet) as Postmaster-General in January 1916, a position which he held until the advent of Lloyd George's coalition government at the end of the year. In January 1917 he was raised to the peerage as Baron Gainford of Headlam in the county of Durham.[8]

It is outside the scope of this book to examine Jack's political career except to note that although he surpassed his father's ambitions as a politician his relative obscurity within the Liberal hierarchy prevented him from attaining the status of one of the great men in British public life. As far as it is possible to judge, Asquith regarded him as a loyal colleague of acceptable competence whose dismissal from Cabinet office was necessitated by the exigencies of wartime politics.[9] If the diaries of his friend Charles Hobhouse are to be believed, Jack had been considered for promotion to the thankless post of Chief Secretary for Ireland at the end of 1914 and when the political crisis of May 1915 erupted Asquith had assured him that his position at the Board of Education was secure.[10] He was, however, replaced by Arthur Henderson who joined Asquith's coalition Cabinet in the Labour interest.

When his active political career ended Jack was nearly sixty years old but a new lease of life awaited him. The background of Quakerism, his days as a senior Liberal politician, the acquisition of a peerage and the possession of a genial personality – all of these in combination were to equip him with a number of useful attributes for the role of an 'elder statesman' of industry in inter-war Britain. As vice-chairman of Pease and Partners he was chosen by the Mining Association of Great Britain for the difficult task of presenting the employers' case to the Sankey Commission of Inquiry on the coal industry in 1919. The Sankey Commission ultimately proved to be a successful attempt by Lloyd George to neutralise the miners' strong bargaining position inherited from the war, but the latter were able to use the proceedings as an effective vehicle for advancing their case for the nationalisation of the coal industry. Thus, much of the burden of defending the private-enterprise system in mining fell on Jack. It is generally agreed by historians that the miners were far more effective in presenting their case than the employers and Jack's evidence is chiefly remembered for its blunt rejection of public ownership.[11] In the new circumstances of labour relations in the coal industry, with the miners advancing political as well as economic demands, the principles of conciliation and arbitration so persistently advocated by Sir Joseph Whitwell Pease and Sir David Dale had no place.[12] In the years after 1900 two mutually incompatible views had emerged in the industry, mainly as a result of the miners' campaign for a minimum wage and the resistance of colliery owners to this demand in the face of declining labour productivity and mounting costs of production.[13] Confrontation was replacing compromise and as employers and trade union organisations began to mobilise on a national basis the old Liberal traditions of industrial and political partnership withered. In Pease and Partners itself the change in status to a public company, whose primary duty was to safeguard the interests of shareholders, no doubt widened the gulf between capital and labour.[14] After 1906 Jack's public statements and those of Arthur Francis on the conduct of labour relations were entirely in accordance with the policy of the Mining Association, whose leadership was irrevocably committed to the view that the objective economic conditions of the industry dictated that wage reductions were no longer a matter for negotiation and that in the event of trade-union opposition colliery owners should resort to the tactics of the lock-out.[15] This policy was to lead directly to the General Strike and miners' lock-out of 1926 and in Jack's case it was exemplified by his reaction to 'Mondism' – the desire on the part of a group of employers led by Sir Alfred Mond (later Lord Melchett) for a *rapprochement* with the trade union movement in general and the TUC in particular. Mond's initiative coincided with Jack's period of office as president of the Federation of British Industries (1927–8) and as a member of the Mining Association central council, one of the principal sources of opposition to national negotiations with the TUC, his response was predictably hostile.[16]

It was the close association with the corrosive politics of the mining industry which in all likelihood robbed Jack of the opportunity of crowning his public career by becoming the first chairman of the British Broadcasting Corporation. In 1922 he had accepted an invitation to become the independent chairman of the newly established British Broadcasting Company on the rather tenuous basis of his experience as Postmaster-General in 1916.[17] In July 1926, when the Baldwin government accepted the recommendations of the Crawford Committee for a change in the company's constitution, Jack could legitimately have expected to retain his position as chairman. He had, after all, been closely associated with the successful launching of broadcasting in Britain and his claims were strongly pressed by John Reith, the managing director of the old company and director-general-designate of the BBC.[18] Instead the then Parliamentary Under-Secretary for the Dominions, Lord Clarendon, was appointed chairman whilst Jack was offered and accepted the vice-chairmanship of the board of governors, a position which he occupied until 1933. His Liberal affiliations may have played a part in the apparent snub, but his position as a leading colliery owner in the year of the General Strike was probably sufficient by itself to render him an unsuitable candidate as chairman.[19]

As for Pease and Partners, it must have been a poignant moment for Jack when he succeeded his cousin as chairman of the company in 1927 – twenty-five years after he had been obliged temporarily to vacate his directorship. In fact, his elevation could not have taken place at a worse moment in the company's fortunes. The export trade and the heavy industries which provided the principal markets for Durham coal had been seriously depressed since 1921 and as inter-district competition within the industry intensified, especially after the revival of German coal production at the end of 1924, profit levels dwindled. Pease and Partners paid no dividend in 1924–5 and, even with the aid of a government subsidy in the following year, severe wage reductions at the end of 1926 and the inauguration of a statutory marketing scheme in 1931, this state of affairs persisted.[20] By the early 1930s the company had a cumulative deficit at profit and loss of £1,174,139 and under pressure from their bankers the board agreed to a moratorium scheme and the appointment of a committee to examine the company's finances.[21] The result of this initiative was that in February 1933 a thoroughgoing reorganisation of the capital and managerial structure of the company took place. This provided for a reduction in capital from £3 million to £1.5 million and, much to Jack's disappointment, his removal from office as chairman. The newly constituted four-man board headed by J. Frater Taylor, the former managing director of the Securities Management Trust, did, however, contain two Peases – Jack himself and Sir Richard Pease, the son of Arthur Francis.[22] Thereafter, aided by general economic recovery and the beginnings of rearmament, Pease and Partners' financial record improved. By 1939 all bank loans had been repaid and with average trading profits well in excess of £400,000 for the two years to March 1939 the company entered the war in a strong financial position.[23] Jack was by then in virtual retirement although he did serve as an arbitrator for the Ministry of Labour and National Service in assessing cases for exemption from military service until his death in February 1943.

With Jack's death the Pease dynasty, based upon extensive interests in the heavy trades of north-east England, was at an end. The nationalisation of railways and the coal industry by the postwar Labour government merely confirmed this fact. But if the Peases were no longer identified with those industries which had provided the mainspring of their wealth and influence in the nineteenth century, new career and business opportunities had presented themselves. These were successfully exploited not by the sons and grandsons of Sir Joseph Whitwell Pease but by the descendants of his brother Arthur. The critical factor was the decision taken by Arthur Francis and Herbert Pike in 1898 not to take up their father's interest in J. and J. W. Pease (see above, p. 100). Their fortunes and directorships had not been forfeited as a result of the failure and while Arthur Francis and his youngest brother Claude occupied senior positions in Pease and Partners for the greater part of the 1920s they had begun to accumulate important directorships elsewhere. By 1922 Arthur Francis was serving as a director of Lloyds Bank and in the following year he was elected to the board of the London and North Eastern Railway, the successor to the NER. More significant, however, was Claude's appointment in 1920 as local director and advisory director of Barclays Bank in succession to Sir Jonathan Backhouse.[24] In 1924 Claude was elected to the London board and it was due to his influence that in 1946 his great nephew Sir Richard Thorn Pease was offered employment by the bank after completing his military service.[25] At the time of writing Sir Richard is vice-chairman of Barclays Bank and executive local director for the Newcastle upon Tyne district, whilst his younger brother Derrek Allix Pease, is a director of Morgan Grenfell Holdings and Alexanders Discount Company, both of them leading financial houses in the City of London. In many ways, however, the most spectacular manifestation of the Peases' growing involvement in the tertiary sector of the economy is provided by the career of John William Beaumont Pease, the great-great-nephew of Edward Pease. When J. and J. W. Pease failed, Beaumont Pease, as he was called, was a partner in the private banking firm of Hodgkin, Barnett, Pease, Spence and Co. of Newcastle upon Tyne. This concern had been founded in 1859 to fill the void created by the collapse of the Northumberland and Durham District Bank,[26] and in 1902 it too was in the process of being taken over, not by Barclays but by Lloyds, another of the country's leading joint stock banks which had also embarked upon a policy of expansion by the absorption of private banking firms.[27] Unlike J. and J. W. Pease, however, the Newcastle-based concern possessed an extensive branch net-

work and was in a prosperous condition. Thus, when the formal amalgamation took place in 1903 Beaumont Pease was elected to the London
board of Lloyds. There then followed a distinguished career in banking
– deputy chairman of Lloyds in 1909, chairman in 1922 – culminating
in the chairmanship of the Committee of London Clearing Bankers
and the presidency of the British Bankers' Association. Between the
wars Beaumont Pease was probably better known to the general public
as an amateur golfer, but in 1936 his services to banking were officially
recognised by his elevation to the peerage as Baron Wardington of
Alnmouth in the county of Northumberland.[28] It is noteworthy that
Beaumont Pease's association with the world of finance has been perpetuated in the career of his elder son, the present Lord Wardington,
who is a partner in the stockbroking firm of Hoare Govett Ltd.

As for other members of the Pease family, their careers display a
remarkable diversity. After completing his education at Eton in 1905
Jack's only son Joseph worked at the coalface in one of Pease and
Partners' collieries near Crook and by 1914 had qualified as a colliery
manager. After the war he too served on the board of Pease and Partners until 1931, when he resigned and opened a sports equipment shop
in Darlington. Unlike his father, Joseph was not attracted to politics
and although he took his seat in the House of Lords after inheriting the
Gainford peerage he never attended Parliament. His elder sister Miriam
was appointed to the Factory Inspectorate of the Home Office in 1916,
a position which she retained until her resignation in 1941.[29] Of Jack's
grandsons the present Lord Gainford became a land surveyor in East
and Central Africa after wartime service in the RAF and joined Soil
Mechanics Ltd, part of the Mowlem Group of civil engineering companies, in the early 1950s. From 1958 he served in the architect's
department of the London County Council and retired from the equivalent department of the Greater London Council in 1978. His younger
brothers, George and John, are currently living in Scotland. The
former is a qualified architect and town planner and now works as a
consultant, while the latter, after farming in Argyllshire, is engaged in
the building construction industry.[30] Alfred's surviving sons, Sir Vincent Pease and his younger brother Gurney, are at present living in
Cumbria. Sir Vincent attended an agricultural college in Co. Durham,
but never farmed on his own account, and Gurney, after a period of
service with the Owners of the Middlesbrough Estate, opted for the
hazardous occupation of running an inn in one of the remoter parts of
the Lake District.

Whilst several members of the Pease family were able to make the
transition from its traditional involvement in the industrial economy to
distinguished employment in the tertiary sector and the professions,
their political influence within the north-east of England had been
eliminated all but completely by the end of the 1920s. The last Pease to

sit in the House of Commons was William Edwin, who succeeded his cousin, Herbert Pike, as the Conservative member for Darlington in 1923, when the latter was raised to the peerage as Baron Daryngton of Witley for his services to Unionism. On William's death in 1926, his younger brother Ernest was adopted as the Conservative candidate, but in the ensuing by-election he was defeated by a margin of 329 votes by the Labour candidate.[31] In a very real sense, William Edwin was the last of the old-style Peases, a resident of Darlington in his spacious mansion at Mowden and serving consecutively as councillor, mayor and alderman on the town council. As a director of the Darlington-based Cleveland Bridge and Engineering Company and the Consett Iron Company, his career was therefore not untypical of those of several members of the family before 1900. By the mid-1920s, however, the time had passed when local politics could be dominated by one family. In 1915 Darlington had become a county borough, the number of council wards had been increased from six to eight, and after successive extensions to the franchise the personalised and highly partisan electioneering of the third quarter of the nineteenth century was no longer possible in a town with a population well in excess of 60,000. But these were not the only reasons for the decline of the family's political influence. Other important factors were the erosion of economic power as a result of stagnation in the staple industries and, more symbolically, the liquidation of the family's interests in Henry Pease and Co. and Robert Stephenson and Co. The increasing scale of business may also have played a part in that it undermined the direct and paternalistic relationship between employers and their workforce that was typical in the years before 1890. By the 1920s, moreover, few members of the family resided in the town or the surrounding district and for those who remained there was neither the desire nor the opportunity to sustain an outmoded form of political hegemony. Above all, new political forces were at work. Unionism may have split the family in the 1880s, but in its Darlington context it had perpetuated the Peases' political influence for a generation after 1900 at a time when the first serious challenges to the traditional Liberal domination of north-east England had begun to appear. Although these should not be overstated for the pre-1914 period, it was a sign of things to come when the by election in the Barnard Castle division of Co. Durham which followed the death of Sir Joseph Whitwell Pease in 1903 was won not by the Liberal candidate (who came bottom of the poll in a three-cornered contest) but by Arthur Henderson, representing the recently established Labour Representation Committee (LRC).[32] Henderson, who was to serve as secretary of the Labour Party from 1911 to 1934 and rise to the position of Foreign Secretary in Ramsay MacDonald's second Labour government, had been employed as Sir Joseph's political agent since 1895. Although he would have preferred to have retained his Liberal ties by standing as a

Lib-Lab candidate, it is significant that by the summer of 1903 four other LRC candidates had been selected for constituencies in Co. Durham, including Darlington and Stockton. The national Liberal Party undoubtedly retained the initiative as an agency of radical social change during its period of office between 1906 and 1914, but the fact remains that the rise of the Labour Party was a partial consequence of the unwillingness of constituency Liberal associations in Co. Durham and elsewhere either to adopt Lib-Lab working-class candidates or to leave the field clear for LRC candidates in accordance with the wishes of the national leadership.[33]

By the time of Jack's death little also remained of the Peases' Quaker antecedents. Whilst he remained a member of the Society of Friends all his life, the decisive break with tradition had taken place in Jack's own generation. It is true that Sir Joseph Whitwell Pease was the first Quaker to accept an honour from the Crown and that he had perpetuated the growing 'conformity to the world' that was so disturbing to Edward Pease, but he was, nevertheless, a fervent upholder of a number of established Quaker principles and reforming agitations. His opposition to the Chinese opium trade and to capital punishment were cases in point, as was his presidency of the Peace Society, an organisation whose pacifist principles were as much articles of faith for Sir Joseph as they had been for his father and uncle. As Alfred recalled, Sir Joseph 'revelled in military history and deeds of battle on sea and land . . . yet such was the influence of his environment and upbringing that he would advocate and support proposals in public and parliament to reduce our navy and even our little army'.[34] In 1900 he even went so far as to inform Alfred of his intention to alter his will in favour of Jack in view of the attempted enlistment in the army of Alfred's elder son, Edward, for service in South Africa.[35] The alteration did not take place, but Sir Joseph's acceptance of Jack's extravagant expenditure on Nunthorpe Hall in the succeeding two years was an indication of deep dissatisfaction with the family of his elder son and heir.[36] On Sir Joseph's death Alfred declined the presidency of the Peace Society and though Jack accepted the position he resigned in 1914 as a result of his support for the government's decision to declare war on Germany.[37] Thereafter, military service was accepted in the Pease family as a matter of honour and duty. During the First World War Edward Pease was employed in various branches of the army in Europe and the Middle East, while his younger brother Christopher served in the Yorkshire Hussars until he was killed in action in 1918. Similarly, Jack's son Joseph enlisted in the Lovat Scouts in 1914, served with distinction at Gallipoli and retained his military links after the war as a territorial, retiring with the rank of major in 1935. Arthur Francis's son Richard served throughout the war in the Northumberland Yeomanry and Arthur himself had no hesitation in accepting the position of Second

Civil Lord of the Admiralty in January 1918, being rewarded for his services to the war effort with a baronetcy in 1920.

Enlistment in the armed forces was only one aspect of the decline of old-style Quakerism in the Pease family. Other indications were provided by changing patterns of education and marriage. In the former case it was commonplace up to the 1870s for male children in the family to be educated at Quaker boarding schools, principally Grove House, Tottenham, with extra private tuition after leaving school.[38] But following the removal of religious tests by the Universities of Oxford and Cambridge in 1871, a new pattern of education rapidly emerged. Virtually all male Peases of Alfred's and Jack's generation attended university with the family exhibiting a particular preference for Trinity College, Cambridge, the largest of the university's colleges and one which had tolerated the attendance of Dissenters even before the reform of 1871.[39] This set a precedent for the future, except that succeeding generations received their earlier education from within the English public school system. Thus, Alfred's elder son was at Winchester before proceeding to Cambridge, Jack's son at Eton, and Claude Pease at Harrow, whilst Beaumont Pease was educated at Marlborough before going on to New College, Oxford. By the end of the nineteenth century, therefore, the Peases were already well into the second generation of those whose education, wealth and social position had ensured their assimilation into the nationwide upper class. Inevitably, this was increasingly reflected in the choice of marriage partners. For Sir Joseph Whitwell Pease and his generation the choice was almost as restricted as it had been for Edward Pease sixty years earlier – from within the Society of Friends, but augmented in the third quarter of the nineteenth century by the increasing acceptability of intermarriage within the family itself. Alfred and Jack, however, were the first Peases to marry non-Quakers (see above, p. 59) and well before the end of the century their relatives were marrying into the established church. In 1887, for example, Beaumont Pease's elder brother Howard married the daughter of Herbert Kynaston, a Canon of Durham Cathedral, and a decade later Herbert Pike Pease married the second daughter of Herbert Mortimer Luckock, the former Dean of Lichfield Cathedral.

By 1914 few members of the Pease family retained their affiliation to the Society of Friends and fewer still were practising Quakers. The nineteenth century had witnessed considerable changes in the world of Quakerism, principally in favour of the relaxation of 'discipline' as pressure for 'conformity to the world' mounted after 1850. The secular forces that were at work within the Society of Friends in general were reinforced in the case of the Peases by their educational backgrounds, wealth and social and political status. In its most extreme form the process of 'conformity to the world' entailed far more than the rejection of Quaker formalism and exclusiveness. It is in fact to be interpreted in

its most literal sense – the abandonment of the Society of Friends for
the established church – and this too was part of the experience of the
Pease family, where the most notable converts to Anglicanism were
Alfred and Herbert Pike. In 1907 Alfred wrote a long introduction to
the edited diaries of Edward Pease, fulsome in its admiration of Quakerism and in 1910, on the occasion of his daughter Lavender's baptism
by the Archbishop of York, a journal entry recorded his contempt for
the established church's 'pretensions to magic and supernatural control
of the destinies of souls'.[40] In July 1916, however, after Christopher
Pease had been disowned by the Guisborough Monthly Meeting
because of his enlistment for military service, Alfred resigned from the
Society of Friends and two years later, following his son's death in
action, joined the Church of England.[41] At a time of intense personal
grief he was motivated primarily by a desire for closer spiritual links
with the Anglican families of Christopher and Lavender. Another factor was that even before his resignation he had been attending 'low
church' services in Guisborough and he now wished to identify himself
formally with 'the general and national recognition of religious and . . .
Christian ideals' as represented by the established church.[42] Alfred was
never an enthusiastic member of the Church of England, unlike his
cousin Herbert Pike, whose devotion to Anglicanism was fervent
enough to lead to his appointment as president of the Church Army in
1917 and as vice-chairman of the House of Laity of the National
Assembly of the Church of England. After his elevation to the peerage
Herbert Pike was invited to join other prestigious Anglican institutions
– the Ecclesiastical Commission in 1923, the Church Estates Commission in 1926, and Queen Anne's Bounty in 1935. Herbert Pike's commitment to the established church, therefore, proved to be as absolute
as that of his Irish Dissenting mother to the discipline of the Society of
Friends. Taking the Pease family as a whole only two generations had
been required for the obliteration of Joseph Pease's radical Quakerism
and its replacement by a growing commitment to the established
order.[43]

The waning of political influence and the decline of Quakerism are
important elements in the history of the Pease family. The main purpose of this study, however, has been to chart the rise and fall of an
industrial dynasty based upon coal, iron and transport. The rise to
industrial power in the north-east of England was, of course, facilitated
by Quakerism – by the relative ease of obtaining finance capital and the
inheritance by Joseph and Henry Pease of an established entrepreneurial ethic. But this is only part of the explanation for their success. In the
early nineteenth century the Peases were able and willing to take advantage of an economic, commercial and technological environment that
was conducive to expansion: the process of industrialisation was firmly
established and the coming of the railway gave a major impetus to

regional economic growth by facilitating the exploitation of key industrial raw materials. It was the railway which opened up the south
Durham coalfield, established the Tees as a major coal-shipping river,
and in the period after 1850 laid the foundations for the expansion of
the Cleveland iron trade with the boom town of Middlesbrough as its
focal point. Joseph and Henry were men of foresight and imagination,
driven onwards by the desire for material success, and, unlike earlier
generations of their family, capable of reconciling their religious beliefs
with business speculations that entailed substantial financial risks and
rewards. By the early 1870s the Peases were heavily involved in railway
enterprise, coal and ironstone mining, limestone quarrying, locomotive
building and the textile industry. This was the rich and diverse legacy
that was passed on to the generation of Sir Joseph Whitwell Pease. It
was Sir Joseph's misfortune, however, that his elevation to the leadership of the Pease dynasty coincided with the onset of the 'Great Depression' in 1873, closely followed by the 'iron smash' of the later 1870s in
the north-east of England. If the adverse commercial conditions of the
final quarter of the nineteenth century render a judgement on Sir
Joseph's entrepreneurial capabilities extremely difficult in the light of
the achievements of his forebears, the task is made even more formidable by the special problems he encountered as a result of rapidly
succeeding deaths in the family after 1872 and his predilection for
introducing non-entrepreneurial considerations into business conduct.
It is this latter factor which makes it impossible to offer an objective
judgement on Sir Joseph's policy of sustaining loss-making enterprises
from the resources of J. and J. W. Pease for a period of nearly twenty
years. With the benefit of hindsight the family interests in Henry Pease
and Co., Robert Stephenson and Co. and Wilsons, Pease should have
been liquidated at the latest by the end of the 1880s since their survival
contributed significantly to the failure of J. and J. W. Pease. Even so, it
is likely that Sir Joseph's financial ruin could have been avoided had it
not been for the disastrous consequences of the Portsmouth case. Sir
Joseph's handling of Lady Portsmouth's affairs was not underhand, but
after the intervention of Sir Richard Nicholson his conduct was less
than exemplary when judged from a commercial standpoint. But once
again the influence of subjective factors was uppermost. Sir Joseph was
the head of the dynasty – the 'Prophet in Israel' whose judgement was
not to be questioned: the 'common stock' was to be retained intact
against the depredations of Lord Portsmouth. Sir Joseph's imprudence
in 1898, especially in the public flotation of Pease and Partners, was
that of a tired and inflexible old man who was determined to make one
of the greatest of all errors of judgement for an entrepreneur – to retain
effective control of a business dynasty in the mistaken belief of his own
indispensability.

Appendix

THE PEASE ANCESTRY

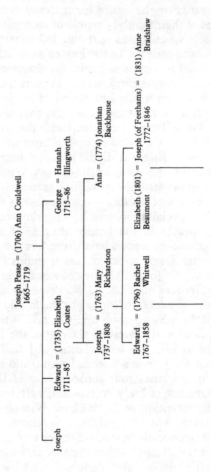

Joseph Pease = (1706) Ann Couldwell
1665–1719

Edward = (1735) Elizabeth
1711–85   Coates

George = Hannah
1715–86   Illingworth

Joseph

Joseph = (1763) Mary
1737–1808   Richardson

Ann = (1774) Jonathan
         Backhouse

Edward = (1796) Rachel
1767–1858   Whitwell

Elizabeth (1801) = Joseph (of Feethams) = (1831) Anne
Beaumont   1772–1846   Bradshaw

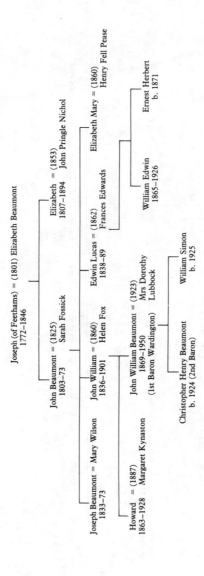

Joseph (of Feethams) = (1801) Elizabeth Beaumont
1772–1846

John Beaumont = (1825) Sarah Fossick
1803–73

Elizabeth = (1853) John Pringle Nichol
1807–1894

Joseph Beaumont = Mary Wilson
1833–73

John William = (1860) Helen Fox
1836–1901

Edwin Lucas = (1862) Frances Edwards
1838–89

Elizabeth Mary = (1860) Henry Fell Pease

Howard = (1887) Margaret Kynaston
1863–1928

John William Beaumont = (1923) Mrs Dorothy Lubbock
1869–1950
(1st Baron Wardington)

William Edwin
1865–1926

Ernest Herbert
b. 1871

Christopher Henry Beaumont
b. 1924 (2nd Baron)

William Simon
b. 1925

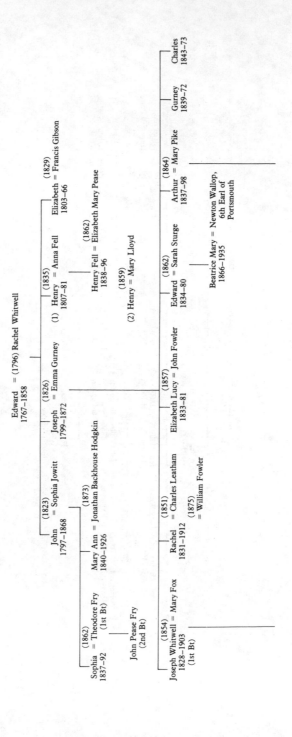

Edward = (1796) Rachel Whitwell
1767–1858

(1823)   (1826)   (1829)
John = Sophia Jowitt   Joseph = Emma Gurney   (1) Henry = Anna Fell   Elizabeth = Francis Gibson
1797–1868   1799–1872   1807–81   1803–66

                                                                                              (1862)
(1862)   (1873)   Henry Fell = Elizabeth Mary Pease
Sophia = Theodore Fry   Mary Ann = Jonathan Backhouse Hodgkin   1838–96
1837–92   (1st Bt)   1840–1926

                                                                                (1859)
John Pease Fry   (2) Henry = Mary Lloyd
(2nd Bt)

(1851)   (1857)   (1862)   (1864)
Rachel = Charles Leatham   Elizabeth Lucy = John Fowler   Edward = Sarah Sturge   Arthur = Mary Pike   Gurney   Charles
1831–1912   1833–81   1834–80   1837–98   1839–72   1843–73
(1875)
= William Fowler

(1854)
Joseph Whitwell = Mary Fox
1828–1903
(1st Bt)

Beatrice Mary = Newton Wallop,
1866–1935   6th Earl of
                        Portsmouth

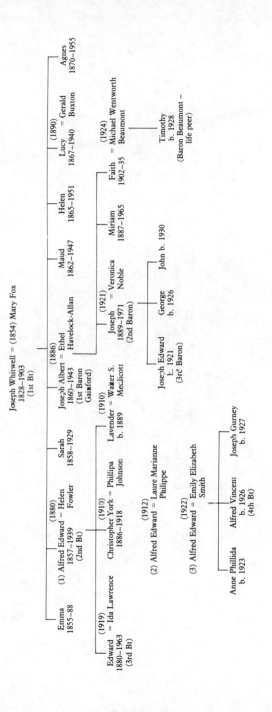

Joseph Whitwell = (1854) Mary Fox
1828–1903
(1st Bt)

- Emma 1855–88
- (1) Alfred Edward = Helen Fowler (1880) 1857–1939 (2nd Bt)
  - Edward = Ida Lawrence (1919) 1880–1963 (3rd Bt)
  - (1) Alfred Edward = Phillipa Johnson / Christopher York 1886–1918 (1910)
  - (2) Alfred Edward = Laure Marianne Philippe (1912)
  - (3) Alfred Edward = Emily Elizabeth Smith (1922)
    - Anne Phillida b. 1923
    - Alfred Vincent b. 1926 (4th Bt)
    - Joseph Gurney b. 1927
- Sarah 1858–1929
- Lavender = Walter S. Meclicott (1910) b. 1889
- Joseph Albert = Ethel Havelock-Allan (1886) 1860–1943 (1st Baron Gainford)
  - Joseph = Veronica Noble (1921) 1889–1971 (2nd Baron)
    - Joseph Edward b. 1921 (3rd Baron)
    - George b. 1926
    - John b. 1930
  - Miriam 1887–1965
- Maud 1862–1947
- Helen 1865–1951
- Faith = Michael Wentworth Beaumont (1924) 1902–35
  - Timothy b. 1928 (Baron Beaumont – life peer)
- Lucy = Gerald Buxton (1890) 1867–1940
- Agnes 1870–1955

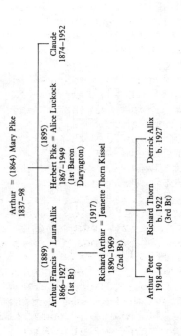

Arthur = (1864) Mary Pike
1837–98

(1889) Arthur Francis = Laura Allix — Herbert Pike = Alice Luckock (1895) — Claude
1866–1927   1867–1949   1874–1952
(1st Bt)   (1st Baron
                          Daryngton)

(1917) Richard Arthur = Jeanette Thorn Kissel
1890–1969
(2nd Bt)

Arthur Peter — Richard Thorn — Derrick Allix
1918–40   b. 1922   b. 1927
               (3rd Bt)

Notes

The place of publication of works is London unless otherwise stated.

Chapter 1

1 Foster, Joseph, *Pease of Darlington* (privately published, 1891), p. 4; Pease, Sir Alfred E. (ed.), *The Diaries of Edward Pease: The Father of English Railways* (1907), p. 43. The descent of the Pease family since 1665 is set out in the Appendix, pp. 128–32.
2 Pease, Sir Alfred E., *The Diaries of Edward Pease*, p. 43.
3 J. Gurney Pease (JGP) Papers, Pease, Sir Alfred E., 'Autobiographical Record' (1916–18).
4 Foster, op. cit., p. 29.
5 Smailes, A. E., *North England* (1st edn, 1960), p. 111.
6 ibid., p. 122.
7 McCord, Norman, *North East England: The Region's Development, 1760–1960* (1979), p. 57.
8 Rimmer, W. G., *Marshalls of Leeds, Flax Spinners, 1788–1886* (Cambridge, 1961), p. 9.
9 Deane, P., 'The output of the British woollen industry in the 18th century', *Journal of Economic History*, vol. 17, no. 2 (1957), pp. 207–23; Ponting, K. G., and Jenkins, David, *The British Wool Textile Industry, 1770–1914* (1982), pp. 57–61.
10 Pease, Henry and Company Ltd, *Bi-centenary 1752–1952, Priestgate Mills, Darlington* (Darlington, 1952), *passim*.
11 Pease, M. F., *A Chronicle of the Pease Family of Leeds, Cote Bank, Westbury-on-Trym, Bristol* (Street, 1949).
12 Pease, Sir Alfred E., *The Diaries of Edward Pease*, p. 46.
13 ibid., pp. 361–2.
14 Pressnell, L. S., *Country Banking in the Industrial Revolution* (Oxford, 1956), p. 15.
15 ibid., pp. 18, 23, 26; Lloyd, Humphrey, *The Quaker Lloyds in the Industrial Revolution* (1975); Windsor, David Burns, *The Quaker Enterprise: Friends in Business* (1980), pp. 22–4.
16 Raistrick, Arthur, *Quakers in Science and Industry* (Newton Abbot, 1968), pp. 74–6, 326–8; Grubb, Isabel, *Quakerism in Industry Before 1800* (1930), pp. 165–6.
17 Phillips, Maberley, *A History of Banks, Bankers and Banking in Northumberland, Durham and North Yorkshire* (1894), pp. 134–54.
18 Birthright membership was adopted in 1737 and was derived from the Apostolic principle that children should share the religious 'status' of their parents. See Grubb, Edward, *What is Quakerism?* (1917), p. 99.
19 See Weber, M., *The Protestant Ethic and the Spirit of Capitalism* (1930); Tawney, R. H., *Religion and the Rise of Capitalism* (2nd edn, 1937); McLelland, D. C., *The Achieving Society* (Princeton, New Jersey, 1961); Samuelsson, Kurt, *Religion and Economic Action* (New York, 1962); Flinn, M. W., 'Social theory and the industrial revolution', in Burns, Tom, and Saul, S. B. (eds), *Social Theory and Economic Change* (1967), pp. 9–34; Thompson, Allan, *The Dynamics of the Industrial Revolution* (1973), pp. 122–40; Marshall, Gordon, *Presbyteries and Profits: Calvinism and the Development of Capitalism in Scotland, 1560–1707* (Oxford, 1980).

20 Braithwaite, William C., *The Second Period of Quakerism* (2nd edn prepared by Henry Cadbury, Cambridge, 1961), p. 206. For similar comment see Sykes, John, *The Quakers: A New Look at their Place in Society* (1958), pp. 162–243, *passim.*

21 Sykes, John, op. cit., pp. 178–9. See also Grubb, Isabel, op. cit., pp. 44, 53, 165–7, and Mullett, Michael, *Radical Religious Movements in Early Modern Europe* (1980), pp. 33–54.

22 Raistrick, op. cit., pp. 34, 45, 335.

23 On the interrelatedness of Quaker families see Anderson, Verily, *Friends and Relations: 3 Centuries of Quaker Families* (1980); Brett, R. L. (ed.), *Barclay Fox's Journal* (1979). On the Peases in particular see Foster, op. cit., *passim*, and Benson, R. Seymour, *Photographic Pedigree of the Descendants of Isaac and Rachel Wilson* (Middlesbrough, 1912).

24 Mullett, op. cit., pp. 41–6; Sykes, op. cit., p. 171. The figure for Darlington Friends is taken from Longstaffe, E. Hylton Dyer, *The History and Antiquities of the Parish of Darlington in the Bishoprick* (1854), pp. 160, 248.

25 On the Quaker 'cousinhood' see Corley, T. A. B., *Quaker Enterprise in Biscuits: Huntley and Palmers of Reading, 1872–1972* (1972), pp. 3–10.

26 For straightforward accounts of Quaker business dynasties see Emden, Paul H., *Quakers in Commerce: A Record of Business Achievement* (1939); Windsor, op. cit.

27 To be precise, Dissenters were barred from entry to the University of Oxford and from taking a degree at the University of Cambridge as a result of their refusal to attend compulsory chapel.

28 Raistrick, op. cit., p. 338; Mathias, Peter, *The First Industrial Nation: An Economic History of Britain 1700–1914* (1st edn, 1969), p. 158.

29 Page, William (ed.), *The Victoria County History of the Counties of England: A History of Durham*, vol. 2 (original edn, 1907, reprinted 1968), p. 318.

30 Pease, Sir Alfred E., *The Diaries of Edward Pease*, p. 47.

31 ibid.

32 See Smiles, Samuel, *Lives of the Engineers*, vol. 3 (*George and Robert Stephenson*) (1862), pp. 149–50.

33 It is a matter for regret that the author has been unable to trace the location of Edward Pease's original diaries. They were probably lost after the death of Sir Alfred E. Pease in 1939 when his home and most of its contents were sold.

34 Pease, Sir Alfred E., *The Diaries of Edward Pease*, pp. 131–260, *passim.*

35 ibid., pp. 48–9.

36 'Schumpeterian' entrepreneurs are endowed with the ability to break out of the trend towards constant equilibrium in the economy by introducing 'new combinations' of processes, products and markets. The core of Schumpeter's thesis is to be found in Schumpeter, J. A., *The Theory of Economic Development* (1934), pp. 74–83. See also Schumpeter, J. A., 'The creative response in economic history', *Journal of Economic History*, vol. 7, no. 2 (1947), pp. 149–59.

37 *Memoir of Fra: Mewburn, Chief Bailiff of Darlington and First Railway Solicitor, by His Son* (Darlington, 1867), p. 63.

38 Pease, Sir Alfred E., *The Diaries of Edward Pease*, p. 202; Loukes, Harold, *The Discovery of Quakerism* (1960), p. 134–5.

39 *The Railway News* (Supplement), 2 October 1875.

40 Perkin, H., *The Age of the Railway* (1970), p. 56.

41 On the 'Grand Allies' see Galloway, R., *Annals of Coal Mining and the Coal Trade*, vol. 1 (1898, reprinted 1971), p. 248; Dendy Marshall, C. F., *History of British Railways down to the Year 1830* (1938), p. 21. For the role of landowners generally in promoting mineral development in the eighteenth century see Mingay, G. E., *English Landed Society in the Eighteenth Century* (1963); Ward, J. T., 'Landowners and mining' in Ward, J. T., and Wilson, R. G. (eds), *Land and Industry: The Landed Estates and the Industrial Revolution* (1971), pp. 63–116.

42 Tomlinson, W. W., *The North Eastern Railway: its rise and development*

(1915, reprinted with an introduction by K. Hoole, Newton Abbot, 1967), pp. 4–32.

43 Longstaffe, op. cit., pp. 359–60.
44 Sunderland, Norman, *A History of Darlington* (Manchester, 1967), pp. 62–3.
45 Tomlinson, op. cit., p. 40.
46 Smailes, op. cit., pp. 158–9.
47 Tomlinson, op. cit., p. 40.
48 The following account is based on Tomlinson, op. cit., pp. 40–74, Jeans, J. S., *Jubilee Memorial of the Railway System: A History of the Stockton and Darlington Railway and a Record of its Results* (1875, reprinted Newcastle, 1974), and McDougall, C. A., *The Stockton and Darlington Railway 1821–1863* (Durham, 1975).
49 See Phillips, op. cit., p. 232.
50 Tomlinson, op. cit., p. 48.
51 ibid.
52 ibid., p. 50.
53 Jeans, *Jubilee Memorial*, pp. 21–2.
54 *Durham County Advertiser*, 21 November 1818.
55 Jeans, *Jubilee Memorial*, p. 24.
56 Tomlinson, op. cit., p. 50.
57 The following figures are taken from Public Record Office (PRO), RAIL 667/233, 'List of subscribers to the project for the purpose of constructing a rail or tramway from Stockton by way of Darlington to the Collieries and the interior of the County of Durham'. They are consistent with those for the 1821 subscription list presented in Cottrell, P. L., and Ottley, G., 'The beginnings of the Stockton and Darlington Railway: people and documents, 1813–25: a celebratory note', *Journal of Transport History*, new series, vol. 3, no. 2 (1975), p. 90.
58 Jeans, *Jubilee Memorial*, p. 25.
59 On Thomas Richardson see Lee, S. (ed.), *Dictionary of National Biography*, vol. 44 (1895), pp. 178–9; Boyce, A. O., *Records of a Quaker Family: The Richardsons of Cleveland* (1889); Emden, op. cit., p. 105.
60 Reed, M. C., *Investment in Railways in Britian, 1820–1844: A Study in the Development of the Capital Market* (Oxford, 1975), pp. 169–78.
61 Cited in Davies, Hunter, *George Stephenson: A Biographical Study of the Father of the Railways* (1975), p. 60.
62 Cited in *Memoir of Fra: Mewburn*, p. 53.
63 Mewburn, Francis, *The Larchfield Diary: Extracts from the Diary of the Late Mr Mewburn, First Railway Solicitor* (1876), p. 8.
64 Smiles, Samuel, op. cit., vol. 3, p. 164.
65 Phillips, op. cit., pp. 148–9; Matthews, P. W. and Tuke, A. W., *A History of Barclays Bank Limited* (1926), p. 206.
66 Jeans, *Jubilee Memorial*, pp. 35–6.
67 Durham Country Record Office (DCRO), Darlington, U415j, Pease, Henry, 'George and Dragon' (1823).
68 Tomlinson, op. cit., p. 69.
69 See Davies, *George Stephenson*, pp. 62–5.
70 Smiles, Samuel, vol. 3, op. cit., pp. 163–5; Tomlinson, op. cit., pp. 75–105, *passim*.
71 Pease, Sir Alfred E., *The Diaries of Edward Pease*, pp. 117–24.
72 *Darlington and Stockton Times*, 24 October 1857.
73 See for example Smiles, Samuel, *Lives of the Engineers*, vols. 1–5 (1861–2, reprinted 1904); *Henry Mayhew's 1851* (1851).
74 See Tomlinson, op. cit., p. 75; Simmons, Jack, 'Rail: 1975 or 1980?', *Journal of Transport History*, new series, vol. 7, no. 1 (1980), pp. 1–7.
75 Jeans, *Jubilee Memorial*, p. 121; Tomlinson, op. cit., p. 69. For an early statement

of the company's limited objectives see DCRO, Darlington, U415j, Chaytor, William Jun., *Observations on the Proposed Rail-Way or Train-Way from Stockton to the Collieries by way of Darlington* (Durham, 1818).

76 See Warren, J. G. H., *A Century of Locomotive Building by Robert Stephenson and Co., 1823–1923* (Newcastle upon Tyne, 1923), pp. 53–61; Bailey, Michael R., 'Robert Stephenson and Co. 1823–1829', *Transactions of the Newcomen Society*, vol. 50 (1980), p. 109.

77 Pease, Sir Alfred E., *The Diaries of Edward Pease*, p. 264; Warren, op. cit., p. 53. Pease's holding included that of Thomas Richardson but the latter did not attend partners' meetings and left it to his cousin to look after his interests in the firm. See Bailey, op. cit., p. 109.

78 Almost from the outset the partners were dissatisfied with George Stephenson's management in the light of his growing commitment to other railway projects. This helps to explain Longridge's appointment as executive partner in December 1824. Bailey, op. cit., p. 115.

79 Pease, Sir Alfred E., *The Diaries of Edward Pease*, p. 363.

80 ibid., pp. 238, 242, 261–2, 264.

81 Davies, *George Stephenson*, p. 89.

82 Tomlinson, op. cit., pp. 87–8; Reed, M. C., 'Investment in railways in Britain, 1820–1844' (D.Phil. thesis, University of Oxford, 1970), p. 295.

83 Warren, op. cit., p. 50.

84 Tomlinson, op. cit., p. 357.

85 Sweezy, P. M., *Monopoly and Competition in the English Coal Trade, 1550–1850* (1938), table 3, p. 47; Jeans, *Jubilee Memorial*, pp. 122–3.

86 Tomlinson, op. cit., p. 117; McCord, op. cit., p. 53.

87 Warren, op. cit., p. 50.

88 Pease, Sir Alfred, E., *The Diaries of Edward Pease, passim*.

89 ibid., p. 145.

90 ibid., p. 184.

Chapter 2

1 Lillie, William, *The History of Middlesbrough: An Illustration of the Evolution of English Industry* (Middlesbrough, 1968), p. 47.

2 Postgate, Charles, *Middlesbrough: its History, Environs and Trade* (Middlesbrough 1899), p. 8; Jeans, *Jubilee Memorial*, p. 123; Tomlinson, op. cit., p. 165.

3 Jeans, J. S., *Pioneers of the Cleveland Iron Trade* (Middlesbrough, 1875), p. 136.

4 ibid., p. 129; Fenwick, Thomas, 'Joseph Pease', *Practical Magazine* (1873), p. 208.

5 JGP Papers, Joseph Pease Diary, 28 October 1827, 30 October 1827, 10 December 1827.

6 ibid., 18 August 1828. The Darlington branch of the Durham County Record Office and the Cleveland County Archives Department, Middlesbrough, hold copies of this important diary entry.

7 Gibson was a brewer and Joseph Pease's brother-in-law, having married his younger sister Elizabeth in 1829. The original Quaker purchasers were themselves assisted by London bankers Francis Baring, Nathan Meyer Rothschild, Samuel Gurney and Moses Montefiore.

8 JGP Papers, Joseph Pease Diary, 15 December 1828. The estate was purchased from William Chilton who had paid £15,750 for the property in 1808. The shareholdings were as follows: Thomas Richardson, 2/10; Henry Birkbeck, 2/10; Joseph Pease, 2/10; Simon Martin, 2/10; Edward Pease Junr, 1/10; Francis Gibson, 1/10. By 1841 the pattern of shareholdings had become more concentrated: Thomas Richardson, 3/10; Henry Birkbeck 3/10; Joseph Pease 3/10; Henry Pease 1/10. By then each one-tenth share was worth £9,789. See Lillie, op. cit., p. 55.

9 Jeans, *Jubilee Memorial*, pp. 175–7. These figures include shipments from Stockton and Middlesbrough up to 1850 and from Hartlepool to 1844.
10 Sweezy, op. cit., pp. 89–90, 94–5.
11 Tomlinson, op. cit., p. 181.
12 Mewburn, *Larchfield Diary*, p. 25; Sweezy, op. cit., pp. 96–8.
13 Taylor, A. J., 'Combination in the mid-nineteenth century coal industry', *Transactions of the Royal Historical Society*, vol. 3 (1953), pp. 26, 31; Sweezy, op. cit., pp. 105–8.
14 Tomlinson, op. cit., p. 278.
15 ibid.
16 PRO RAIL, SAD 1/31, *Stockton and Darlington Railway Sub-Committee Minutes*, 30 October 1835.
17 Tomlinson, op. cit., p. 167. Tennant, who had once been a sailor, named the company after the Duke of Clarence, Lord High Admiral of the Navy.
18 Tomlinson, op. cit., pp. 236–40.
19 ibid., p. 281.
20 ibid., pp. 288–9; Mewburn, *Larchfield Diary*, pp. 43–4.
21 Tomlinson, op. cit., pp. 72–3.
22 The pattern of shareholdings in the Great North of England Railway was far more geographically dispersed than that of its Stockton and Darlington counterpart. It was therefore a more typical example of nineteenth-century railway financing. See Reed, *A Study in the Development of the Capital Market*, pp. 184–92 and Brooke, D., 'The promotion of four Yorkshire railways and the share capital market', *Transport History*, vol. 5, no. 3 (1972), pp. 256–64.
23 Tomlinson, op. cit., p. 357.
24 Perkin, *The Age of the Railway*, pp. 101–2.
25 The record of share transfers can be traced in PRO RAIL, 667/234.
26 Briggs, Asa, *Victorian Cities* (Pelican edn, 1968), pp. 244–5.
27 Lillie, op. cit., p. 55.
28 Tomlinson, op. cit., p. 437; Jeans, *Jubilee Memorial*, p. 110.
29 Briggs, *Victorian Cities*, pp. 245–6.
30 Reid, H. G., *Middlesbrough and its Jubilee* (Middlesbrough, 1881), pp. 85–6.
31 ibid., p. 146. The Middlesbrough site was purchased from the estate company for £1,800. Lillie, op. cit., p. 70.
32 Ord, J. W., *The History and Antiquities of Cleveland* (1846), p. 107.
33 Ranger, William, *Report to the Public Health Board in regard to the Inquiry into the Adoption of the 1848 Act by Middlesbrough* (1854); Pease, Sir Alfred E., *The Diaries of Edward Pease*, p. 194; Lillie, op. cit., p. 71. The early stages of urban growth in Middlesbrough are expertly analysed in Leonard, J. W., 'Urban development and population growth in Middlesbrough 1831–71 (unpublished D.Phil. thesis, University of York, 1976). Leonard concludes, with considerable justification, that as an early exercise in idealistic town planning the development of Middlesbrough was a notable failure.
34 Harrison, J. K., 'The production of pig iron in north east England 1577–1865' in Hempstead, C. A. (ed.), *Cleveland Iron and Steel: Background and Nineteenth Century History* (British Steel Corporation, 1979), p. 58.
35 Bullock, I., 'The origins of economic growth on Teesside, 1851–81', *Northern History*, vol. 9 (1974), pp. 83–4.
36 Brooke, David, 'The North Eastern Railway, 1854–80: A study in railway consolidation and competition' (unpublished PhD thesis, University of Leeds, 1971), p. 57.
37 In 1840, when 426,304 tons of coal were shipped from Middlesbrough the equivalent figure for Hartlepool was already 441,707 tons. See Barton, Peter, 'The port of Stockton on Tees and its creeks 1825 to 1861', *Maritime History*, vol. 1, no. 2, (1971), p. 129. On the dock proposal see DCRO, Darlington, U415j, D/XD/35/7,

Stockton and Darlington Management Committee Reports 1839 and 1840: The Report of the Stockton and Darlington Railway Company to the General Meeting (12 August 1840). These reports (D/XD/35/1–16), which cover the financial years from 1832/3 to 1848/9, contain handwritten reviews of the company's operations and also balance sheets showing revenue and expenditure.

38   Postgate, op. cit., pp. 15–16.
39   Kenwood, A. G., 'Capital investment in north eastern England, 1800–1913' (unpublished PhD thesis, University of London, 1962), pp. 139–40; Pease, Joseph Albert and Pease, Alfred Edward, *An Historical Outline of the Association of Edward Pease, Joseph Pease, and Sir Joseph Whitwell Pease, with the Industrial Development of South Durham and North Yorkshire, and with the creation of the Railway System* (privately published, c. 1903), p. 8.
40   DCRO, Darlington, U415j, D/XD/35/12, *Stockton and Darlington Management Committee Report* (August 1845).
41   *Report of the Committee appointed to Inquire into the State of the Population in the Mining Districts*, Parliamentary Papers (PP), 1846, vol. 24, p. 410.
42   JGP Papers, Joseph Pease Diary, preface for 1851.
43   Brooke (thesis), p. 59.
44   Pease, Sir Alfred E., *The Diaries of Edward Pease*, pp. 230, 250.
45   ibid., p. 248. The report presented to shareholders in 1848 described the financial year 1847/8 as one of 'unprecedented commercial difficulties'. DCRO, Darlington, U415j, D/XD/35/15, *Stockton and Darlington Management Committee Report* (August 1848).
46   Pease, Sir Alfred E., *The Diaries of Edward Pease*, pp. 275, 292.
47   JGP Papers, Joseph Pease Diary, 19 February 1849; concluding remarks, December 1849.
48   ibid., 16 February 1849.
49   Sweezy, op. cit., pp. 122–3; Kenwood, op. cit., pp. 86, 88, 90.
50   Galloway, op. cit., p. 364.
51   Tomlinson, op. cit., p. 488.
52   Smiles, Aileen, *Samuel Smiles and his Surroundings* (1956), p. 107.
53   Church, Roy (ed.), *The Dynamics of Victorian Business: Problems and Perspectives to the 1870s* (1980), pp. 38–43.
54   *First Report from the Select (Secret) Committee on Commercial Distress*, PP, 1847–8, vol. 8, Q. 4690, p. 395.
55   JGP Papers, Joseph Pease Diary, concluding remarks, December 1850.
56   Bullock, op. cit., pp. 83–4.
57   ibid.; Lillie, op. cit., pp. 96–7.
58   Owen, J. S., 'The Cleveland ironstone industry', in Hempstead (ed.), p. 21.
59   Tomlinson, op. cit., p. 509.
60   Kenwood, op. cit., p. 173.
61   Tomlinson, op. cit., p. 558. In the half-year ending in December 1849, 27,712 tons of ironstone were carried on the Stockton and Darlington network. The equivalent figure for 1852 was 230,873 tons. The company's gross revenue in the half-year to June 1849 had been £147,367. For the same period in 1853 it amounted to £241,314. See PRO RAIL 667/180, *Report to the Directors of the Stockton and Darlington Railway concerning the increase in traffic, 1853 over 1849* (February 1854).
62   Briggs, *Victorian Cities*, p. 241.
63   JGP Papers, Joseph Pease Diary, random entry, 1857. In view of his central role in Middlesbrough's early development it is surprising (and disappointing) that Joseph Pease's surviving diaries shed no light on his reactions to the growth of the town, in particular the abandonment by the Owners of the Middlesbrough Estate of the original 'gridiron' conception.
64   Harrison, 'The Production of pig iron', pp. 60–1; Reid, op. cit., p. 87; Barber, B.,

'The concept of the railway town and the growth of Darlington 1801–1911: a note', *Transport History*, vol. 3, no. 3 (1970), pp. 287–8.

65 Briggs, *Victorian Cities*, p. 252.
66 Owen, op. cit., p. 44.
67 Harrison, J. K. 'The development of a distinctive "Cleveland" blast furnace practice 1866–1875', in Hempstead (ed.), op. cit., pp. 81–115.
68 Pease, Sir Alfred E., *The Diaries of Edward Pease*, p. 299.
69 ibid., p. 300.
70 Tomlinson, op. cit., p. 509.
71 ibid., pp. 520–1.
72 Brooke (thesis), pp. 64–5.
73 ibid., p. 66.
74 ibid., p. 67.
75 ibid.
76 ibid., p. 68.
77 ibid., p. 72.
78 ibid., p. 70.
79 Tomlinson, op. cit., p. 524.
80 Brooke (thesis), p. 72.
81 *Fortunes made in Business*, vol. 1, 'The Peases of Darlington' (1884), p. 334.
82 Kenwood, op. cit., p. 269.
83 Tomlinson, op. cit., p. 561.
84 Brooke (thesis), p. 81.
85 Henry Pease was elected deputy chairman of the new railway and John Wakefield, a Kendal banker, chairman.
86 Tomlinson, op. cit., p. 596.
87 McDougall, op. cit., pp. 33–4.
88 Pease, Mary, *Henry Pease: A Short Story of His Iife* (1897), p. 72.
89 Brooke (thesis), pp. 83–4.
90 See Brooke, D., 'Railway consolidation and competition in north east England, 1854–80', *Transport History*, vol. 5, no. 1 (1972), pp. 256–64.
91 Brooke (thesis), p. 88.
92 Kenwood, op. cit., p. 232.
93 Kennedy, William P., 'Institutional response to economic growth: capital markets in Britain to 1914', in Hannah, Leslie (ed.), *Management Strategy and Business Development: An Historical and Comparative Study* (1976), p. 160.
94 Phillips, op. cit., pp. 335–45; Cottrell, P. L., *Industrial Finance, 1830–1914: The Finance and Organisation of English Manufacturing Industry* (1980), p. 211.
95 DCRO, Darlington, U415j, 37744, *Stockton and Darlington Railway: Half-Yearly Meeting* (9 August 1861): statement by Joseph Whitwell Pease.
96 The greater portion – £160,000 – was advanced by the Stockton and Darlington Company. See PRO RAIL 667/1475A, 'T. McNay to Official Liquidators of the Northumberland and Durham District Bank', 27 August 1858.
97 See Wilson, A. S., 'The Consett Iron Company, Limited: a case study in Victorian business history' (unpublished M. Phil. thesis, University of Durham, 1973), pp. 26–34.
98 Richardson, H. W., and Bass, J. M., 'The profitability of the Consett Iron Company before 1914', *Business History*, vol. 7, no. 2 (1965), pp. 71–93.
99 PRO RAIL 667/1475A, 'Derwent Affairs: Note by J. W. Pease', 30 December 1857; Backhouse Papers, Barclays Bank, Darlington, D9, 'Agreement for financial assistance to Derwent and Consett Iron Company', August 1859.
100 Dale was born in India on 11 December 1829. His father (a civil servant with the East India Company), who died in 1830, was a nephew of the David Dale who was father-in-law to Robert Owen, both of whom were responsible for the creation and direction of the model industrial community at New Lanark. On their return to

Scotland Dale and his mother were looked after by Darlington Quakers. They settled permanently in the town in 1841 when Ann Dale was admitted into the Society of Friends. See Grey, Sir Edward, *Sir David Dale: Inaugural Address Delivered to the Dale Memorial Trust* (1911); Jeans, *Pioneers*, pp. 196–7.
101 See Tomlinson, op. cit., p. 560.
102 ibid., pp. 563–4.
103 ibid., p. 566.
104 ibid., pp. 570–6.
105 ibid., p. 621.
106 ibid., p. 588.
107 ibid., pp. 586–8, 594–5; Brooke (thesis), p. 90.
108 PRO RAIL 667/97, *Negotiations between the NER and the S & DR Co*. The following account is based upon this volume.
109 *Report of the Select Committee on Railway Companies Amalgamations*, PP, 1872, vol. 13, p. 27.
110 JGP Papers, Joseph Pease Diary, 26 March 1860; Mewburn, *Larchfield Diary*, p. 186.
111 *The Northern Echo*, 28 September 1895.
112 'The Peases of Darlington', *The British Workman* (February 1892).
113 JGP Papers, Joseph Pease Diary, concluding remarks, 1860.
114 Owen, op. cit., pp. 33–4. For further details on the company's ironstone interests see Burt, R., *et al.*, *The Yorkshire Mineral Statistics: Metalliferous and Associated Minerals 1845–1913* (Exeter, 1982), pp. 20, 36, 40–2, 75–6.
115 Jeans, J. S., *The Iron Trade of Great Britain* (1877), p. 63.
116 *An Historical Outline of the Association of Edward Pease, Joseph Pease, and Sir Joseph Whitwell Pease*.
117 For discussion of the Peases' interest in Wilsons, Pease and Co., iron founders of Middlesbrough, see below, pp. 79–80.
118 See Lillie, op. cit., p. 159; Leonard (thesis), pp. 34–5. The Peases (Henry in particular) were also instrumental in developing the seaside resort of Saltburn after 1860. The focal point of their endeavours was the Saltburn Improvement Company, founded in 1861. See Harrison, J. K., and Harrison, A., 'Saltburn-by-the-Sea: the early years of a Stockton and Darlington Railway Company venture', *Industrial Archeology Review*, vol. 4 (1980), pp. 135–59; Leonard, J. W., 'Saltburn: the northern Brighton', in Sigsworth, Eric (ed.), *Ports and resorts in the regions* (Conference Papers, Hull College of Higher Education, July 1980), pp. 191–200.
119 Pease Papers, MS Gainford (MSG) 125, 'The Affairs of J. and J. W. Pease'.
120 See Church, R. A., *The Great Victorian Boom 1850–1873* (1975).
121 Bullock, op. cit., pp. 86–7.
122 Gourvish, T. R., *Railways and the British Economy 1830–1914* (1980), pp. 32, 40.
123 Rubinstein, W. D., 'The Victorian middle classes: wealth, occupation, and geography', *The Economic History Review*, second series, vol. 30, no. 4 (1977), pp. 666–7.
124 *Darlington and Stockton Telegraph*, 2 March 1872. For the fullest contemporary appreciation of Joseph's life and works see *Northern Echo*, 9 February 1872.
125 See Ure, Andrew, *Philosophy of Manufactures* (1835).
126 Quoted in Thomson, David, *England in the Nineteenth Century* (Harmondsworth, 1950), p. 52.
127 *Northern Echo*, 28 September 1895. Up to the age of twelve Joseph Whitwell was educated at the Friends' School, York. Thereafter, he received private tuition from Mr Ritchie, a minister of the Free Church of Scotland, and Dr Stevenson of Glasgow. The latter subsequently became a missionary in Jamaica.

Chapter 3

1 Tomlinson, op. cit., p. 673.

2 *Northern Echo*, 28 September 1875.
3 ibid. See also PRO RAIL 667/414, *Railway Jubilee Celebration at Darlington, 27 September 1875*.
4 In commemoration of the jubilee the NER presented the mayor of Darlington with a portrait of Joseph Pease to be hung in the council chamber.
5 Isichei, Elizabeth, *Victorian Quakers* (Oxford, 1970), pp. 144–65.
6 ibid., p. 162.
7 ibid., p. 163.
8 On the activities of Elizabeth Pease see Stoddart, Anna M., *Saintly Lives: Elizabeth Pease Nichol* (1899); Fladeland, Betty, 'Our cause being one and the same: Abolitionists and Chartism', in Walvin, James (ed.), *Slavery and British Society 1776–1846* (1982), pp. 69–99. Rice, C. Duncan, *The Scots Abolitionists 1833–1861* (Baton Rouge, 1981), pp. 105–7.
9 Details of the philanthropic career of Joseph Pease of Feethams are to be found in Stoddart, op. cit., pp. 1–167, *passim*; Bell, John Hyslop, *British Folks and British India Fifty Years Ago: Joseph Pease and his Contemporaries* (1891), pp. 32–62, 50–60, 72, 83, 86, 105–11; Temperley, Howard, *British Antislavery 1833–1870* (1972), pp. 212–14. On the Peases' involvement in other reforming agitations see below, p. 58.
10 Stoddart, op. cit., pp. 188–9.
11 JGP Papers, Pease, Sir Alfred E., 'Autobiographical Record'.
12 DCRO, Darlington, D/XD/24/3, Francis Mewburn Diary, vol. 5, 24 August 1861, 23 December 1861.
13 Robinson, William (ed.), *Friends of a Half Century* (1891), p. 252.
14 Pease, Mary, op. cit., pp. 45–66; *Illustrated London News*, 11 March 1854.
15 Pease, Sir Alfred E., *The Diaries of Edward Pease*, p. 214.
16 Chapman, Vera, *Rural Darlington: Farm, Mansion and Suburb* (Durham, 1975), p. 33. This work provides excellent descriptions of the Peases' residences and their lifestyle.
17 JGP Papers, Pease, Sir Alfred E., 'Autobiographical Record'.
18 Chapman, op. cit., p. 51.
19 *Gardeners' Chronicle* (August 1879). Henry also possessed two other properties, both of them acquired after his father's death. Stanhope Castle in Weardale and a large house in Balmoral Terrace, Saltburn, served a similar function to that of Cliffe House. The Pease family acquired the right to a coat of arms in March 1879.
20 Longstaffe, op. cit., p. 388.
21 Cited in Chapman, op. cit., p. 28.
22 JGP Papers, Pease, Sir Alfred E., 'Autobiographical Record'.
23 ibid.
24 ibid.
25 Pease, Sir Alfred E., *The Diaries of Edward Pease*, p. 270.
26 Mewburn, *Larchfield Diary*, p. 99.
27 Pease, Sir Alfred E., *The Diaries of Edward Pease*, p. 270.
28 ibid., p. 271.
29 Mewburn, *Larchfield Diary*, p. 106.
30 Chapman, op. cit., p. 53.
31 ibid.
32 Isichei, op. cit., p. 187.
33 Boyson, Rhodes, *The Ashworth Cotton Enterprise: the rise and fall of a family firm* (Oxford, 1970), p. 240.
34 Fox, Elton, *Two Homes, by a Grandson* (Plymouth, 1925). This was not the first time that a Pease had attempted to marry into the Fox family. Joseph Pease of Feethams had earlier made the journey to Falmouth but was unable to propose to the lady in question at the appointed hour due to the effects of intoxication. See Pease, Sir Alfred E., *The Diaries of Edward Pease*, p. 193. John William Pease, the

younger son of John Beaumont Pease of North Lodge, was also to marry one of Alfred Fox's daughters in 1860.

35 JGP Papers, Alfred Edward Pease (AEP) Journal, 1902, p. 151. The estate consisted of the following properties:

Hutton Hall Estate	1626 acres
Pinchinthorpe Estate	278 acres
Nunthorpe Hall Estate	197 acres
Morton Farm	585 acres
Galley Hill Farm	85 acres
Ayton Bank Farm	141 acres

The freehold of the Pinchinthorpe and Nunthorpe estates was ultimately vested in Joseph Whitwell's sons, Alfred and Jack respectively.

36 JGP Papers, Sylvia Calmady-Hamlyn to J. Gurney Pease, 22 June 1957.
37 Hare, A. J. C., *The Story of My Life*, vol. 4 (undated), p. 269.
38 Information supplied by J. Gurney Pease.
39 JGP Papers, Joseph Whitwell Pease (JWP) Diary, 28 November 1882.
40 Nossiter, T. J., *Influence, Opinion and Political Idioms in Reformed England: Case Studies from the North-East, 1832–74* (Hassocks, 1975), p. 21.
41 At this time Backhouse was senior partner in the family bank. Theodore Fry was the second son of Francis Fry of Bristol, antiquary and bibliographer. After his marriage to Sophia Pease in 1862 he founded the Rise Carr Rolling Mills in Darlington and subsequently became a director of the Weardale and Shildon Water Company. He was created a baronet in 1894. See Emden, op. cit., p. 195 and *The Times* (obituary), 6 February 1912.
42 Isichei, op. cit., p. 206.
43 Nossiter, op. cit., pp. 62–3.
44 JGP Papers, Joseph Pease's election address, 16 August 1832. See also DCRO, Darlington, U415c, for a collection of election addresses by various members of the Pease family. Perhaps in deference to the interests of a substantial proportion of the electorate Joseph declared himself in favour of agricultural protection.
45 It is highly likely that Joseph's decision to retire from parliamentary politics was taken as a result of the desire of his elder brother John to give up the management of the Pease industrial interests so that he could embark upon overseas ministry on behalf of the Society of Friends. There is considerable evidence of John Pease's heavy involvement in the affairs of the Stockton and Darlington Railway Company and the family woollen business throughout the 1830s. See, for example, DCRO, Hodgkin Papers, D1/0/C52/196; D/HO/C48/104; D/HO/C48/103; D/HO/X/11. On John Pease's religious activities see London Friend's Institute, *Biographical Catalogue* (1888), pp. 495–500.
46 Nossiter, op. cit., p. 62.
47 Pease, Sir Alfred E., *The Diaries of Edward Pease*, pp. 64–6; Loukes, op. cit., p. 135.
48 *Random Recollections of the House of Commons, from the year 1830 to the Close of 1835 . . . by one of No Party* (1836), p. 289.
49 JGP Papers, Sylvia Calmady-Hamlyn to J. Gurney Pease, 6 April 1957.
50 Isichei, op. cit., p. 203.
51 ibid., p. 205.
52 For further details on the Pike family see Pease, Sir Alfred E., *The Diaries of Edward Pease*, pp. 137–8; Grubb, Isabel, op. cit., pp. 102–3.
53 JGP Papers, AEP Journal, 4 July 1886.
54 ibid., 5 July 1886.
55 For further details see Isichei, op. cit., pp. 204–6.
56 ibid., p. 205; Alderman, Geoffrey, *The Railway Interest* (Leicester, 1973), *passim*; MacCoby, S., *English Radicalism, 1886–1914* (1953), pp. 433–4.

57 Hamer, D. A., *The Politics of Electoral Pressure: A Study in the History of Victorian Reform Agitations* (Hassocks, 1977), pp. 165–304, *passim*.
58 Pease, Sir Alfred E., *Elections and Recollections* (1932), p. 105.
59 Isichei, op. cit., p. 204.
60 JGP Papers, AEP Journal, 31 May 1894, 1 June 1894.
61 ibid., 30 August 1892.
62 ibid., 27 October 1902.
63 Fowler resigned from the Society of Friends in 1858. In 1860 he was elected MP for Penryn and Falmouth and in 1880 for the City of London. He was an alderman and sheriff of the City and its Lord Mayor in the years 1883–5, and was created a baronet in 1885. Fowler was himself married to Sarah Fox, sister-in-law to Joseph Whitwell Pease. See Lane, Michael R., *The Story of the Steam Plough Works: Fowlers of Leeds* (1980), pp. 19–20.
64 Havelock-Allan was recommended for the Victoria Cross on three occasions and was awarded the medal in 1859. For details of his career see Wooler, Edward and Boyde, Alfred Caine, *Historic Darlington* (1913), pp. 223–45.
65 Dunkley, Peter James, 'The New Poor Law and County Durham' (unpublished MA thesis, University of Durham, 1971), pp. 115–24.
66 Smith, H. John, *Public Health Act: Report to the General Board of Health on Darlington, 1850*, introduced and discussed by H. John Smith (Durham, 1967), p. 3. The following account has benefited greatly from Dr Smith's work.
67 ibid., pp. 3–4; Smith, H. J., 'The water supply of the industrial north-east, 1850–1920', in Sturgess, R. W. (ed.), *The Great Age of Industry in the North-East, 1700–1920* (Durham, 1981), pp. 114–33.
68 McCord, op. cit., p. 164.
69 *Memoir of Fra: Mewburn*, p. 31.
70 Smith, *Public Health Act*, pp. 4–5.
71 ibid., p. 18.
72 ibid., p. 12.
73 ibid., pp. 6–7.
74 *Durham Chronicle*, 20 December 1850.
75 Smith, op. cit., p. 12.
76 *Darlington and Stockton Times*, 9 September 1865.
77 Smith, op. cit., pp. 12–13.
78 'The Peases of Darlington', *The British Workman*, February 1892.
79 *Northern Echo*, 11 September 1981.
80 Moore, Robert, *Pit-Men, Preachers and Politics: The effects of Methodism in a Durham mining community* (Cambridge, 1974), pp. 82, 84.
81 *Darlington Telegraph*, 20 October 1860.
82 ibid.
83 Sunderland, op. cit., p. 92. Henry had, of course, participated in the Quaker peace mission to Russia in 1854.
84 *Darlington Telegraph*, 21 September 1861.
85 DCRO, Darlington, U418c, *Poll Book of the Darlington Local Board of Health Election, September 1862*.
86 Smith, *Public Health Act*, p. 15.
87 ibid.
88 Sunderland, op. cit., p. 92.
89 ibid.
90 DCRO, Darlington, U418f, Pease, Joseph, *Ought Darlington to have a Municipal Corporation? To the Ratepayers of Darlington* (printed handbill), 29 March 1866.
91 Smith, *Public Health Act*, p. 16.
92 Greenbank was the former home of Alfred Backhouse, Quaker banker and member of the board of health, 1855–67.

93   *Darlington and Stockton Times*, 5 October 1867. See also Nossiter, op. cit., pp. 136–7.
94   DCRO, Darlington, U418f, *Letter to the inhabitants of Darlington from John Pease of East Mount*, 10 November 1866.
95   Sunderland, op. cit., p. 94.
96   *Darlington and Stockton Times*, 23 November 1867.
97   Henry served as mayor for the first two years after incorporation.
98   Sunderland, op. cit., p. 95.
99   Nossiter, op. cit., p. 137.
100 cf. Joyce, Patrick, *Work, Society and Politics: The Culture of the Factory in Later Victorian England* (Brighton, 1980).
101 *Darlington Telegraph*, 5 October 1867, 12 October 1867.
102 DCRO, Darlington, U418c, *Darlington Municipal Election 1867: Notice from John Pease*, 2 December 1867.
103 Nossiter, op. cit., pp. 138–9.
104 DCRO, Darlington, U418c, Spark, Henry King, *Election Address, Greenbank*, 14 July 1868.
105 Nossiter, op. cit., pp. 139–41.
106 ibid., pp. 140–1.
107 DCRO, Darlington, U415e, *The Durham Thirteen: Biographical Sketches of the Members of Parliament returned for the City, Boroughs, and County of Durham at the General Election of 1874*.
108 Although the Trade Union Act of 1871 endowed trade unions with a secure legal status as registered societies, the Criminal Law Amendment Act of the same year contained stringent penal clauses against picketing.
109 Nossiter, op. cit., pp. 141–2.
110 *Northern Echo*, 9 March 1874.
111 *Darlington and Richmond Herald*, 3 April 1880.
112 *Northern Echo*, 2 June 1880.
113 Steel, John W., *Friendly Sketches: Essays illustrative of Quakerism* (Darlington, 1876). See also Wallis, Amy E., 'Darlington: the English Philadelphia', *Journal of the Friends Historical Society*, vols 47–8 (1956–8), pp. 55–69.
114 Nossiter, op. cit., p. 131.
115 For five of the first ten years of incorporation members of the Pease family served as mayor. This figure does not include their relative Theodore Fry (1877–8). In 1889–90 Sir Joseph Whitwell Pease's younger son Jack served as mayor. He was then only twenty-nine and possibly the youngest holder of the office in England.
116 Nossiter, op. cit., p. 131.

Chapter 4

1   McCord, op. cit., pp. 111–46.
2   Birch, Alan, *The Economic History of the British Iron and Steel Industry 1784–1879* (1967), pp. 331–6.
3   Bullock, op. cit., pp. 91–2.
4   Bell, Lady Florence, *At the Works: A Study of a Manufacturing Town* (1907).
5   The following analysis is based on Irving, R. J., *The North Eastern Railway Company 1870–1914: an economic history* (Leicester, 1976), pp. 21–41.
6   Harrison, J. K., 'The production of malleable iron in north east England and the rise and collapse of the puddling process in the Cleveland district', in Hempstead (ed.), op. cit., p. 152; McCord, op. cit., p. 122.
7   Taylor, A. J., 'The coal industry', in Aldcroft, D. H. (ed.), *The Development of British Industry and Foreign Competition, 1875–1914* (1968), p. 42.

8 Kirby, M. W., *The British Coalmining Industry 1870–1946: A Political and Economic History* (1977), pp. 13–15.

9 The exception was the great dispute of 1892 when the Durham Miners' Association unsuccessfully opposed the owners' demand for a 10 per cent reduction in wages.

10 Garside, W. R., *The Durham Miners, 1919–1960* (1971), p. 26.

11 Bell, R., *Twenty Five Years of the North Eastern Railway, 1898–1922* (1951), chapter 2, *passim*; Irving, op. cit., pp. 130–2.

12 Both Sir David Dale and Sir Joseph Whitwell Pease wielded considerable influence over the company's labour relations policy. See Irving, op. cit., pp. 53–74, *passim*. For further consideration of their views on labour relations see below, pp. 83–4.

13 Irving, op. cit., p. 138. In his evidence before the parliamentary committee on railway companies' amalgamations Sir Joseph Whitwell Pease had vigorously defended the NER's regional monopoly by reference to local shareholders and directors such as himself who, as traffic senders, had a vested interest in keeping rates as low as possible. See *Joint Select Committee of the House of Lords and the House of Commons on Railway Companies' Amalgamation: Proceedings of the Committee and Minutes of Evidence*, 1872, Qs 5100–5163.

14 Pease Papers, MSG 13, 'J. W. Pease's Overdraft: How Arisen from January 1879 to October 1902'.

15 Pease Papers, MSG 47, 'Some Reminiscences of Lord Gainford' (typescript, 1932).

16 JGP Papers, JWP Diary, 17 June 1872.

17 See Odber, A. J., 'The manufactured iron trade of the north of England', *Oxford Economic Papers*, vol. 3, no. 2 (1951), pp. 201–20; Porter, J. H., 'David Dale and conciliation in the northern manufactured iron trade, 1869–1914', *Northern History*, vol. 5 (1970), pp. 157–71; Dale, David, *Thirty Years Experience of Industrial Conciliation and Arbitration* (Darlington, 1899). For his services to commerce and to the maintenance of industrial peace Dale received a baronetcy in 1895.

18 *Durham Chronicle*, 15 January 1875.

19 JGP Papers, JWP Diary, 8 July, 9 July 1872.

20 JGP Papers, AEP Journal, 10 April 1882. Henry died in 1881: his estate was valued at £430,000.

21 JGP Papers, JWP Diary, 27 June 1882, 8 August 1882, 22 September 1882.

22 ibid., 31 December 1890.

23 ibid., 31 December 1892.

24 Pease Papers, MSG 26, 'Statement of Facts Relating to the Case of Portsmouth vs. Pease, High Court of Chancery, November 1900'.

25 Grey, op. cit., p. 26.

26 JGP Papers, JWP Diary, 2 February 1877, 31 December 1886, 3 March 1888, 31 December 1890, 31 December 1891, 11 April 1892, 20 February 1894, 14 September 1894, 31 December 1894.

27 ibid., 11 January 1883.

28 ibid., 24 October 1885, 4 November 1885; Pease Papers, MSG 125, 'The Affairs of J. and J. W. Pease'.

29 Warren, op. cit., p. 417.

30 Pease Papers, MSG 125, 'The Affairs of J. and J. W. Pease'.

31 Harrison, 'The production of pig iron', p. 60; Reid, op. cit., p. 81.

32 Pease Papers, MSG 13, 'J. W. Pease's Overdraft: How Arisen'.

33 Pease Papers, MSG 125, 'The Affairs of J. and J. W. Pease'.

34 Pease Papers, MSG 13, 'Memorandum on the Financial Position of J. and J. W. Pease', 20 December 1902.

35 Pease Papers, MSG 13, 'J. W. Pease's Overdraft: How Arisen'.

36 JGP Papers, Joseph Whitwell Pease to Alfred E. Pease, 13 May 1880.

37 JGP Papers, JWP Diary, 9 May 1888, 2 March 1892.

38 Pease Papers, MSG 125, 'The Affairs of J. and J. W. Pease'.

39 JGP Papers, JWP Diary, 6 May 1897; Pease Papers, MSG, 'The Affairs of J. and J. W. Pease'.
40 Pease Papers, MSG 125, 'The Affairs of J. and J. W. Pease'; MSG 13, 'Losses Made by Failures 1876–1880 by J. and J. W. Pease and Co.'.
41 Pease Papers, MSG 9/80.
42 JGP Papers, JWP Diary, 29 January 1892, 3 February 1892, 12 March 1892.
43 ibid., 15 May 1894, 28 May 1894, 21 June 1894, 18 December 1894.
44 ibid., 21 August 1895.
45 ibid., 6 February 1896.
46 Pease Papers, MSG 16, 'Loans from Messrs. Gurney and Co. and Barclay and Co. secured by Middlesbrough Estate Shares'.
47 JGP Papers, AEP Journal, 31 July 1886.
48 Pease Papers, MSG 125, 'The Affairs of J. and J. W. Pease'.
49 ibid.
50 After he was elected chairman of the new company in July 1899 Sir Joseph was censured by fellow Quakers for his association with an armaments manufacturer – Sir William Armstrong – when he was president of the Peace Society. The dry dock was eventually sold to Palmers' Shipbuilding and Iron Co. of Jarrow in 1911.
51 JGP Papers, AEP Journal, 14 June 1901.
52 See Hamer, D. A., *Liberal Politics in the Age of Gladstone and Rosebery: A Study in Leadership and Policy* (Oxford, 1972), pp. 12–18.
53 Harrison, R., *Before the Socialists* (1965), p. 4.
54 Porter, J. H., 'Wage bargaining under conciliation agreements, 1860–1914', *The Economic History Review*, second series, vol. 23, no. 3 (1970), p. 464.
55 *Durham Chronicle*, 2 May 1879; Moore, op. cit., p. 87.
56 Hamer, *Liberal Politics*, p. 13.
57 JGP Papers, AEP Journal, 10 April 1882, 13 April 1882.
58 ibid., 9 June 1888.
59 The financing of the newspaper was taken over by Sir Christopher Furness. After 1900 it came under the control of the Joseph Rowntree Social Service Trust.
60 These included *Biskra and the Oases and Desert of the Zibans* (1893); *Antelopes of Algeria and Abyssinia* (1896); *Hunting Reminiscences* (1898); *The Badger* (1899); *Loders and Doreas Gazelle* (1899); *Abyssinian and Somaliland Antelopes* (1901). For an appreciation of Alfred's activities as a sportsman see *Baily's Magazine of Sports and Pastimes*, vol. 101, no. 649 (1914).
61 JGP Papers, 'The Affairs of Sir J. W. Pease in 1900 and 1902: Note by his Grandson Edward Pease, summer 1940'.
62 JGP Papers, Pease, Sir Alfred E., 'Autobiographical Record'.
63 JGP Papers, JWP Diary, 19 November 1873, 31 December 1873. Wilsons, Pease and Co. was known as Gilkes, Wilsons, Pease and Co. at this time.
64 JGP Papers, Joseph Whitwell Pease to Alfred E. Pease, 13 May 1880.
65 To be fair to Sir Joseph no evidence has come to light in support of this interpretation.
66 For an illustration of this point in another context see Boswell, Jonathan S., 'Hope, inefficiency or public duty? The United Steel Companies and West Cumberland 1919–1939', *Business History*, vol. 22, no. 1 (1980), pp. 35–50.
67 JGP Papers, Pease, Sir Alfred E., 'Autobiographical Record'.
68 Pease, Sir Alfred E., *The Diaries of Edward Pease*, p. 151.
69 JGP Papers, JWP Diary, 28 August 1898.
70 In the early 1880s Alfred believed that he would be fortunate to reach his fortieth birthday as a result of recurring 'heart palpitations and a disordered stomach' (JGP Papers, AEP Journal, 23 April 1882). Like his father and paternal grandfather he was an inveterate hypochondriac – if diary entries are to be believed.
71 This conclusion is in accord with the views presented in Payne, Peter L., *British Entrepreneurship in the Nineteenth Century* (1974).

Chapter 5

1 JGP Papers, Pease, Sir Alfred E., 'Autobiographical Record'.
2 Pease Papers, MSG 125, 'The Affairs of J. and J. W. Pease'.
3 Pease Papers, MSG 26, 'Statement of Facts Relating to the Case of Portsmouth vs Pease'.
4 At Cambridge Jack was captain of his college football team, played polo against Oxford and was master of the university draghounds. Before entering Parliament he was a popular member of the Durham County Cricket Club.
5 JGP Papers, Sylvia Calmady-Hamlyn to J. Gurney Pease, 3 March 1957.
6 JGP Papers, JWP Diary, 26 November 1884.
7 ibid., 8 December 1884.
8 ibid., 9 December 1884.
9 ibid., 31 December 1884.
10 ibid., 3 November 1888, 10 November 1891.
11 ibid., 14 February 1893. Despite recession in the coal trade Beatrice had received an average income from the trust estate of £4,500 per annum in the period 1885–91. At the same time Sir Joseph and Arthur Pease advanced £200,000 on their own accounts as guarantees to meet the liabilities of the estate. See Pease Papers, MSG 26, 'Statement of Facts Relating to the Case of Portsmouth vs. Pease'.
12 JGP Papers, Beatrice Pease to Sir J. W. Pease, 28 October 1893; JWP Diary, 31 October 1893.
13 ibid., 20 November 1893.
14 JGP Papers, Sir J. W. Pease to Sir Richard Nicholson, 20 January 1895.
15 JGP Papers, Sir R. Nicholson to Arthur Lucas, 20 August 1896.
16 JGP Papers, Sir R. Nicholson to A. Lucas, 10 September 1896.
17 Pease Papers, MSG 26, 'Statement of Facts Relating to the Case of Portsmouth vs. Pease'.
18 Pease Papers, MSG 125, 'The Affairs of J. and J. W. Pease'.
19 JGP Papers, JWP Diary, 8 October 1897.
20 ibid., 24 February 1898.
21 ibid., 6 May 1898, 12 May 1898, 24 May 1898, 27 May 1898.
22 Cottrell, op. cit., p. 167.
23 JGP Papers, Sir J. W. Pease to Sir David Dale, 25 May 1898; JWP Diary, 20 July 1898.
24 ibid., 18 September 1898.
25 The following account is based on JGP Papers, *High Court of Justice, Chancery Division, Royal Courts of Justice, December 11, 1900 before Mr Justice Farwell in re Edward Pease (Deceased): The Earl of Portsmouth v. Pease: Judgment*.
26 This point was subsequently stressed by Jack Pease. See Pease Papers, MSG 145, J. A. Pease to A. E. Pease, 27 January 1901.
27 *The Times*, 17 December 1900.
28 Pease Papers, MSG 125, 'The Affairs of J. and J. W. Pease'.
29 JGP Papers, AEP Journal, 23 April 1901.
30 Pease Papers, MSG 145, J. A. Pease to A. E. Pease, 27 January 1901. Jack's view of the original agreement was that although the shares in the old company were ultimately realised at a profit the assets in the trust estate had been purchased 'as a whole', and both parties, not least the Portsmouths' accountant, had accepted that a significant proportion of the securities in the estate were being acquired at an overvalued rate. See MSG 26, 'Statement of Facts Relating to the Case of Portsmouth vs. Pease'.
31 JGP Papers, JWP Diary, 31 December 1901.
32 JGP Papers, Sylvia Calmady-Hamlyn to J. Gurney Pease, 17 November 1957.
33 Pease Papers, MSG 145, J. A. Pease to A. E. Pease, 27 January 1901.

34 Sir Joseph subsequently agreed to meet all losses accruing to his nephews as a result of the Portsmouth case. JGP Papers, JWP Diary, 16 August 1901.
35 JGP Papers, 'The Affairs of Sir J. W. Pease in 1900 and 1902: Note by his Grandson'.

Chapter 6

1 Sayers, R. S., *Lloyds Bank in the History of English Banking* (Oxford, 1957), pp. 189, 252, 256–7; Clapham, J. H., *An Economic History of Modern Britain*, vol. 3 (Cambridge, 1938), p. 280.
2 Matthews and Tuke, op. cit., pp. 3–10. For comment on the merger movement generally see Sykes, J., *The Amalgamation Movement in English Banking, 1825–1924* (1925) and Cottrell, op. cit., pp. 197–8.
3 Pease Papers, MSG 125, 'J. and J. W. Pease: Negotiations with Barclay and Company'.
4 JGP Papers, JWP Diary, 22 April 1902. Sir Jonathan was the son of Edmund Backhouse, the former Liberal MP for Darlington. Jonathan had received a baronetcy for services to Liberal Unionism in 1901.
5 JGP Papers, AEP Journal, 13 July 1902, 24 July 1902.
6 JGP Papers, JWP Diary, 7 August 1902.
7 JGP Papers, AEP Journal, 8 August 1902; JWP Diary, 8 August 1902.
8 Pease Papers, MSG 125, 'The Affairs of J. and J. W. Pease'.
9 JGP Papers, AEP Journal, 16 August 1902.
10 ibid., 18 August 1902.
11 Buxton, who was to extend considerable personal help to the Pease family during the ensuing months, was directly connected with the London brewing company Truman, Hanbury and Buxton.
12 JGP Papers, JWP Diary, 18 August 1902.
13 ibid., 20 August 1902.
14 Pease Papers, MSG 13b, 'Memorandum for Barclay and Company Limited in regard to the affairs of J. and J. W. Pease'.
15 *The Times*, 26 August 1902.
16 Pease Papers, MSG 125, 'J. and J. W. Pease: Negotiations with Barclay and Company'. In September 1901 Pease and Partners ordinary shares were valued at £17 15s 0d and a year later at £13 2s 6d.
17 Details of Barclays' policy with regard to J. and J. W. Pease after August 1902 are to be found in J. and J. W. Pease Papers, Box 21, Barclays Bank Historical Records (BBHR), Lombard Street, London.
18 Pease Papers, MSG 125, 'Negotiations with Barclay and Company'.
19 JGP Papers, JWP Diary, 28 August 1902.
20 See Pease Papers, MSG 19, 'Outline of Suggested Scheme by Sir Christopher Furness, M.P.', and *Deed of Assignment and Conveyance*, December 1902.
21 Pease Papers, MSG 125, 'Memorandum for the information of Barclay and Co. Ltd. in regard to the affairs of J. and J. W. Pease'.
22 Pease Papers, MSG 17, 'J. and J. W. Pease: Analysis of Credit Balances in Books, 22 August 1902'.
23 BBHR, Box 21, 'J. and J. W. Pease, Darlington: Proposals of W. B. Peat, 24 September 1902'.
24 PRO RAIL 527/1776, NER, 8/42, 'Memorandum re J. and J. W. Pease'.
25 In 1922 Peat revealed that the unsecured creditors with claims amounting to £749,484 had received 9s 2.631d. in the pound, leaving a deficiency of £399,148. JGP Papers, 'The Affairs of Sir J. W. Pease, 1900 and 1902: Note by his Grandson'.
26 ibid.
27 JGP Papers, JWP Diary, 25 September 1902, 26 September 1902.

28 Pease Papers, MSG 78, W. B. Peat to Sir J. W. Pease, 7 February 1903.
29 JGP Papers, JWP Diary, 31 January 1903, 7 February 1903.
30 JGP Papers, R. L. Harrison to A. E. Pease, 27 November 1902; Pease Papers, MSG 19, 'J. and J. W. Pease: Assets to be Retained', 18 December 1902.
31 Pease Papers, MSG, Box 9, Henry Tennant to Sir J. W. Pease, 13 September 1902; R. L. Harrison to Sir J. W. Pease, 12 November 1902.
32 The house had at one time been occupied by Isaac Wilson, one of Joseph Pease's early industrial protégés.
33 JGP Papers, R. L. Harrison to A. E. Pease, 27 November 1902.
34 JGP Papers, AEP Journal, 18 December 1902.
35 ibid., 9 March 1903. Alfred had earlier been offered a minor diplomatic post with the British Legation in Siam.
36 JGP Papers, AEP Journal, 10 April 1903.
37 Pease Papers, MSG 79, J. B. Paulton to J. A. Pease, 9 March 1903.
38 Pease Papers, MSG 79, Herbert Gladstone to J. A. Pease, 18 April 1903.
39 Pease Papers, MSG 80, David Denbigh to J. A. Pease, 16 August 1903.
40 Pease Papers, MSG 145, J. A. Pease to A. E. Pease, 5 August 1904.
41 Pease Papers, MSG 80, Maud Pease to J. A. Pease, 4 June 1903; MSG 50, 'Father's last days, written by his daughter, Maud Pease, June 1903'.
42 See, for example, *North Eastern Daily Gazette*, 20 December 1902; *Northern Echo*, 22 December 1902; *Daily Mail*, 22 December 1902; *Western Mail*, 23 December 1902. In his first speech as chairman of Robert Stephenson and Company Ltd, Sir Christopher Furness stressed this aspect of the bank's failure (*North Eastern Daily Gazette*, 15 April 1903). Less flattering comment on Sir Joseph can be found in *The Financial Times*, 24 December 1903 and the *Investors' Review*, 27 December 1902.
43 *South Durham and Cleveland Mercury*, 26 June 1903.
44 Kirby, op. cit., pp. 12–13.
45 Perkin, Harold, *The Origins of Modern English Society 1780–1880* (1969), p. 431.
46 Pease Papers, MSG 11, Gerald Buxton to A. E. Pease, 12 June 1903; JGP Papers, Sylvia Calmady-Hamlyn to J. Gurney Pease, 10 March 1957.
47 Pease Papers, MSG 11, Sir J. W. Pease to Gerald Buxton, 15 June 1903.

Chapter 7

1 Pease, Sir Alfred E., *Elections and Recollections* (1932), p. 301.
2 See Wiener, Martin, *English Culture and the Decline of the Industrial Spirit, 1850–1980* (Cambridge, 1981).
3 JGP Papers, AEP Journal, 6 October 1881.
4 Cited in Wiener, op. cit., p. 106.
5 This was *Elections and Recollections*, a work which provides some fascinating insights into late nineteenth-century electoral politics.
6 Pease Papers, MSG 80, A. E. Pease to J. A. Pease, 23 August 1925.
7 Coincidentally, Asquith dismissed Lord Portsmouth as Under-Secretary for War after promptings from Edward VII. See Koss, Stephen, *Asquith* (1976), p. 95.
8 During and after the war Jack also served as a member of the Allied Claims Commissions in France and Italy charged with the task of assessing compensation for military damage to private property.
9 In May 1915 Asquith, inspired by the Cambridge tripos examinations, drew up a rank list of his ministers. Jack was placed second in the lowest rank behind Herbert Samuel. Koss, op. cit., p. 190.
10 Davies, Edward (ed.), *Inside Asquith's Cabinet: From the Diaries of Charles Hobhouse* (1977), pp. 249–50. Jack too was a cabinet 'diarist'. An edited version of his political papers prepared by Cameron Hazelhurst and Christine Woodland awaits publication.

11 Coal Industry Commission, *Reports and Minutes of Evidence*, vol. II, Q. 19,671, Cmd. 360 (1919).

12 Moore, op. cit., pp. 79–81, 87, 157.

13 In his speech to shareholders in 1907 Arthur Francis Pease pointed out that 911 men were now necessary to raise 1,000 tons of coal in a working day, compared with 858 in the previous decade. Pease and Partners, *Report of Proceedings at the Ordinary General Meeting of Shareholders*, 1907.

14 This is amply demonstrated in the field notes of Professor Robert Moore, in which retired miners formerly in the company's employment made frequent reference to the harsher managerial regime which had emerged after the demise of Sir Joseph Whitwell Pease. I am grateful to Professor Moore for drawing this point to my attention. In this respect there is a parallel with the South Wales coalfield, where the growth of Lord Rhondda's Cambrian Combine is reported to have contributed to a deterioration in labour relations in the coalfield. See Commission of Inquiry into Industrial Unrest, *Report of the Commissioners for Wales including Monmouthshire*, Cd. 8668 (1917).

15 Pease and Partners, *Report of Proceedings at the Ordinary General Meeting of Shareholders*, 1907 and 1923; Lord Gainford, 'The coal problem', *Contemporary Review*, vol. 119 (June 1921).

16 See MacDonald, G. W., and Gospel, H. F., 'The Mond-Turner talks, 1927–1933', *The Historical Journal*, vol. 16 (1973), pp. 807–29.

17 Briggs, Asa, *The History of Broadcasting in the United Kingdom*, vol. 1, *The Birth of Broadcasting* (1961), p. 123.

18 Boyle, Andrew, *Only the Wind Will Listen: Reith of the BBC* (1972), p. 210.

19 Briggs, *The History of Broadcasting*, pp. 353–4; Reith, J. C. W., *Into the Wind* (1949), p. 105.

20 The company's ordinary dividend had averaged 11 per cent in the years 1904–13. In 1920, at the peak of the postwar boom, it reached 18 per cent, but by 1922 had fallen to 5 per cent.

21 *The Economist*, 26 November 1932, p. 1045.

22 ibid., 25 February 1933, p. 440.

23 ibid., 20 May 1939, p. 469; 3 June 1939, p. 571.

24 Matthews and Tuke, op. cit., p. 206.

25 Personal information from Sir Richard Pease.

26 Phillips, op. cit., p. 384.

27 Sayers, op. cit., pp. 12–30.

28 ibid., pp. 260, 351; Winton, J. R., *Lloyds Bank 1918–1969* (Oxford, 1982), p. 35. Beaumont Pease served four terms as chairman of the Committee of London Clearing Bankers. He retired from Lloyds Bank in 1945 after 'one of the longest tenures of such an office in English banking that there had been' (ibid.).

29 Miriam then joined the personnel section of Barclays Bank, and after her retirement in 1947 moved to North Berwick, where she served on the burgh council and played an active role in the organisation of civil defence in south-east Scotland. In 1924 her younger sister, Faith, married Michael Wentworth Beaumont (a descendant of the Beaumonts of Allandale who had made their fortune from the London Lead Company's mining activities in Weardale).

30 Jack's other grandson, Timothy Wentworth Beaumont Pease, was chairman of the Liberal Party in 1967–8 and president of the Party in 1970. He was created a life peer in 1967 and took the title Baron Beaumont of Whitley.

31 The sitting Labour MP, Arthur Lewis Shepherd, was himself defeated in the 1931 general election by the Conservative candidate, Charles Urie Peat, the son of the accountant who had presided over the liquidation of the assets of J. and J. W. Pease.

32 The Barnard Castle division had been carved out of the old South Durham constituency following the redistribution of parliamentary seats in 1885.

33 See Purdue, A. W., 'Parliamentary elections in north east England, 1900–1906: the revolt of Labour' (unpublished M.Litt. thesis, University of Newcastle upon Tyne, 1974); 'Arthur Henderson and Liberal, Liberal-Labour and Labour politics in the north-east of England, 1892–1903', *Northern History*, vol. 11 (1976 for 1975), pp. 195–217. The last Pease to engage in parliamentary elections was Joseph Gurney Pease, the younger surviving son of Sir Alfred Edward Pease. Between 1959 and 1974 Gurney Pease unsuccessfully contested a number of seats in the north of England (including Darlington in 1964) in the Liberal interest.

34 JGP Papers, Pease, Sir Alfred E., 'Autobiographical Record'.

35 JGP Papers, AEP Journal, 15 October 1902.

36 JGP Papers, Sylvia Calmady-Hamlyn to J. Gurney Pease, 29 March 1957.

37 After Jack's resignation Sir John Pease Fry, the son of Theodore and Sophia Fry, accepted the presidency of the Peace Society.

38 On Grove House see Brown, S. W., *Leighton Park: A History of the School* (1952), pp. 6–31.

39 See Winstanley, D. A., *Later Victorian Cambridge* (Cambridge, 1947).

40 JGP Papers, AEP Journal, 2 October 1910.

41 JGP Papers, *Minute of Guisbro' Monthly Meeting, Held 31 August 1916*. The minute noted that whilst Sir Alfred still revered 'those principles which have bound his family to the Society for more than 200 years', there was now 'a divergence of view regarding the employment of force'.

42 JGP Papers, Sir Alfred E. Pease to Edward Pease, 15 September 1918.

43 For the experience of other Quaker families in all of these respects see Boyson, op. cit., pp. 252, 256; Corley, *Quaker Enterprise in Biscuits*, p. 131; Corley, T. A. B., 'How Quakers coped with business success: Quaker industrialists, 1860–1914' (paper read to the Christianity and Business Seminar, London School of Economics, March 1982); Musson, A. E., *Enterprise in Soap and Chemicals: Joseph Crosfield and Sons Limited, 1815–1965* (Manchester, 1965), p. 119. The Backhouse family provides an extreme and fascinating example of 'conformity to the world'. The activities of Edmund, the oldest son of Sir Jonathan Backhouse, are revealed in Trevor-Roper, Hugh, *A Hidden Life: The Enigma of Sir Edmund Backhouse* (1976). Sinologist, pornographer and British secret service agent, Edmund was eventually converted to Roman Catholicism. His younger brothers, Oliver and Roger, joined the Royal Navy and achieved high rank, the latter retiring as Admiral of the Fleet.

Bibliography

The place of publication is London unless otherwise stated.

1 Unpublished Sources

Papers in the Public Record Office
RAIL 527   Records of the North Eastern Railway Company.
RAIL 667   Records of the Stockton and Darlington Railway Company.

Private Papers
Backhouse Papers, Barclays Bank, Darlington
Hodgkin Papers, Durham County Record Office, Durham
Francis Mewburn Diary, Durham County Record Office, Darlington
Pease Papers (MS Gainford), Nuffield College, Oxford
Pease Family Papers, Durham County Record Office, Darlington
J. Gurney Pease Papers
J. and J. W. Pease Papers, Barclays Bank Historical Records, Lombard Street, London
Stockton and Darlington Railway Papers, Durham County Record Office, Darlington

2 Official Publications

Report of the Committee appointed to Inquire into the State of the Population in the Mining Districts, PP, 1846, vol. 24.
First Report from the Select (Secret) Committee on Commercial Distress, PP, 1847–8, vol. 8
Report to the Public Health Board in regard to the Inquiry into the Adoption of the 1848 Act by Middlesbrough (1854).
Joint Select Committee of the House of Lords and the House of Commons on Railway Companies Amalgamation: Proceedings of the Committee and Minutes of Evidence, PP, 1872, vol. 13.
Commission of Inquiry into Industrial Unrest, *Report of the Commissioners for Wales including Monmouthshire*, Cd. 8668, 1917.
Coal Industry Commission, *Reports and Minutes of Evidence*, vol. 2, Cmd. 360, 1919.

3 Theses

Brooke, David, 'The North Eastern Railway, 1854–80: A Study in Railway Consolidation and Competition' (PhD thesis, University of Leeds, 1971).

Dunkley, Peter James, 'The New Poor Law and County Durham' (MA thesis, University of Durham, 1971)

Kenwood, A. G., 'Capital Investment in North Eastern England, 1800–1913' (PhD thesis, University of London, 1962).

Leonard, J. W., 'Urban Development and Population Growth in Middlesbrough, 1831–71' (D.Phil. thesis, University of York, 1976).

Purdue, A. W., 'Parliamentary Elections in North East England, 1900–1906: The Revolt of Labour' (M. Litt. thesis, University of Newcastle upon Tyne, 1974).

Reed, M. C., 'Investment in Railways in Britain, 1820–1844' (D.Phil. thesis, University of Oxford, 1970).

Wilson, A. S., 'The Consett Iron Company Limited: A Case Study in Victorian Business History' (M. Phil. thesis, University of Durham, 1973).

4 Periodicals

Baily's Magazine of Sports and Pastimes
British Workman
Contemporary Review
Daily Mail
Darlington and Richmond Herald
Darlington and Stockton Telegraph
Darlington Telegraph
Darlington and Stockton Times
Durham Chronicle
Durham County Advertiser
The Economist
Financial Times
Gardeners' Chronicle
Illustrated London News
Investors' Review
North Eastern Daily Gazette
Northern Echo
Railway News
South Durham and Cleveland Mercury
The Times
Western Mail

5 Published Secondary Sources

Aldcroft, D. H. (ed.), *The Development of British Industry and Foreign Competition, 1875–1914* (1968).

Alderman, Geoffrey, *The Railway Interest* (Leicester, 1973).

Anderson, Verily, *Friends and Relations: 3 Centuries of Quaker Families* (1980).

Bailey Michael R., 'Robert Stephenson and Co. 1823–1829', *Transactions of the Newcomen Society*, vol. 50 (1980).

Barber, B., 'The concept of the railway town and the growth of Darlington 1801–1911: a note', *Transport History*, vol. 3, no. 3 (1970).

Barton, Peter, 'The port of Stockton on Tees and its creeks 1825 to 1861', *Maritime History*, vol. 1, no. 2 (1971).

Bell, Lady Florence, *At the Works: A Study of a Manufacturing Town* (1907).

Bell, John Hyslop, *British Folks and British India Fifty Years Ago: Joseph Pease and His Contemporaries* (1891).

Bell, R., *Twenty Five Years of the North Eastern Railway, 1898–1922* (1951).

Benson, R. Seymour, *Photographic Pedigree of the Descendants of Isaac and Rachel Wilson* (Middlesbrough, 1912).

Birch, Alan, *The Economic History of the British Iron and Steel Industry 1784–1879* (1967).

Boswell, Jonathan S., 'Hope, inefficiency or public duty? the United Steel Companies and West Cumberland 1919–1939', *Business History*, vol. 22, no. 1 (1980).

Boyce, A. O., *Records of a Quaker Family: The Richardsons of Cleveland* (1889).

Boyle, Andrew, *Only the Wind Will Listen: Reith of the BBC* (1972).

Boyson, Rhodes, *The Ashworth Cotton Enterprise: the rise and fall of a family firm* (Oxford, 1970).

Braithwaite, William C., *The Second Period of Quakerism* (2nd edn prepared by Henry Cadbury, Cambridge, 1961).

Brett, R. L. (ed.), *Barclay Fox's Journal* (1979).

Briggs, Asa, *The History of Broadcasting in the United Kingdom*, vol. 1, *The Birth of Broadcasting* (1961).

Briggs, Asa, *Victorian Cities* (Pelican edn, 1968).

Brooke, D., 'The promotion of four Yorkshire railways and the share capital market', *Transport History*, vol. 5, no. 3 (1972).

Brooke, D., 'Railway consolidation and competition in north east England, 1854–80', *Transport History*, vol. 5, no. 1 (1972).

Brown, S. V., *Leighton Park: A History of the School* (1952).

Bullock, I., 'The origins of economic growth on Teesside, 1851–81', *Northern History*, vol. 9 (1974).

Burns, Tom, and Saul, S. B. (eds.), *Social Theory and Economic Change* (1967).

Burt, R., *et al.*, *The Yorkshire Mineral Statistics: Metalliferous and Associated Minerals 1854–1913* (Exeter, 1982).

Chapman, Vera, *Rural Darlington: Farm, Mansion and Suburb* (Durham, 1975).

Church, Roy (ed.), *The Dynamics of Victorian Business: Problems and Perspectives to the 1870s* (1980).

Church, R. A., *The Great Victorian Boom 1850–1873* (1975).

Clapham, J. H., *An Economic History of Modern Britain*, vol. 3 (Cambridge, 1938).

Corley, T. A. B., 'How Quakers coped with business success: Quaker industrialists, 1860–1914' (paper read to the Christianity and Business Seminar, London School of Economics, March 1982).

Corley, T. A. B., *Quaker Enterprise in Biscuits: Huntley and Palmers of Reading, 1872–1972* (1972).

Cottrell, P. L., *Industrial Finance, 1830–1914: The Finance and Organisation of English Manufacturing Industry* (1980).

Cottrell, P. L. and Ottley, G., 'The beginnings of the Stockton and Darlington Railway: people and documents, 1813–25: a celebratory note', *Journal of Transport History*, new series, vol. 3, no. 2 (1975).

Dale, David, *Thirty Years Experience of Industrial Conciliation and Arbitration* (Darlington, 1899)

Davies, Edward (ed.), *Inside Asquith's Cabinet: From the Diaries of Charles Hobhouse* (1977).

Davies, Hunter, *George Stephenson: A Biographical Study of the Father of the Railways* (1975).

Deane, P., 'The output of the British woollen industry in the eighteenth century', *Journal of Economic History*, vol. 17, no. 2 (1957).

Dendy Marshall, C. F., *History of British Railways down to the Year 1830* (1938).

Edwards, K. H. R., *Chronology of the Development of the Iron and Steel Industries of Tees-side* (Wigan, 1955).

Emden, Paul H., *Quakers in Commerce: A Record of Business Achievement* (1939).

Fenwick, Thomas, 'Joseph Pease', *Practical Magazine* (1873).

Fladeland, Betty, 'Our cause being one and the same: Abolitionists and Chartism', in Walvin, James (ed.), *Slavery in British Society 1776–1846* (1982).

Flinn, M. W., 'Social theory and the industrial revolution', in Burns, Tom, and Saul, S. B. (eds.), *Social Theory and Economic Change* (1967).

Fordyce, William, *The History and Antiquities of the County Palatine of Durham*, vol. 2 (1857).

Fortunes Made in Business, vol. 1, *The Peases of Darlington* (1884).

Foster, Joseph, *Pease of Darlington* (privately published, 1891).

Fox, Elton, *Two Homes, by a Grandson* (Plymouth, 1925).

Galloway, R., *Annals of Coal Mining and the Coal Trade*, vol. 1 (1898, reprinted 1971).

Garside, W. R., *The Durham Miners, 1919–1960* (1971).

Gourvish, T. R., *Railways and the British Economy 1830–1914* (1980).

Grey, Sir Edward, *Sir David Dale: Inaugural Address Delivered to the Dale Memorial Trust* (1911).

Grubb, Edward, *What is Quakerism?* (1917).

Grubb, Isabel, *Quakerism in Industry before 1800* (1930).

Hamer, D. A., *Liberal Politics in the Age of Gladstone and Rosebery: A Study in Leadership and Policy* (Oxford, 1972).

Hamer, D. A., *The Politics of Electoral Pressure: A Study in the History of Victorian Reform Agitations* (Hassocks, 1977).

Hannah, Leslie (ed.), *Management Strategy and Business Development: An Historical and Comparative Study* (1976).

Hare, A. J. C., *The Story of My Life*, vol. 4 (undated, c. 1880).

Harrison, Brian, 'The British Prohibitionists 1853–72', *International Review of Social History*, vol. 15, no. 3 (1970).

Harrison, J. K., 'The development of a distinctive "Cleveland" blast furnace practice 1866–1875', in Hempstead, C. A. (ed.), *Cleveland Iron and Steel: Background and Nineteenth Century History* (British Steel Corporation, 1979).

Harrison, J. K., 'The production of malleable iron in north east England and the rise and collapse of the puddling process in the Cleveland district', in Hempstead (ed.), op. cit.

Harrison, J. K., 'The production of pig iron in north east England 1577–1865', in Hempstead (ed.), op. cit.

Harrison, J. K., and Harrison, A., 'Saltburn-by-the-Sea: the early years of a

Stockton and Darlington Railway Company venture', *Industrial Archeology Review*, vol. 4 (1980).

Harrison, R., *Before the Socialists* (1965).

Hempstead, C. A. (ed.), *Cleveland Iron and Steel: Background and Nineteenth Century History* (British Steel Corporation, 1979).

Henry Mayhew's 1851 (1851).

Hoole, K., *A Regional History of the Railways of Great Britain*, vol. 4, *North East England* (Dawlish, 1965).

Irving, R. J., *The North Eastern Railway Company 1870–1914: an economic history* (Leicester, 1976).

Isichei, Elizabeth, *Victorian Quakers* (Oxford, 1970).

Jeans, J. S., *The Iron Trade of Great Britain* (1877).

Jeans, J. S., *Jubilee Memorial of the Railway System: A History of the Stockton and Darlington Railway and a Record of its Results* (1875, reprinted, Newcastle upon Tyne, 1974).

Jeans, J. S., *Pioneers of the Cleveland Iron Trade* (Middlesbrough, 1875).

Joyce, Patrick, *Work, Society and Politics: The Culture of the Factory in Later Victorian England* (Brighton, 1980).

Kennedy, William, P., 'Institutional response to economic growth: capital markets in Britain in 1914', in Hannah, Leslie (ed.), *Management Strategy and Business Development: An Historical and Comparative Study* (1976).

Kenwood, A. G., 'Transport capital formation and economic growth on Teesside, 1820–50', *Journal of Transport History*, vol. 11 pt 2 (1981).

Kirby, M. W., *The British Coalmining Industry 1870–1946: A Political and Economic History* (1977).

Koss, Stephen, *Asquith* (1976).

Lane, Michael R., *The Story of the Steam Plough Works: Fowlers of Leeds* (1980).

Lee, S. (ed.), *Dictionary of National Biography*, vol. 44 (1895).

Leonard, J. W., 'Saltburn: the Northern Brighton', in Sigsworth, Eric (ed.), *Ports and Resorts in the Regions* (Conference Papers, Hull College of Higher Education, July 1980), pp. 141–200.

Lillie, William, *The History of Middlesbrough: An Illustration of the Evolution of English Industry* (Middlesbrough, 1968).

Lloyd, Humphrey, *The Quaker Lloyds in the Industrial Revolution* (1975).

Longstaffe, W. Hylton Dyer, *The History and Antiquities of the Parish of Darlington in the Bishoprick* (1854).

Louckes, Harold, *The Discovery of Quakerism* (1960).

Maccoby, S., *English Radicalism, 1886–1914* (1953).

McCord, Norman, *North East England: The Region's Development, 1760–1960* (1979).

MacDonald, G. W., and Gospel, H., 'The Mond-Turner talks, 1927–1933', *The Historical Journal*, vol. 16 (1973).

McLelland, D. C., *The Achieving Society* (Princeton, New Jersey, 1961).

Marshall, Gordon, *Presbyteries and Profits: Calvinism and the Development of Capitalism in Scotland, 1560–1707* (Oxford, 1980).

Mathias, Peter, *The First Industrial Nation: An Economic History of Britain 1700–1914* (1st edn, 1969).

Matthews, P. W., and Tuke, A. W., *History of Barclays Bank Limited* (1926).

Memoir of Fra: Mewburn, Chief Bailiff of Darlington and First Railway Solicitor, by His Son (Darlington, 1867).

Mewburn, Francis, *The Larchfield Diary: Extracts from the Diary of the Late Mr Mewburn, First Railway Solicitor* (1876).

Mingay, G. E., *English Landed Society in the Eighteenth Century* (1963).

Moore, Robert, *Pit-Men, Preachers and Politics: the effects of Methodism in a Durham mining community* (Cambridge, 1974).

Mullett, Michael, *Radical Religious Movements in Early Modern Europe* (1980).

Musson, A. E., *Enterprise in Soap and Chemicals: Joseph Crosfield and Sons Limited, 1815–1965* (Manchester, 1965).

Nossiter, T. J., *Influence, Opinion and Political Idioms in Reformed England: Case Studies from the North East 1832–74* (Hassocks, 1975).

Odber, A. J. , 'The manufactured iron trade of the north of England', *Oxford Economic Papers*, vol. 3, no. 2 (1951).

Ord, J. W., *The History and Antiquities of Cleveland* (1846).

Owen, J. S., 'The Cleveland ironstone industry', in Hempstead (ed.), op. cit.

Page, William (ed.), *The Victoria County History of the Counties of England: A History of Durham*, vol. 2 (original edn 1907, reprinted 1968).

Payne, Peter, *British Entrepreneurship in the Nineteenth Century* (1974).

Pease, Alfred E., *Biskra and the oases and desert of the Zibans* (1893).

Pease, Alfred E., *Hunting Reminiscences* (1898).

Pease, Alfred, E., *The Badger* (1899).

Pease, Alfred E., *Loders and Dorleas Gazelle* (1899).

Pease, Alfred E., *Abyssinian and Somaliland Antelopes* (1901).

Pease, Sir Alfred E., *A Private Memoir of Sir Thomas Fowler, Bart.* (privately published, *c*. 1905).

Pease, Sir Alfred E. (ed.), *The Diaries of Edward Pease: The Father of English Railways* (1907).

Pease, Sir Alfred E., *My Son Christopher: being the story of the childhood of Christopher York Pease* (Middlesbrough, 1919).

Pease, Sir Alfred E., *Elections and Recollections* (1932).

Pease, Henry, and Company, *Bi-Centenary 1752–1952, Priestgate Mills Darlington* (Darlington, 1952).

Pease, J. A., and Pease, A. E., *An Historical Outline of the Association of Edward Pease, Joseph Pease and Sir Joseph Whitwell Pease, with the Industrial Development of South Durham and North Yorkshire, and with the Creation of the Railway System* (privately published, *c*. 1903).

Pease, Mary, *Henry Pease: A Short Story of His life* (1897).

Pease, M. F., *A Chronicle of the Pease Family of Leeds, Cote Bank, Westbury-on-Trym, Bristol* (Street, 1949).

Perkin, H., *The Age of the Railway* (1970).

Perkin, Harold, *The Origins of Modern English Society, 1780–1880* (1969).

Phillips, Maberley, *A History of Banks, Bankers and Banking in Northumberland, Durham and North Yorkshire* (1894).

Ponting, K. G., and Jenkins, David, *The British Wool Textile Industry 1700–1914* (1982).

Porter, J. H., 'David Dale and conciliation in the northern manufactured iron trade, 1869–1914', *Northern History*, vol. 5 (1970).

Postgate, C., *Middlesbrough: its History, Environs and Trade* (Middlesbrough, 1899).

Pressnell, L. S., *Country Banking in the Industrial Revolution* (Oxford, 1956).

Raistrick, Arthur, *Quakers in Science and Industry* (Newton Abbott, 1968).

Random Recollections of the House of Commons, from the year 1830 to the Close of 1835 . . . by one of No Party (1836).

Reed, M. C., *Investment in Railways in Britain, 1820–1844: A Study in the Development of the Capital Market* (Oxford, 1975).

Reid, H. G., *Middlesbrough and its Jubilee* (Middlesbrough, 1881).

Reith, J. C. W., *Into the Wind* (1949).

Rice, C. Duncan, *The Scots Abolitionists 1833–1861* (Baton Rouge, 1981).

Rimmer, W. G., *Marshalls of Leeds, Flax Spinners, 1788–1886* (Cambridge, 1961).

Robinson, William (ed.), *Friends of a Half Century* (1891).

Rounthwaite, T. E., *The Railways of Weardale* (1965).

Rubinstein, W. D., 'The Victorian middle classes: wealth, occupation and geography', *The Economic History Review*, second series, vol. 30, no. 4 (1977).

Samuelsson, Kurt, *Religion and Economic Action* (New York, 1962).

Sayers, R. S., *Lloyds Bank in the History of English Banking* (Oxford, 1959).

Schumpeter, J. A., 'The creative response in economic history', *Journal of Economic History*, vol. 7, no. 2 (1947).

Schumpeter, J. A., *The Theory of Economic Development* (1934).

Sigsworth, Eric (ed.), *Ports and Resorts in the Regions* (Conference Papers, Hull College of Higher Education, July 1980).

Simmons, Jack, 'Rail: 1975 or 1980', *Journal of Transport History*, vol. 7, no. 1 (1980).

Smailes, A. E., *North England* (1st edn, 1960).

Smiles, Aileen, *Samuel Smiles and His Surroundings* (1956).

Smiles, Samuel, *Lives of the Engineers*, vol. 3, *George and Robert Stephenson* (1862).

Smith, H. John, *Public Health Act: Report to the General Board of Health on Darlington 1850*, introduced and discussed by H. John Smith (Durham, 1967).

Smith, H. J., 'The water supply of the industrial north-east 1850–1920', in Sturgess, R. W. (ed.), *The Great Age of Industry in the North-East, 1700–1920* (Durham, 1981).

Steel, John W., *Friendly Sketches: Essays illustrative of Quakerism* (Darlington, 1876).

Stoddart, Anna M., *Saintly Lives: Elizabeth Pease Nichol* (1899).

Sturgess, R. W. (ed.), *The Great Age of Industry in the North-East, 1700–1920* (Durham, 1981).

Sunderland, Norman, *A History of Darlington* (Manchester, 1967).

Sweezy, Paul M., *Monopoly and Competition in the English Coal Trade, 1550–1850* (1938).

Sykes, John, *The Quakers: A New Look at their Place in Society* (1958).

Sykes, J., *The Amalgamation Movement in English Banking, 1825–1924* (1925).

Tawney, R. H., *Religion and the Rise of Capitalism* (2nd edn, 1937).

Taylor, A. J., 'The coal industry', in Aldcroft, D. H. (ed.), *The Development of British Industry and Foreign Competition, 1875–1914* (1968).

Taylor, A. J., 'Combination in the mid-nineteenth century coal industry', *Transactions of the Royal Historical Society*, vol. 3 (1953).

Temperley, Howard, *British Antislavery 1833–1870* (1972).

Thompson, Allan, *The Dynamics of the Industrial Revolution* (1973).

Thomson, David, *England in the Nineteenth Century* (Harmondsworth, 1950).
Tomlinson, W. W., *The North Eastern Railway: its rise and development* (1915, reprinted with an introduction by K. Hoole, Newton Abbott, 1967).
Trevor-Roper, Hugh, *A Hidden Life: The Enigma of Sir Edmund Backhouse* (1976).
Ure, Andrew, *Philosophy of Manufactures* (1835).
Walvin, James (ed.), *Slavery and British Society 1776–1846* (1982).
Wallis, Amy E., 'Darlington: the English Philadelphia', *Journal of the Friends Historical Society*, vols 47–8 (1956–8).
Ward, J. T., and Wilson, R. G. (eds.), *Land and Industry: The Landed Estates and the Industrial Revolution* (1971).
Ward, J. T., 'Landowners and mining', in Ward J. T., and Wilson, R. G. (eds.), *Land and Industry* (1971).
Wardell, John W., *The Economic History of Tees-side* (Stockton-on-Tees, 1960).
Warren, J. G. H., *A Century of Locomotive Building by Robert Stephenson and Company, 1823–1923* (Newcastle upon Tyne, 1923).
Weber, M., *The Protestant Ethic and the Spirit of Capitalism* (1930).
Wiener, Martin, *English Culture and the Decline of the Industrial Spirit, 1850–1980* (Cambridge, 1981).
Windsor, David Burns, *The Quaker Enterprise: Friends in Business* (1980).
Winstanley, D. A., *Later Victorian Cambridge* (Cambridge, 1947).
Winton, J R., *Lloyds Bank 1918–1969* (Oxford, 1982).
Wooler, Edward and Boyde, Alfred Caine, *Historic Darlington* (1913).

INDEX